TOWN ON THE TELLY

TOWN ON THE TELLY

By Karl Fuller

Foreword by Matt Holland

First published 2022 by DB Publishing, an imprint of JMD Media Ltd,
Nottingham, United Kingdom.

ISBN 9781780916378

Printed in the UK

CONTENTS

Foreword by Matt Holland   7

Introduction   9

Chapter 1: Full circle   13
Sir Bobby Robson, John Duncan, John Lyall

Chapter 2: Portman Road to WemBurley   23
George Burley

Chapter 3: The 'nearly' men   60
Joe Royle

Chapter 4: It starts and ends at QPR   78
Jim Magilton

Chapter 5: From Arsenal joy to Posh woes   89
Roy Keane, Ian McParland, Paul Jewell

Chapter 6: The not so Famous Five   108
Mick McCarthy

Chapter 7: Down and out   127
Paul Hurst, Paul Lambert, John McGreal

Chapter 8: A new hope   137
Kieran McKenna

The Games   139

STATISTICS SECTION

Abidallah to Zuiverloon   197
A to Z of Town's live TV appearances and goals

Town's TV Ten   206
Town's top ten players for live TV appearances

Goals   207
Town's top ten players for live TV goals scored

Sir Bobby to McKenna   208
Town managers' live TV record

The opposition   209
A list of opponents that Town have faced live on TV

Town's TV highlights   211
Records from Town on the Telly

Town's TV milestones   213
Key moments from Town on the Telly

Acknowledgements   216

FOREWORD

by Matt Holland

Ipswich Town Football Club is one of the most respected, historic, admired, and prestigious clubs in the land. Represented by so many talented players and managers, it is a friendly, family club that invests heavily in the local community. We are unique and special and play such a big part in people's lives. And did you know that we have been live on TV 171 times and counting?

I did not until Karl approached me to write the foreword for this book. Whenever I am asked to do anything Ipswich Town-related I find it difficult to say no, but this was an easy one to agree to. He dangled the carrot by saying that I had appeared in exactly 50 live games and (although he had not finished his research) that he thought this was the record for an individual. Naturally, I was thrilled with this news and jumped at his offer. Subsequently after concluding his analysis, and as you will read, it is in fact Jim Magilton that holds the record with 54 appearances on TV. It is too late to change your mind though Karl – I have said yes!

Football has forever been and will always be my life. Growing up I always had a ball at my feet and my passion for the game has never waned. Saturday was, without doubt, and continues to be my favourite day of the week. I used to watch my dad play in the afternoon while listening to the scores on the radio, but the highlight of the day was when dad would wake me up to watch *Match of the Day*. Live games were rare at that time, but it was such a treat to be able to watch football on television.

Of course, with the advent of Sky and them acquiring the rights to the Premier League in 1992 and the Football League in 1995, live matches are more frequent and accessible which is a good thing. Nothing can beat going to a game. The anticipation, excitement and buzz you get from walking to the ground. The smell, the atmosphere, and the sense of belonging. But it is not always possible to go to the match. You may not be able to get a ticket, or your health might not allow, so the opportunity to watch on TV can be a welcome alternative.

Looking back at some of the games I have been involved in on TV with the Town has provoked some incredible memories. No one will forget 29 May 2000 as we beat Barnsley at Wembley to reach the Premier League, or 22 November 2001, as an Alun

Armstrong header put paid to Inter Milan at Portman Road. We even sent Manchester City (whatever happened to them) down on 7 May 2001. More forgettable, in fact I have got no recollection of, was the 0-0 draw at Grimsby on 9 August 1998!

I am sure that this book will induce some of your own recollections as you take a nostalgic look back at our rich history and reminisce about where you were when some of these games took place.

As we enter a new chapter under the leadership of Kieran McKenna, I am absolutely convinced that we are set for a successful period which will mean that we quickly add to the 171 games we have already played live on TV. And maybe a Sam Morsy or Conor Chaplin will break Jim Magilton's record!

Matt Holland
Ipswich Town
August 1997 to May 2003

INTRODUCTION

For those of you who know me well, you will be aware that since September 2012 I have written a column in the *East Anglian Daily Times* and *Ipswich Star* newspapers, as well as writing feature articles for the *Kings of Anglia* magazine. Those of you who know me more than well, will also be aware that prior to that, I wrote a non-league column for the *Green 'Un* as well as being the Clacton Town scribe for the same newspaper. I have also written for the *Non League Paper* and was matchday programme editor for seven years for Clacton Town and FC Clacton. I have also written two FC Clacton books.

Despite being involved with those publications I have always had a strong urge to write an Ipswich Town-related book. I have just never known where to start. Sure, I could have written purely about my memories of watching the Tractor Boys since August 1978, but I wanted to do something a bit more niche.

Town on the Telly, on the face of it, might seem a bit of a miserable choice given that we do not have the best of records when screened live on television. But each time a live TV game comes around, I see the same old questions on social media pertaining to our record on screen. The questions are like: How bad is our record? When was the last time this or that happened? And so many more are asked. I usually then step in and refer those folk to my website – www.thefullerflavour.co.uk – and the 'ITFC on TV' page. I have one of the few comprehensive lists of all games screened live which answers those questions.

After a screened match in December 2021, I had a lightbulb moment. I thought that I could put all the details into a book, share my memoirs of watching some of those games, whether on TV or by being at the ground itself, and add a bit of flavour of the season surrounding the games too. And that is how *Town on the Telly* was born.

When the singer Robbie Williams said, 'No regrets, they don't work,' I disagree with him. As far as supporting Ipswich Town is concerned, I have had a few regrets which have worked, and they will unravel themselves during this book.

The first regret I have cannot be helped though. That is, I wish that I had been born about 15 years earlier. Then I would have been able to watch the very first full Ipswich game to be shown live on TV, which was of course the 1978 FA Cup Final. Had I been of an older age, I would like to think that I would have been at Wembley itself. But at the very least it would have been nice to have watched it on television. You will see what happened to me on the day when we get to that game in the opening chapter.

A little over three months after we won the FA Cup, I saw my first Ipswich match – a 3-0 home defeat to Liverpool on 22 August 1978. It was also the day Arnold Muhren made his debut for the club. I remember snippets of that game. I was only six years old though. Yet, I am sure I would have remembered some of the cup final had I have been allowed to watch it.

When I was old enough to start going to games on my own without a responsible adult, my dad, or my brother, I tended to go on the Clacton branch of the Ipswich supporters' club coach, picking it up outside the cinema across the road to what used to be a market site in Clacton's Pier Avenue.

I was one of the youngest to travel in those days and I soon got to meet and make friends for life with some of the guys around ten years older than me. Don Welsh was later to become my best man at my wedding, Phil 'Moped' Corton is one of the loveliest people I have ever met, Kevin Mitchell would become a great travelling companion to away games, as did Chris Hayes, while Mark Snow and Andy Smith also became great companions from time to time.

The branch owes much to sisters Jill Lewis and Pat Edwards who for far longer than I can remember have organised the coaches to both home and away games, looking after their members for so many trips in the process.

Nearly, if not all of those mentioned, had the privilege of watching the FA Cup Final win over Arsenal, as well as being in Amsterdam in 1981 to see the UEFA Cup being lifted by Mick Mills. They have travelled to numerous games across Europe too. I envy their Ipswich Town-supporting lives and would quite happily be in my 60s now if I had those memories too.

That is not to say that I have had it bad though. I caught the end of the Sir Bobby Robson era, I saw us win the old Division Two Championship in 1991/92 which is my favourite season as a Town fan, and I was at Wembley when we beat Barnsley in the play-off final in 2000. I also have the wonderful memories of travelling into Europe to watch a couple of UEFA Cup games in Sweden and Luxembourg.

I have two sons, Karl who is in his early 30s and Craig who is in his late 20s, who have seen nothing as Ipswich fans. I feel for fans of their ages and younger. They travel all over the country in good numbers to watch a team that has delivered next to nothing in terms of real joy and history to revel in forever. I hope one day that their time will come.

In total, Ipswich have played 171 live TV games at the time of writing; 84 at home and 85 have been away. The other two were played at Wembley. I have seen 67 of the 84 home games (the last three were played behind closed doors due to COVID-19 restrictions). I had a good run which saw me present at the first 53 consecutive home games that were screened during a spell of 11 seasons where I did not miss a single Portman Road match. I then went on a shameful run of 11 consecutive home TV games where I was not present, and more on that later. It is even more galling to think that of the first five I missed, we won them all!

As well as my memoirs, this book contains details of every single live TV game, complete with match line-ups for both Ipswich and the opposition. After that, the book then moves on to some statistics and milestones which will hopefully be of interest.

I hope that some of my memories of watching the live games will bring back memories for you too. But before I go any further, there is a little bit of housekeeping to bring to your attention.

The fixtures featured in this book are all full games and thus, the first, as previously mentioned, is the 1978 FA Cup Final. I am aware that the second half of our Charity Shield defeat to Tottenham in 1962 was screened live. But as it was not the whole game, it does not qualify for the book. What also do not qualify are the games that we have been able to watch outside of what I call your normal television. By that, I mean BBC, ITV, Channel 5, and your traditional Sky Sports. So, no red button stuff or iFollow games. Nor are there any other type of streamed matches, illegal or otherwise. That is the criteria.

Nowadays, it is all too easy to watch a live game every day of the week. For a club like Ipswich, to be shown live on a terrestrial channel or Sky Sports, it is still a rare moment and carries more of a feeling than watching on iFollow just because I can.

When I was growing up in the 1970s and '80s, the only live TV game outside of major tournaments would have been the FA Cup Final. Highlights were even special in those days. *Match of the Day* on BBC One on a Saturday night was something to look forward to, especially if Ipswich were one of the main games. *Match of the Week* on Anglia TV on a Sunday afternoon was even better. Being regionalised, Ipswich were on most weeks. You just had to suffer getting through *Farmers Weekly* first. I love watching *The Big Match Revisited* these days on ITV4 on a Saturday morning. When Ipswich feature on there, Brian Moore will tell us that the pictures come from Anglia TV and the commentator would be Gerry Harrison. I still enjoy his dulcet tones. The whole thing puts me in a timewarp and takes me back over 40 years.

Town on the telly in that era, other than those weekend programmes, would often be highlights of our midweek games either on *Sportsnight* on BBC One presented by Harry Carpenter, or *Midweek Sports Special* on ITV presented, again, by Brian Moore.

There were two reasons why I enjoyed these programmes, Firstly, my mum worked part-time as a barmaid back then and Wednesday was one of her working evenings. If she had been at home, I would have no doubt been sent to bed at my usual bedtime of around 8pm. But dad would let me stay up and watch these programmes – if I could stay awake.

The other reason is that you never knew which games would be shown. As the matches would often be highlights of European ties, Ipswich of course would feature a fair bit.

You would not always know the score either. This was in the day before Ceefax and Teletext, never mind mobile phones. Even local radio would not have match commentary. The best you could hope for on Radio Orwell was updates by Peter Slater every 15 minutes and when there was a goal, midway through whatever song was being played at the time, a jingle would cut over the top with a cry of 'goal action' and then you were left on tenterhooks as the jingle finished before crossing over to Slater to find out if Ipswich had scored or if it was the opposition.

So, the highlights really were worth watching. You were going into the complete unknown almost every Wednesday night.

I have only ever shed a tear twice for an Ipswich matter. Most recently when the great Kevin Beattie passed away, and once as a nine-year-old over a game that I watched on television on one of those Wednesday evenings.

In fact, it was 7 November 1980, and it was the second leg of a second-round tie, with Ipswich hosting Grasshoppers of Zürich. The first leg in Switzerland had finished 0-0. Kevin Beattie put Ipswich 1-0 up in the first half and Claudio Sulser equalised in the second half. The final whistle went with the score at 1-1 and I thought that although it was late and my mum would be home from work soon, we had extra time to look forward to.

The commentator then stated that Ipswich were out of Europe. Why? I quizzed when we had not lost. My dad tried his best to explain the away goals rule to me, but it just would not sink into my head. I claimed that to win a game, one team had to put the ball in the net more times than the other team and Grasshoppers had not done this. I insisted that penalties would have been fairer as one team has to score more than the other to win a shoot-out. My poor dad, as hard as he tried, could not get me to understand and put me to bed where I cried my eyes out and fell asleep. I have never liked the away goals rule, and it would return to haunt me again later in life.

To round up the housekeeping, as far as any mentions of what stands I have watched games from at Portman Road, they will be called as I knew them at the time that I first watched games from each stand, ie Churchmans, Cobbold, Pioneer and North Stand.

Right, let's crack on.

Karl Fuller
Twitter: @fullerflavour

CHAPTER 1: FULL CIRCLE

Sir Bobby Robson, John Duncan, John Lyall (16 games)

Aged just six years, seven months, and 11 days, it was deemed by female members of my family, that I was too young to be around my dad and grandad who would no doubt want to watch the 1978 FA Cup Final in peace.

I was therefore dragged around the shops on that glorious Saturday afternoon by my mum and my nan with no knowledge at all that Ipswich Town, who I would fall in love with for life just over three months later, were winning the FA Cup. If ever there was a case for me to call the NSPCC in my childhood that was probably the day to do it.

I have watched Town's first live TV game back on numerous occasions, both on video and DVD. I have also listened to the game several times on the *Bobby's Dazzlers* LP with the succinct radio commentary of the BBC's Alan Parry and Peter Jones. Who will ever forget Jones's immortal words describing the moment that a cross by David Geddis led to Town's goal, 'Willie Youngs there, the chance is there, it's there! Roger Osborne has done it for Ipswich Town. They have scored, 1-0.'

Anyone growing up in that era will know that the FA Cup Final was the football TV highlight of the year. It was the only game shown live on TV. The day's coverage would start around 10am and would include cameras at each of the team hotels at breakfast, to following fans who were Wembley-bound, before boarding the team buses and taking in the atmosphere en route to the twin towers.

Even if it was not your team in the final, you were still engrossed in it all. The lack of live football in those days is a mark of sadness to say that the 1978 FA Cup Final was to be Sir Bobby Robson's only live TV game in charge of Ipswich. Even all those matches in Europe, including the home ties in which we never lost and the UEFA Cup that we won in 1981, were not screened live.

When you think of the 'Boys of 81', the likes of Frans Thijssen, Russell Osman, Terry Butcher, Arnold Muhren, Alan Brazil, Eric Gates, Steve McCall, and Kevin O'Callaghan never played live on TV for Town. It is criminal that such talent never had the opportunity to display their skills into British households for 90 minutes.

How many teams can claim that their first live TV game occurred on such a high as winning the FA Cup?

While I missed out on watching the final on TV, I will share with you all, the experience that my older brother Shaun had when he had the privilege of seeing it:

'Back in the 1970s, as Karl states, live football games were rare. Besides any major tournament or occasional England international, the FA Cup Final represented the sole live television game for domestic clubs and, the most important match in the calendar.

'As a football-mad youngster, I vividly remember watching Southampton pull off one of the great FA Cup Final shocks in 1976 with Bobby Stokes scoring late on to beat hot favourites Manchester United. It was an entire year until my next live game, with Manchester United successful that time around in beating Liverpool 2-1 and all the goals were scored in a frenetic four minutes early in the second half. My third live television game came mid-November 1977, with a Kevin Keegan-inspired England beating a strong Italian side in a failed bid to reach the 1978 World Cup finals in Argentina.

'Close to six months later and now ten years old, 6 May 1978, brought the next opportunity. Just my fourth live game in those first couple of years and arguably the greatest day in the history of Ipswich Town Football Club.

'In reaching Wembley for the first time, Town had overcome a much-fancied West Bromwich Albion in the semi-finals. With it some years prior to these matches being broadcast live, I remember being glued to a radio set alongside family in my grandparents flat. Ron Atkinson (commonly known as Big Ron), the flamboyant manager for the opposition, had done them few favours in being filmed at Wembley on the morning of the game alongside the FA Cup and dismissing an Ipswich Town scarf with words along the lines of it having no place there.

'The build up to the final itself was typical of many at the time. There was the obligatory music single, 'Ipswich, Ipswich (Get That Goal)', we played out the final in the primary school playground every break-time ahead of the big day, and then on to the day itself with the coverage starting in the morning.

'My memories include the *Road to Wembley*, *Cup Final Mastermind* and the coach journey for the teams from their hotels to the stadium itself. Of note, this would be the 50th Wembley FA Cup Final and the last with commentary from David Coleman for the BBC as part of their *Grandstand* show (ITV also showed the match live as part of their *World of Sport* programme).

'It was a gloriously sunny day on the back of lots of rain with the bookmakers clearly positioning Ipswich as underdogs, a label which the late great Sir Bobby Robson was content with, "Being the underdogs helps ease the tension and that suits us fine. Arsenal seem to be most people's choice this time, but that does not worry us in the least."

'This was on the back of a season, where we narrowly fought off relegation to finish 18th and it was the only year in 11 where Town finished outside the top six.

'Back to the game itself. I watched with my West Ham-supporting best friend who became a staunch Town fan for the day in hoping that the Hammers would remain the latest London club to win the cup following their success three years earlier.

'Arsenal wore their second kit of yellow and blue, following previous cup final successes, and had a real Irish influence with Pat Jennings, Pat Rice, Sammy Nelson, David O'Leary, Liam Brady, and Frank Stapleton, plus manager Terry Neill (himself a former Northern Ireland international). Leading the line was talisman Malcolm Macdonald (aka Supermac). Ipswich, making our Wembley debut, wore traditional blue and white.

'I vaguely remember Arsenal starting the brighter, but from Paul Mariner hitting Arsenal's crossbar after 11 minutes it really was one-way traffic. By the time John Wark had rattled the post after 52 minutes, then struck the same spot on the same post once more after 72 minutes, and George Burley having a point-blank header superbly saved by Pat Jennings a couple of moments later, we really should and could have been 4-0 up. I wondered whether this was going to be Arsenal's day.

'I need not worry for long as in the 77th minute, Willie Young diverted a cross from David Geddis for Roger Osborne to be in the right place at the right time and the rest is history. Coleman's commentary, 'Osborne, 1-0', lives long in the memory.

'I clearly remember Osborne being overcome with exhaustion and emotion and then substituted. There was a late scare when Arsenal's Supermac got a sniff of goal with just six minutes left on the clock. But he shot straight at Paul Cooper and Town saw out time.

'It was left for Mick Mills to lead the triumphant Town team up those famous 39 steps to the Royal Box and be presented with the FA Cup for the first time in our history by HRH Princess Alexandra. Then, at some point, Mills collected a floppy blue hat for a lap of honour and photos on the pitch.

'All that remained was a trip to our local playing fields with my West Ham buddy to re-enact the afternoon's events of that wonderful day.'

* * *

While Shaun had the great experience of watching that final on television, my good friend Don was at Wembley, and I just had to ask him to share with us his FA Cup memories and of course being at Wembley for our win:

'In the early hours of Sunday, 7 May 1978, I returned home from Wembley to my parents' house where I was still living. I had the privilege of being at Wembley Stadium the day before to watch Ipswich win the FA Cup. My dear mum and dad were still awake and had waited up to celebrate my triumphant return home. Dad had drunk several whiskies by way of his own celebration and said to me, "Son, what you have experienced has been a once-in-a-lifetime day." How true those words have been for me ever since that day.

'My love for the FA Cup competition began many years earlier, before I had even visited Portman Road for the first time. I grew up in a football-loving family and the cup final was one of only two live games shown on TV back then. My brother and I would watch all the build-up programmes before the game kicked off. Guests would come to our house to share the experience with us and at half-time, Mum would provide sandwiches, cakes, biscuits, and tea.

'In 1971, we got a colour television, and I can still recall Charlie George laying on his back in celebration after scoring the winner for Arsenal when they beat Liverpool 2-1 after extra time.

'To be at Wembley seven years later to watch my beloved Ipswich was to be a dream come true when I was lucky enough to have secured a much-coveted ticket. I went to the game on a coach with members of the Clacton branch of Ipswich supporters. The excitement was tangible and somehow, I felt that despite being the underdogs, it was going to be our day.

'Three years earlier, in 1975, I cried my first tears over Ipswich when we were cruelly beaten in an FA Cup semi-final replay by West Ham at Chelsea's Stamford Bridge. That sad memory made me appreciate the special day at Wembley even more.

'Hundreds of vehicles headed to London displaying various forms of blue and white scarves, flags, and banners. The scene was like an ancient army on the march. As soon as I saw the iconic twin towers, that was the point when the nerves really started to kick in.

'Arsenal fans soon came into view, and I felt that they were walking with a swagger as if they expected an easy victory. Town fans were simply enjoying the glorious experience, taking everything in. I stood in the tunnel end of the grand stadium and boy, was the atmosphere electric. The players emerged into the red-hot throng like gladiators of old about to go into combat.

'My memory of the game itself is slim these days, although I do remember Town hitting the woodwork on three occasions. There was also a world-class save by Pat Jennings to deny George Burley. I began to wonder if we would score despite outplaying the Gunners.

'Then came the moment late in the second half I will never forget. We attacked down the right through Clive Woods and David Geddis, who had tormented the Arsenal defence all afternoon, which led to a low cross from Geddis pinging off Willie Young to Roger Osborne who shot, and the net bulged. Our fans erupted into a maelstrom of noise and pure joy. I recall being swept off my feet in a dance of celebration. Strangers clutched each other like soldiers in a fearful retreat. The mass of humanity began to bounce up and down singing "We shall not be moved".

'I had no fear of an Arsenal equaliser. I was not worried at all. We had been that good. The final whistle blew tears from my eyes as we had won the FA Cup. Mick Mills climbed the stairs to the Royal Box and then one could see the silver trophy gleaming as he lifted it above his head. We were now a "big club".

'I began my tale with wise words from my dad. We often talked about whether there was life after death. On a visit to see him, which was to be the last time, he said to me, "See you later, son." My dad always kept his promises.'

* * *

Each of Town's first four live TV games were all FA Cup ties. There was a gap of almost ten years between that 1978 cup final and Town's next live game – the first live match to be played at Portman Road, with Manchester United as the visitors. This was also the first in a successive run of 53 live TV games where I would be present at Portman Road. There are few things that I do not remember about my time of watching Ipswich. I am often referred to as the memory man, or statto by some family and friends. But I cannot for the life of me remember who I attended this game with. What is noticeably clear though was the excitement that surrounded this game. We were a Division Two team at home to the mighty Manchester United. The BBC cameras were present, and we were going to be on the television.

I took up my seat in the lower tier of the Cobbold Stand full of excited anticipation, complete with a red, white, and blue Ipswich flat cap that one could purchase from the club shop. I am sure that I looked very fetching as a 16-year-old. From what I recall, it was a decent game that United won 2-1. Mich d'Avray had the misfortune of scoring Ipswich's first own goal on live television to give United the lead. Then a minute before half-time, Tony Humes restored parity and sent us into raptures going into the break. But the dream of reaching the fourth round was over when another defender scored the winning goal as United's Viv Anderson sealed a 2-1 win.

Liverpool were the visitors on 16 February 1992, for what was another FA Cup tie to catch the imagination of Town fans, as over 26,000 filled Portman Road. This was our first live game to be shown on Sky Sports and John Lyall's first TV game in charge of Ipswich. It was probably the windiest match that I have ever been to as well.

The 1991/92 season is about my favourite as a Town fan. It holds so many memories from many different games which culminated in winning promotion and ensuring that we were founder members of the inaugural Premier League.

I did not have a season ticket in 1991/92. Instead, I held a membership card which then reduced the cost of a matchday ticket to the royal sum of £5 for the North Stand. In those days, it was of course a terraced stand and thinking about that season, and all the celebrations that we had after each goal and win passed us by, was like nothing else that I have experienced since. This was due to the following season the North Stand became all-seated and for home fans only. There was no dividing fence anymore for us to peer through and throw obscenities at visiting supporters.

If I was not in the North Stand that season, then I could be found seated in the upper tier of the Pioneer Stand and that is exactly where I was on this day. The build-up and excitement matched that of the visit of Manchester United almost ten years previously. We were in the second tier and we welcomed a massive club to Portman Road. Only this time there was a quarter-final at stake.

I think Liverpool would have been happier with the draw, especially when they saw John Wark meet a corner superbly and his fierce header cannoned back off the crossbar. The wind played a massive part that day and made free-flowing football almost impossible to play. Still, we were worthy of our draw and were on our way to Anfield for a replay.

Regret number two was to be had from the replay – one that has haunted me for all the years since. It is not very often that you have regrets for not being at a game when your team has lost. Town were majestic that night. We took Liverpool to extra time in their back yard, and I was not there. I have no idea why I did not go. I was 20 years old, old enough to go on my own but for some reason, it just did not happen.

Four years previously, I was still at school and my work experience saw me spend a couple of weeks at a local branch of Midland Bank in Frinton-on-Sea. Yes, I got all the free Griffin stuff that the kids got when opening a bank account. A chap by the name of David Jones took me under his wing. Apart from being a Leeds United fan, he was a good guy who loved his Formula One motor racing.

At the time, he still lived at home with his parents. He invited me along with some of his other friends to watch the Liverpool v Ipswich replay. He was the only person I knew at that time who had Sky Sports. I was thrilled to think that I would get to see the game. But it meant that I would have to be on my best behaviour. No swearing when Liverpool scored and no jumping around like a lunatic when Town scored.

When I think of that game, it all comes flooding back. Firstly, when Gavin Johnson equalised with eight minutes to go with a bullet of a header, and secondly, when Jason Dozzell put us in front five minutes into extra time. On the night, I could not contain myself and went nuts. OK, so the lead only lasted for three minutes, but this was an immense performance. It took a Steve McManaman winner in the 100th minute to finally beat us. But boy was I proud of all the lads.

The following day, one of the national newspapers had a picture of Dozzell celebrating his goal. He was pointing upward with one arm and had both feet off the ground. It was a performance that had me feeling like I was walking on air too.

I know that some fans blame our FA and UEFA Cup runs in 1980/81 for taking their toll on our 66-game season, thus preventing us from winning the league, but every year we go out of the FA Cup now, to concentrate on the league – which never works – I always look back to 1992 and think how much confidence we got from that FA Cup run which ultimately would have helped us to win Division Two.

The first Ipswich league game to be screened live was at Portman Road – an FA Premier League match against Tottenham. That day will only ever be remembered for one thing – Jason Cundy's goal from the halfway line to give Tottenham a 29th-minute lead. I was in the North Stand that day, almost right behind the goal. The moment that the ball left Cundy's foot you knew it was going in. Poor Craig Forrest had no chance and I doubt he has ever conceded another goal like it. No doubt it was wind-assisted and Cundy just struck the ball with perfection.

I got to know Jason a little a few years down the line. When he discovered that he had testicular cancer, I later helped him raise awareness for a charity when he had his head shaved. The event took place at Portman Road. This came after I conducted an interview with him in the bar of what was then known as the Forte Posthouse Hotel, now the Holiday Inn, in London Road on the outskirts of Ipswich.

The interview was for the 50th edition of the fanzine *Those Were The Days*, in April 1999. I asked him what he remembered about that fluke of a goal and here is how he responded,

'Not a great deal! Had it have not been on TV and had I not seen it countless times repeatedly, I do not know what my memories would be of it. I distinctly remember that the moment it left my foot, Neil Ruddock shouted "it's in"! And after a split second, I realised that it was too. You do not score a goal from that sort of distance over the head of Craig Forrest easily!

'It was a combination of everything. Jason Dozzell was going to put his foot into the ball and where it was in midfield, had it gone over my shoulder, I think we would have been a bit exposed at the back. So, I thought get rid of this and regroup. In the end, Dozzell pulled out of the tackle and of course, I went through with the laces and the ball sailed over the goalkeeper's head and it ended up quite a laugh!'

I suppose the last laugh was with Ipswich though when John Wark equalised on the stroke of half-time and the game ended in a 1-1 draw.

After Cundy's goal, *The Sun* challenged him to score one like it again. He accepted the challenge, in a pair of trainers, at a local park.

Town's first live league win was seen on Sky Sports and came at no better venue than Carrow Road as we beat top-of-the-table Norwich City 2-0.

My dad had subscribed to Sky a week or so before this game. Prior to that, he had the old BSkyB subscription and when he got his new dish, he gave me his old dish and box. In those days, you could set up such a thing yourself and I did so all in suitable time for this match, which was screened free by the way before you needed such a thing as a Sky Sports subscription.

The game took place just four days before Christmas Day in 1992. I invited my old mate Adam King round to my flat to watch it with me. Adam likes a drink, and back then, I did not mind one. I bought eight cans of lager from the local off-licence which I figured four cans each would see us through the game nicely. Wrong! They were all gone by half-time. But no problem as the off-licence was only around the corner and we restocked for the second half.

Just seven minutes after the break, Chris Kiwomya scored and the icing on the cake came in the 88th minute with Neil Thompson wrapping up a 2-0 win to present all Town fans with a lovely early Christmas present.

By now, Adam and I were quite merry on the alcohol we had consumed. Nevertheless, we felt the occasion was right to be celebrated and headed off into Clacton's town centre. We found ourselves in the old Lord Nelson pub, ordered a pint each and made our way to the back room where there was a band practising.

I asked if they could play 'Walk of Life' by Dire Straits and they duly obliged. There was Adam and I, on the dance floor, the only two people in the room other than the band, and we were blasting out a rendition of 'And he do the walk, do the walk of life, yeah, he do the Johnny Wark of life!'

We were doing this with what started off with full pints in our hands by the way, of which most was on the floor by the time we had finished strutting our stuff. What a great night that was. I can only imagine what it must have been like for Town fans at the game as we headed into Christmas in sixth place of the Premier League.

By the time Town were next to appear live on TV, there was an alarming slump in form, and we went into a game at Blackburn Rovers on 12 April 1993, without a league victory since beating Manchester United 2-1 at Portman Road on 30 January. The poor run of form, which saw just four points gained from 13 matches, meant that Town would slump from fourth to 17th in the table.

When Stuart Ripley gave Blackburn a sixth-minute lead, the signs were ominous, and fears of another defeat came to fruition. Phil Whelan extended the hosts' lead two minutes before the break with an unfortunate own goal, and despite Simon Milton pulling a goal back for Town in the 68th minute, a 2-1 defeat ensured that we were becoming embroiled in a relegation battle.

Just a week later however, the perfect tonic laid waiting for us all as the double for the season was completed over Norwich. Jason Dozzell had been pushed forward in the starting line-up to partner Chris Kiwomya and the move paid off big time when he opened the scoring on 21 minutes. Chris Sutton scored for the Canaries four minutes before half-time and then two goals in a frantic three-minute spell after the interval had us rocking in the North Stand. Firstly, Micky Stockwell restored our lead in the 54th minute and then Dozzell notched his second of the game on 57 minutes.

This victory gave John Lyall his first live TV win on home soil to back up his first away win on the box – also against Norwich. The result also eased any relegation worries. As the Town players came over to salute us delirious fans, the tannoy system blasted out the music to 'Land of Hope and Glory' and you know the words that would have been sung along to that tune. The misfortune of being the first player to be sent off in a live game featuring Town fell to Colin Calderwood of Tottenham. Our 2-2 FA Premier League draw on 22 September 1993, will always be remembered for what happened five minutes from time.

If it was not strange enough to see former Ipswich favourite Jason Dozzell in Tottenham's line-up, it certainly was to see him score what proved to be the equalising goal and even more bizarre, watching him celebrate wildly in front of the North Stand.

All was looking good for Town after Teddy Sheringham had given Tottenham a 28th-minute lead. Second half goals from Simon Milton (59) and Ian Marshall (69) looked to have been enough to give us all three points until Dozzell intervened. When a player returns to his old club and scores, you never know how they might choose to celebrate. If they have returned to a club which had given them such a distinguished career, you would expect them not to celebrate at all. Dozzell could not have celebrated any more ecstatically if he had tried. Not that I blamed him. It was just surreal to see an ex-favourite celebrate and that was something that I would become accustomed to as my years of supporting Ipswich started to unfold.

Three weeks later, another Portman Road game to be screened live came our way when on Sunday, 17 October 1993, Leeds United were the visitors. A 0-0 draw extended our winless run to eight matches which started to become a concern for the fans after we had won the opening three games of the season. Just eight days later however, a 2-0 win at Wimbledon live on Sky momentarily put any worries to the back of the mind. This game was petering out until the 72nd minute when Paul Mason gave Town the lead having been assisted by Micky Stockwell.

Nine minutes later, we saw a goal that had Maradona similarities. Not only was Stockwell of a similar build to the Argentinian, but his 81st minute goal showed some footwork on the edge of the area that Maradona himself would have been proud of. Stockwell rode the challenges before firing across Hans Segers to inflict the Dons' first home defeat of the season upon them.

It would be the following March before Town were shown live again as Sky selected the FA Cup fifth round replay at home to Wolverhampton Wanderers for viewing. The visitors had future Town defender Mark Venus in their starting XI, while future Portman Road boss Paul Cook came on as an 80th minute substitute.

The tie looked as good as over before half-time. Wolves had cantered into a two-goal lead thanks to goals by Lee Mills in the eighth minute and Andy Thompson seven minutes before the break. A minute after the restart, Town were back in the tie when Steve Palmer scored. But Wolves resisted everything that Town threw at them and advanced to the quarter-final stage.

Our final live game of 1993/94 would be our last home match of the season, against Manchester United. We went into the game on the back of a run of nine winless games that had stretched across seven weeks and saw us languishing 17th and three places above the relegation zone.

Our final games were against the Premier League's top two teams. United were already assured of the title, and our final game was to come six days later at the already confirmed runners-up, Blackburn Rovers.

Chris Kiwomya gave us strong hopes of avoiding relegation when putting Town ahead after 19 minutes. Eric Cantona equalised for United nine minutes before half-time and once Ryan Giggs edged his side in front two minutes into the second half, we never really looked like getting anything out of the game and lost 2-1.

Phil Whelan suffered a broken leg which happened right in front of my row b seat and was a sickening remarkable sight.

Back in the day, it was customary to invade the pitch on the final whistle of the final home game of the season. This proved to be the last time this happened at Portman Road.

As was the norm, thousands of Town fans ran on to the pitch and headed to the away fans where for 20 minutes or so, there was the usual slinging of verbal abuse to one another.

When it came to finally leave the ground, it became a stark reality that we still had a chance of being relegated. In the event we drew 0-0 at Blackburn the following week. This result, coupled with Mark Stein scoring for Chelsea in injury time against Sheffield United, ensured that we were to remain in the Premier League for another season. We survived by one point at the expense of the Blades.

The 1994/95 season saw Town screened live on four occasions with the first three games being the final trio of live matches in the John Lyall era of management. All four ended in defeat and the headline player proved to be John Wark. It was also the season that we were relegated for the first time from the Premier League. It was also the first season in a run of 11 seasons where I would not miss a single home game.

Having beaten Norwich twice in both live games shown to date, 19 September 1994 would be the date that the Canaries would win for the first time against us live on TV. A 2-1 defeat at Portman Road in front of a crowd of just 17,406 sent Ipswich fans home in a miserable mood.

Wark scored an equalising goal on the stroke of half-time, but it proved to be to no avail when Norwich scored their winner eight minutes after the break. This game also saw midfielder Steve Sedgley making his Ipswich debut.

Three weeks later, another Monday night live match saw us visit Coventry City. Wark was on target once more and again, on the stroke of half-time. Only this time it was an own goal to give Coventry the lead.

For the second time, future manager Paul Cook featured against Town on TV and on this occasion he played a full game and scored in the 76th minute to seal Coventry's win.

Defender Leo Cotterell made just the two substitute appearances for Ipswich, and this was his final outing when he came off the bench to replace Stuart Slater on 71 minutes.

Just six days later, a Sunday afternoon clash at home to Sheffield Wednesday was Sky Sports' choice to entertain the watching millions and again, Town conceded twice and lost in what proved to be Lyall's final live TV game.

Mark Bright gave the Owls a ninth-minute lead and Town equalised on 52 minutes through that man Wark once more. Just when we were hopeful of sealing a rare point, David Hirst scored a 90th-minute winner for Wednesday. Even the dismissal of their central defender Des Walker did us no favours. We slipped to 21st in the table and remained in the relegation zone for the rest of the season.

From Town's very first live TV game, that FA Cup success over Arsenal under the guidance of Sir Bobby Robson, to relegation in 1985/86, John Lyall had made sure that during his tenure, we had gone full circle in terms of success by leading us to promotion from the old Division Two in 1991/92. He left at the beginning of December 1994 with the team in a perilous position under the watchful eye of his assistant Mick McGiven. Lyall will always be remembered fondly by Ipswich fans and those of us around at the time will never forget that glorious 1991/92 season.

CHAPTER 2: PORTMAN ROAD TO WEMBURLEY

George Burley (60 games)

George Burley had been in the hotseat at Portman Road for three months by the time it came to his first live TV game. The fans, by now, had given up on survival. But blame could and would not be apportioned to Burley who was therefore in a no-lose situation. Two weeks before this TV fixture, I was present at Old Trafford as Manchester United had beaten us 9-0. I will never forget that day as an Ipswich fan and it was one of my lowest of lows.

A 3-0 defeat followed at Tottenham before the Sky cameras were ready to unleash another poor Ipswich performance at the worst place of all, away at Norwich City. Burley could not have wished for a defeat at a worse place for his first live game. Although as half-time approached, and with the score at 0-0, there may have been a small cause for optimism.

That is until John Wark became the first Ipswich player to be sent off in a live game, in the 44th minute. Norwich took full advantage after the break and ran out comfortable 3-0 winners.

The 1994/95 season concluded in relegation, and Town were condemned to second-tier football once more.

I completed my first season in a run of 11 in a row where I would not miss a game; that sequence would see me go on to attend 303 consecutive home matches.

Even the seven seasons beforehand dating back to 1987/88 saw me miss very few games – all due to valid reasons I will add. I had completed 1991/92 and 1992/93 too. I am gutted to have missed two home games in 1993/94, otherwise I could look back on 14 complete seasons.

Town's first live game of the 1995/96 season saw the Anglia TV cameras at Portman Road on 22 October 1995, for what was considered the new East Anglian derby for the season as Luton Town were the visitors.

In the Hatters ranks were two ex-Ipswich favourites, Gavin Johnson and Bontcho Guentchev, who both appeared as second-half substitutes. A David Oldfield goal after 24 minutes was enough to give Luton a 1-0 win as Town's transition to the Endsleigh League First Division was anything but smooth.

The game was to be the last time we were to see David Linighan in an Ipswich shirt and the attendance figure was a paltry 9,123. The defeat saw us drop to 14th place, while Luton would go on to be relegated that season, finishing bottom – just to compound that defeat further.

My only visit to Carrow Road up to this point of my time watching Ipswich had been a Hospital Cup game which Town won 4-0 in pre-season ahead of 1989/90.

With such a score and a packed away end, that was a wonderful day to remember, and it had me wondering for the next six years if it was always going to be that good at Norwich.

For me personally, it never got any better than that sunny day in 1989. It remains as the only time that I have seen Ipswich win there! It is also the first occasion I can recall meeting another Ipswich fan called Jason Bennett. For over 30 years now, Jason and I have been good mates. We have stood and sat with each other at Ipswich games ever since.

For my first meaningful visit to Carrow Road in November 1995, I made a weekend of it staying, at a friend's guest house in Great Yarmouth.

I took a train on the Sunday morning from there to Norwich and it was horrible. Just yellow and green everywhere I looked. In truth, the day got no better and in fact, it got much worse.

Jon Newsome had given them a ninth-minute lead and when Robert Fleck made it 2-0 on 71 minutes, it looked game over for us. As had become customary by now, John Wark scored, and we were back in it.

With a minute to go, a Town player was fouled in the penalty area and referee Kevin Lynch pointed to the spot. Wark placed the ball down and we were all expecting him to score (which he usually did from 12 yards) to earn a draw.

A good few seconds after the decision had been given, the linesman in front of us raised his flag. It caused confusion among all of us as to why it suddenly went up. Lynch came over and spoke to his assistant and the result was a free kick to Norwich for somebody offside.

TV replays were inconclusive, I later learnt, and to this day I still have no idea why such a decision was formed. That left a very sour taste in our mouths as we left the stadium. If only VAR was around in those days!

That defeat was to be our eighth live TV loss in a row, which remains our longest sequence of successive defeats in any period of all our live TV games.

After three defeats from his first three live games, Burley would have been relieved to stem the flow of poor results as next up on the box was a trip to Wolverhampton Wanderers covered by both ITV Anglia and ITV Central.

Mind you, it took a 90th-minute equaliser by Tony Mowbray to earn a share of the spoils. Ian Marshall had earlier given Ipswich the lead on the half-hour mark, only for Wolves to lead 2-1 going into the latter stages of the game thanks to two goals from Don Goodman. Lining up for the hosts was Mowbray's future central defensive partner and later his long-time assistant once Mowbray became a manager, Mark Venus.

What I recall most about this game was the first and last appearance for Ipswich for goalkeeper Fred Barber. Some of you might recall that when the teams emerged from the tunnel before kick-off, Barber ran on to the field sporting a mask.

Burley finally saw a first live TV win come his way at the fifth attempt, on Sunday 3 March 1996, with a 4-2 win at home to Leicester City. Town got off to a dream start, racing into a 3-0 lead inside the opening 13 minutes.

Wark was on target once again when opening the scoring on six minutes. Simon Milton doubled our lead on 11 minutes and just two minutes later, Ian Marshall scored his first goal of the afternoon.

Leicester threatened to stage a remarkable comeback when Iwan Roberts scored twice on 55 and 75 minutes. But Marshall made sure of the three points with a goal five minutes from time.

What sticks in my mind that day was that Leicester's Steve Claridge had his shorts on the wrong way round. This was picked up by the North Stand and as Claridge came down to our end to defend a corner, a chorus of 'He's got his shorts on, back to front' bellowed out from behind the goal.

Having gained a first win on TV, Burley struck gold once more in the next televised game with Norwich City once more the visitors on 14 April 1996.

Town went into this game sitting in fifth place and with just six games to go, a play-off place looked ever closer. The Canaries were just below mid-table and were ripe for picking off which Town duly obliged with a little help from a Norwich error.

Ian Marshall gave us the lead on 23 minutes, and all was going well for Town. The North Stand was rocking, and we then laughed as Jamie Cureton came off the bench in the 61st minute sporting green hair. A minute later, however, he equalised and was having the next laugh.

Then a truly magnificent moment occurred in the 86th minute which will never be forgotten. Norwich left-back Robert Ullathorne played an innocuous back-pass to Bryan Gunn. With James Scowcroft threatening to close him down, Gunn opted for a first-time clearance only for the ball to hit a divot leaving the goalkeeper with an air kick and the ball rolling into the back of the net. Cue pandemonium.

In what was not one of my finest moments as an Ipswich fan, I must admit to joining the hundreds of supporters who invaded the pitch. In those days away fans were in the upper Cobbold tier at both ends. I found myself on my knees bowing to them in appreciation of their wonderful gift.

Richard Appleby came off the bench for his first TV game but also to make the last of his four Ipswich appearances.

The final match of the season, at home to Millwall, had a lot riding on it for both teams, so much so that Anglia TV chose to show it live. Town were in sixth place knowing victory would seal a place in the play-offs, while Millwall needed a win to avoid relegation.

No goals scored meant that there was no reward for either side. James Scowcroft came agonisingly close to scoring for Town but saw his looping header come back off the post in the 74th minute.

With Leicester winning at Watford, we finished seventh and missed out on the play-offs by two points. Meanwhile, Millwall were relegated on goal difference with Portsmouth surviving. Millwall had led the table just five months earlier.

As mentioned above, the away fans were at both ends in the upper Cobbold stand. As we made our way out of the ground, we had to dodge seats and other missiles being thrown at us as clearly the Millwall fans were upset. Outside the ground was no better either with the sight of plenty of skirmishes. It was a depressing end to the season all round.

For many years, I would travel to away games on the Clacton supporters' branch coach which was fantastically organised by Jill. As an affiliated branch to the club, if you travelled on the coach it would also mean that your match ticket was booked, which was handy for going to the big grounds in our Premier League days.

I would board in Great Clacton, usually armed with a bag of food and drink and a copy of *The Sport*, which would be a source of entertainment for many at the back of the coach on our journey.

Pick-up stops would occur at Weeley, Elmstead Market, Colchester, Witham, Chelmsford, and Brentwood. By which time, we would have a full coach. Getting on first though meant we would commandeer the back seat.

I must mention 'naughty' Stuart Vernon who would join us at Witham. Nobody was safe once he was on board. It usually involved a peg and so often, wherever we were, you would see someone with a peg hanging off the back of their top. I must just say thank you to Stuart for all the laughs that he gave us for so many years.

One such trip was for the opening game of the 1996/97 season away at Manchester City, which was moved to a Friday night to become the first match screened live on the brand-new Sky Sports 3 channel.

This was also our first game wearing our new cream-and-black-striped away kit and Bobby Petta made his debut. A Steve Lomas goal after 25 minutes was enough to give City the win, despite them having Michael Frontzeck sent off with 25 minutes remaining, and we were faced with a long journey home feeling down.

The back of a coach on an away day can be quite a childish place at times. As we were leaving Manchester, there was a bottle fight between a couple of the lads where they were hitting one another over the head with empty plastic bottles.

This was somehow distracting the driver who got on his microphone and kindly asked the pair to stop. We all know that this would not deter them, and the two lads continued. The next thing to happen was that the coach ground to a halt and an angry driver marched his way down the aisle. When he got to the back, he asked whoever the culprits were to stop, citing that it was something he did not need with a long journey home.

Someone then remarked with, 'No, but you need a dentist though!' The driver had a couple of teeth missing but it was a remark that we really did not need to hear at that point. We were lucky to get home at all in the end. The remark did make us laugh though and the defeat seemed not so bad.

The first home game to appear live on television that season came on 20 September 1996, as Charlton Athletic were the visitors. A week before this match, both Stuart Niven and Richard Naylor made their Town debuts in a 3-1 win away at Sheffield United. This would be Naylor's first of the 50 live TV matches that he featured in for Town, and Niven's last appearance overall for the club.

Charlton opened the scoring through Bradley Allen after 34 minutes, a lead which they held until ten minutes after the break. Then the game turned on its head. Jamie Stuart tripped Town's Claus Thomsen on the edge of the area and was sent off for his efforts. Steve Sedgley curled in the resultant free kick to draw Town level and then Alex Mathie scored the winner with the first of just the two goals he would score on TV. The win lifted Town to sixth in the table, but a run of six winless games sent us tumbling back down again.

During this run, the next live TV instalment of the East Anglian derby arrived as Town fell to a 3-1 defeat at Norwich on 11 October. It was the first time that the sides had clashed following Ian Crook's proposed move from Norwich to Ipswich in the summer beforehand.

Crook, for those of you who do not know, was photographed with an Ipswich scarf above his head as the deal was all but done, but returning Norwich boss Mike Walker convinced him to stay in Norfolk.

Two Andy Johnson goals had given Norwich a 2-0 lead before Danny Sonner reduced the arrears less than a minute after the restart. John Polston added a third midway through the second half to give Norwich a comfortable 3-1 win.

It would be a full six months before we saw Ipswich live again and it was for the return fixture against Norwich at Portman Road. By the time this game was upon us, Town's season had taken a dramatic turn for the good. Having fallen as low as 19th in mid-November, we came into this one in the top six and once again, in the hunt for a play-off place.

Goals by Mauricio Taricco (32) and Paul Mason (42) gave us a much-deserved 2-0 win on a calm Friday night. I recall the ground shaking in a tremendous, vibrant atmosphere when Taricco scored past Ipswich's future number one Andy Marshall, and it was in the dying embers of the celebrations for that goal that we were at it again as Mason scored his 15th of the season. We were now up to fifth place and with just three games to go, we were once more dreaming of the play-offs.

We went on to finish the 1996/97 season in fourth place, six points behind runners-up Barnsley. This meant a two-legged semi-final against Sheffield United would decide who would go to Wembley for the play-off final.

We had only ever reached the play-offs once previously. Ten years earlier, we lost a semi-final to Charlton after they had beaten us 2-1 at The Valley following a 0-0 stalemate at Portman Road. I had been present for the home leg that year and was not ready for heartache again this time.

I attended the 1-1 draw at Bramall Lane in the first leg, with Micky Stockwell equalising a goal scored by United's Jan Åge Fjørtoft. The tie was delicately balanced, and we had a crucial away goal in the bag.

I suppose it is fair to say that in general, Ipswich play-off games are never short of drama and this second leg proved to be just that. But before I get on to the game itself, there is a story to be told about the tickets we obtained.

Our season tickets were not valid for this game and the group that I would watch matches with those days had to buy tickets. I was left in charge to obtain them. Back then, the club had agents selling tickets on their behalf, typically newsagents dotted around many areas of East Anglia.

We had one such newsagent to supply us in Clacton-on-Sea. They would normally get ten tickets to sell, and I snapped up at least half of those on this occasion. It was only when I got home and opened the envelope that I discovered that they were tickets in the Churchmans Stand. This may not seem much of a drama as after all, at least we had tickets for the big game. But we were North Stand boys, and we were accustomed to being part of a raucous atmosphere.

So, Churchmans it was and not only was it my first experience in there as an all-seated stand, but it remains to this day the only time I have sat in the lower tier. I have only sat in the upper tier when the old North Stand was demolished and being rebuilt and on one occasion when a friend had complimentary tickets given to him by an ex-player.

Petr Kachuro gave the Blades a ninth-minute lead despite our protests after a linesman deemed the ball had crossed the line after crashing down off the underside of the crossbar.

United's goalkeeper Alan Kelly then got injured and despite lengthy treatment he continued at less than full mobility.

Town took advantage and James Scowcroft equalised on 32 minutes. Ipswich then dominated the second half and deservedly took the lead with 17 minutes remaining through Niklas Gudmundsson. It was at this point that although you could take the boys out of the North Stand, you could not take the North Stand out of the boys. Having seen a few exuberant fans come on to the pitch down the other end, my friend Kevin thought he would do the same from our end. He had only got one leg over the wall when he realised that it would not be a wise thing to do. Moments later, he felt the hands of a couple of stewards on his back and was swiftly removed from the ground.

I started to think that Kevin was going to miss the moment that we were going to get to Wembley. But four minutes later, the bubble of that dream was pricked and burst.

Sheffield United substitute Andy Walker had only been on the pitch for nine minutes before he equalised, and with no further goals either in 90 minutes or after extra time, the Blades progressed to Wembley on away goals to face Crystal Palace.

That night hurt. We were so near yet so far. It was a quiet journey home. For me personally, it was my seventh semi-final heartache as an Ipswich fan. In my time to that point, we had lost an FA Cup semi-final to Manchester City, League Cup semi-finals to Liverpool and Norwich, a Full Members' Cup semi-final to Blackburn, an Anglo-Italian Cup semi-final to Port Vale and now two play-off semi-finals.

Little did I know that night that there would be a lot more heartache to come further down the years.

The first live game of the 1997/98 season proved disastrous all round for Town. It was our next visit to Carrow Road on Friday, 26 September – the day after my 26th birthday. I was hoping for a lovely belated present with an Ipswich win to send me into a weekend of celebrations.

But the first 15 minutes told us all present that it was not going to be our night. Firstly, Darren Eadie gave Norwich an eighth-minute lead and then seven minutes later, James Scowcroft went down in worrying fashion after clashing heads with team-mate Matt Holland. For six minutes Scowcroft laid motionless on the ground and there were concerned looks among the Town faithful. He was stretchered off wearing a neck brace.

To compound the misery of the night, in attempting to head clear a free kick from Eadie, Tony Mowbray's nod-down deflected off the shins of Jason Cundy and into the net for an own goal.

Mark Stein pulled a goal back 17 minutes from the end, heading home David Kerslake's inch-perfect cross from the right. We almost snatched a draw but Andy Marshall made two excellent saves at the death from Mowbray and if memory serves me correctly, Bobby Petta.

It was not to be, and I once again left Carrow Road on the back of a defeat.

Our next live game on 9 November saw yet another sickening injury when we played 'Norwich of the North' Sheffield United at Portman Road. Town conceded yet another early goal with Gareth Taylor putting the visitors ahead on nine minutes, a lead they held until the break. Five minutes after the restart, Andy Legg drew Ipswich level.

Then United lost goalkeeper Simon Tracey after he cracked his ahead against a post. With no substitute goalkeeper in those days, Don Hutchinson took over in goal and substitute Mitch Ward scored in the 79th minute to put the Blades back in front.

With three minutes remaining, Neil Gregory, who had only been on the pitch for eight minutes after replacing Alex Mathie, scored to earn Town a point. In doing so, Gregory became the first Ipswich substitute to score in a live TV game.

The point did little to cheer us up as we had been languishing in the bottom four for much of the season to date. It was all quite different from the season before when we had reached the play-offs.

If ever you think a season is over by Christmas, never give up hope. After that draw with Sheffield United, Town then lost only two games by the time we next appeared live on TV. We had gone from 16th on Boxing Day to sitting fifth on 5 April 1998. The venue of the next live game would be the City Ground, home of Nottingham Forest, who were looking to inflict a double over Town having been the victors in one of those two defeats after the Sheffield United game.

After half-time had reached us with no goals, our good run looked like it might continue when James Scowcroft scored just a minute or so after the restart.

However, Forest had other ideas and two goals in five minutes turned the game around. Colin Cooper scored first, tapping home a rebound after Richard Wright's fantastic save to deny Pierre van Hooijdonk, and then van Hooijdonk fired home the winner but not before Steve Chettle cleared off the line from Alex Mathie in the dying seconds.

Town's 16-match unbeaten run had ended. Forest went on to win the league by finishing three points clear of Middlesbrough.

As for ourselves, we were certainly in for an exciting end to the season.

After that defeat to Forest, we followed with a 0-0 draw at home to Tranmere Rovers before winning our final five matches.

Our penultimate game, at home to Sunderland on 28 April, was the last of our league matches to be screened live that season.

For only the third time in the league in 1997/98, a crowd of over 20,000 turned up. Ipswich's place in the play-offs was already confirmed and Sunderland could still gain automatic promotion, which would only come with victory in this game, and at Swindon on the last day.

To put the attendance figure into context, our average in the league for that season stood at 14,893 and was the 31st-ranked of all 92 clubs. It was also the season in which only 8,938 fans attended the 2-0 defeat at home to Stockport County in the November. This was often cited as being a game that if you had attended, then you were classed as a die-hard with the phrase, 'I was at the Stockport game' often muted.

Sunderland had in their line-up Chris Makin, the full-back who would join Town further down the line in his career.

After a goalless first half, Matt Holland scored his first live TV goal for Ipswich on 48 minutes and Alex Mathie sealed the win with Town's second on 61 minutes after he had not long seen a penalty saved by Lionel Pérez.

This was the first defeat that Sunderland had encountered in 14 matches, and they missed out on automatic promotion at the expense of Middlesbrough by a single point. The question on our minds at this point was would we be facing them again in just a few weeks in the Wembley play-off final.

First, we had to overcome Charlton Athletic who we faced for a second time in the play-offs, with the first leg staged at Portman Road on Sunday, 10 May 1998.

What was served up between two footballing teams was a cagey affair, full of niggly tackles, and little of the beautiful game on offer. Not surprising given the prize that was at stake.

Nine bookings, a sending-off and an own goal were about all this repulsive affair could muster. Jamie Clapham was the unfortunate man to score at the wrong end when diverting a low cross past Richard Wright in front of us North Stand hopefuls. In truth, it was another of those days where we were never going to score, even when Danny Mills was sent off for the Addicks with 16 minutes remaining.

The second leg on the following Wednesday evening was a chance for us to avenge defeat but we lost 1-0 and for the eighth time, I was suffering again from the heartache of a semi-final loss.

The 1998/99 season kicked-off with Town attempting once more to get out of the division, either via the play-offs or otherwise. For the fans, we were hoping for it to be a case of third time lucky.

Our first game of the season was away at Grimsby Town on Sunday, 9 August. Let me tell you about my trips to Grimsby.

The first time I visited Blundell Park was on Easter Monday in 1996. Tony Vaughan was sent off after 36 minutes, and Clive Mendonca, who loved scoring against Town, scored a hat-trick. It was such an unpleasant experience all round that I vowed never to go again.

On Easter Monday the following year, Town were once more playing away from home and for the second year in a row, it was at Grimsby. And like most football fans that follow their team rigidly around the country, when we say we are never going to a particular place ever again, we often do.

So, off I went to Grimsby again, on the supporters' coach from Clacton, and this game practically mirrored the one that took place a year earlier. For Tony Vaughan's sending off in 1996, read James Scowcroft seeing red on this occasion and just a minute away from being the exact time for both red cards. Mendonca scored again, only this time just the once, and we lost 2-1. I have never been back to Grimsby since.

When we drew 0-0 there on the first weekend of 1998/99, it was somewhat of a relief. It also proved to be the only 0-0 game of the opening weekend of the Nationwide League. Four things helped our cause this time. Firstly, I was not there; secondly, there was no Clive Mendonca for Grimsby; thirdly, we kept 11 players on the pitch for the entirety of the game; and lastly, Kingsley Black missed a penalty in the first couple of minutes as Richard Wright saved his spot-kick.

In the days leading up to the game, both Wright and Kieron Dyer had been called up for an England get-together by Glenn Hoddle. As for the match itself, there was a Town debut for Marco Holster.

I had a few moments distraction from watching on TV at a friend's house. They had a pond at the bottom of their garden and my two young sons were outside playing. I will not name which one through not wanting to embarrass him, but one of them fell in the pond and came indoors completely soaked. It gave me a good reason to ignore the game for a short while.

Before August was over, we were back on Sky again. Our opening three fixtures of the new season had seen three 0-0 draws achieved and it was not to get any better when we hosted Sunderland.

Two goals in the first half effectively killed the game off as Paul Mullin scored on 12 minutes and then Kevin Phillips was on target after 36 minutes. Phillips was a player who came so close to joining Town. This was not the last time that we would regret the decision that he chose to go to Sunderland instead. We had now stretched our goalless run in the league to 575 minutes.

In the era of the late 1990s, if there was ever a season that we were not playing Norwich live on TV, then you could almost guarantee that we would be playing Sheffield United instead. I have already dubbed them the 'Norwich of the North' and some of our recent meetings had the feel of a derby type game.

Five days before Christmas Day, it was a Sunday afternoon trip to Bramall Lane and for once, we had plenty to cheer.

Seventeen-year-old Titus Bramble was making his Ipswich debut, while Lee Hodges came off the bench to make his fourth and final appearance for the club.

After no goals were scored in the first period, Town took the lead in the 49th minute through Samassi Abou. This was the only TV game the man from Côte d'Ivoire would play for Ipswich and he is one of only seven Ipswich players to score in the one TV game that they were to appear in. For the record, the other six are Roger Osborne, Tony Humes, Mark Stein, Andy Legg, DJ Campbell, and Andros Townsend.

Paul Devlin came off the bench for United in the 74th minute and took just four minutes to equalise. As the game reached the 89th minute, Richard Naylor stepped up to score the first of his seven live TV goals for Ipswich and a 2-1 win was the perfect early Christmas present for Town fans. It was also Naylor's 50th appearance for the club and was Town's fifth away win in seven away games. We were sitting pretty in second place and went into the new year full of hope that this season would finally be the one.

After the next four games had seen us win, lose, win, lose, we headed into our next live game in mid-January with a third TV date with Sunderland at the Stadium of Light.

Not only did Jim Magilton make his debut in this game, but it was also the first of his 54 live TV appearances for Ipswich, a figure that still stands as the record at the time of publication.

For once, Kevin Phillips failed to find the net against us, but strike partner Niall Quinn did so, twice. His brace came within a six-minute spell between the 27th and 33rd minutes and with the writing on the wall as far as any hope of winning this game was concerned, Matt Holland pulled a goal back just three minutes later. But there was to be no further scoring and a third successive defeat saw us drop to fifth place.

In the process, Sunderland stretched their lead at the top of the table over Bradford City to ten points.

A further three months would pass by until in mid-April, Sky Sports selected our Tuesday night home game against Stockport County for live viewing. An unusual fixture it would seem to screen, but by now we were pushing hard for promotion in third place.

For some of us in the stands, we were trying to erase the memory of Stockport's last visit, which was that game I mentioned in November 1997 when fewer than 9,000 fans had turned up.

On this night there was almost double that in attendance as promotion fever started to rise. Our line-up was boosted by the return of Kieron Dyer who started his first game for seven weeks after recovering from a cracked fibula.

The only goal came six minutes before half-time and it was one of real quality by Jim Magilton that saw us regain the second automatic promotion place. His fierce drive from 30 yards tucked inside the near post. We now held a three-point lead over Bradford with both teams having three games remaining.

Four days later, we inexplicably lost 2-1 at home to Crewe Alexandra who started the day bottom of the league. Bradford won to go above us on goal difference.

Two games to go and Sky were as excited as we were at the prospect of promotion finally being achieved as they were to screen both of our remaining matches. I would not say that I was excited. I was a bag of nerves in truth.

It was becoming ingrained within every ounce of feeling that I have ever held for Ipswich Town that we do not have an exceedingly high success rate with the big occasions. Yes, we had won the UEFA Cup in my time of supporting the club, but remember that up to this point those eight semi-final defeats were weighing heavy on my urges and thirst for success.

First up was our final away game of the season, at Birmingham City on the first Sunday of May. Brum had their own aspirations of reaching the play-offs and would not be an easy nut to crack. And it was Paul Furlong who scored the only goal of the game on the hour to give City the win.

Here we go again. Everything was falling apart, and I was in mental agony. Automatic promotion was fading and yet again, it would be another lottery of the play-offs to contend with. That was unless we won our final game of the season at home to Sheffield United and Bradford had to either lose or draw away at Wolves.

I will never forget the day when a near-capacity packed Portman Road, in desperate hope of beating a Sheffield United side that a year before, had inflicted so much pain on us all. I was worried sick yet I was embodied with excitement. I was an emotional wreck that only football fans could experience on days like this.

Part of me wanted to be at home watching on Sky, but I knew that I would have been hidden behind the sofa for much of the game. I do not think that I was as fearful when watching *Texas Chainsaw Massacre* on video when I was about 12 years old. I still get nervous watching Ipswich on occasions now I am in my 50s.

The sun was shining and the ground was buzzing. If this was going to be our day then it would be an amazing one to be part of. Remember, this was in the day before mobile phones. Instead there were plenty of fans with earphones firmly in place, keeping track of what was going on at Wolves. Could they help us by at least holding Bradford to a draw?

As first halves go, we were simply superb. Despite United hitting the post twice, we were 3-0 up at the break. Jim Magilton, James Scowcroft, and Kieron Dyer all scored to make sure that we were doing our part and 50 per cent of our nerves could now relax. In fact, at the time of Magilton's goal, Wolves were leading Bradford 1-0 and automatic promotion was ours. Bradford then equalised and it was tension time again.

Then disaster, Bradford went 2-1 up and the United fans were taunting us with chants of 'you're not going up'. This was all too much.

Giorgios Donis pulled one back for the visitors just moments after he had hit the woodwork. The ground then fell silent, apart from the pocket of away fans, when news came through that Bradford had gone 3-1 up.

Robert Kozluk was sent off for the Blades before Richard Naylor scored a fourth in the 79th minute to secure a 4-1 win. In the meantime, Bradford missed a penalty, Wolves pulled a goal back and then a cheer circulated around Portman Road when we thought Paul Simpson had brought Wolves level five minutes from time. Instead, his late free kick struck the inside of a post and stayed out. We thought it had gone in and our triumphant cheers were soon drowned out by gasps of disbelief. Bradford held on to win 3-2.

The defeat for Wolves ensured Bolton made the play-offs and I am 100 per cent positive that the emotions of their supporters were an opposite to our feelings for achieving the same finish to the season. Yes, we had the advantage of playing the home leg second, but for now, our season had come to yet another disappointing end. We came so close to finally getting automatic promotion. How could the players lift themselves to go again when the fans were feeling rock bottom? We were soon to find out.

For the third year in a row, it was the play-offs once more to determine if Town were going to make it back to the Premier League. And on Sunday, 16 May 1999, we took on Bolton Wanderers in the first leg at the Reebok Stadium.

Sky Sports in those days, if memory serves me correctly, would show one leg from each tie meaning that the home game against Bolton would not be screened in front of millions anticipating if we would fail once more.

The away leg was heading for a goalless draw, and we would have all taken that heading back to Portman Road. That was until the 84th minute when Michael Johansen gave the Trotters the lead.

Town should have had a penalty as early as the sixth minute when David Johnson was fouled by Mark Fish inside the area and when that was not given, you could already sense that it was going to be another occasion where nothing would go our way.

Only once in the previous nine years had the team that came closest to gaining automatic promotion to the Premier League gone on to win the play-offs. It already felt like that we would not become the second club to do so.

The return leg at Portman Road on the following Wednesday was a night of high-octane drama. Going into the final minute, the score was 2-2 on the night and Bolton looked all but certain to win through 3-2 on aggregate.

Then in the dying seconds, Kieron Dyer looped in a header to force extra time. Bolton then equalised and in the 117th minute, Matt Holland scored his second of the night to put us 4-3 ahead.

The final three minutes saw the home crowd baying for just one more goal. It would not come, and the tie finished 4-4 on aggregate with Bolton going through on the away goals rule. Not only had we come within a whisker of automatic promotion that season, but we had also been so close to finally getting to Wembley.

Talk about a double blow. I felt we were cursed forever, and I would never see a moment of glory again as an Ipswich fan. That night, Kieron Dyer trudged slowly towards the North Stand where he passed his boots over to a fan in the knowledge that he would no doubt be leaving his club (he went on to join Newcastle United) without the success he craved as much as every one of us. We all felt his pain that night.

After this tie, Town chairman David Sheepshanks lobbied the league to get rid of the away goals rule in the play-offs. This motion was passed, and therefore Ipswich became the last club to lose in such a way.

I look back and think how we failed by the thinnest of margins on three fronts that season. I also endured my ninth semi-final defeat. Surely the luck had to change at some point. Would it be in 1999/2000?

The end of the 1990s and going into the 2000s saw Ipswich play live on TV more than any other team. It was testament to how good we were, and Sky thought that we were fair value for their viewers. Either that or they just enjoyed watching us build up to being promotion candidates and falling at the penultimate hurdle.

The 1999/2000 season saw no fewer than ten games screened live. The first of those came in the first midweek of the new season as we visited Griffin Park, home of Brentford, for a League Cup first round, first leg tie.

The trouble with away games in London is that you tend to want to make a day of it, especially for an evening match. And by the time kick-off comes around, you have either had too much of an enjoyable time in the capital, had too much to drink, or both. And as for my travelling companion Jason and I, we became victims of exactly this.

Having arrived in central London around lunchtime, we took in a bit of sightseeing before settling down in the Leicester Square area. A few drinks later, and more sights to be seen had us wondering whether to go to the game, which by now had become a bit of an inconvenience to our fun.

But that was what we were there for and off we went to Griffin Park. After an hour, and with the score at 0-0, concerns crept in that Brentford might hold on for a little bit of a shock draw. Then David Johnson scored followed by a second from Jamie Clapham and Town won 2-0. Hermann Hreidarsson lined up for Brentford in this game.

The game just did not live up to how the rest of the day had been. Jason and I figured that we had plenty of time to get the last train home back from Liverpool Street to Colchester, where my car was parked. We returned to Leicester Square for one last shenanigan to round the day off. However, we were having too much fun before realising that we might struggle to make catching the last train.

Sure enough, when we got to Liverpool Street, it had gone. A guard placed us on a train that was terminating at Chelmsford, but that was the closest he could get us to home.

While we sat waiting for the train to leave, we could hear a group of fans on our platform singing football songs. The same guard who had dealt with us stopped next to our carriage, and told this group that two more of their 'hooligan' group were in the carriage with the same problem. They were Ipswich fans who had a similar idea to us and likewise, had missed the last train.

So, on they got, and we all made it as far as Chelmsford. I then had to use my negotiating skills with a taxi driver to take us to Colchester before about seven of us crammed into my car. This whole group who joined us all lived in Clacton and wanted me to give them a lift home.

If you are reading this, Jason, I have left parts of the day out for our own sake!

Our first live league game of the season was a magnificent sight. Nothing too exciting about Swindon Town away on a Sunday afternoon in mid-August, you might think. But with Town fans packing out both ends and in fine voice, this was one of those great away days. We were excellent that day. And the players were not too shoddy either, winning 4-1. We had won 6-0 at the same venue the season before.

Mind you, we did not really see that coming as half-time approached. Giuliano Grazioli had given the hosts the lead on 16 minutes, and it was not until a minute before the break that we scored our first through David Johnson.

We then turned on the style in the second half as Richard Naylor scored twice and Johnson scored his second and Town's fourth with 16 minutes to go.

Having beaten Nottingham Forest on the opening day of the season, and then following up the win over Swindon with a victory at Bolton Wanderers, a draw at Sheffield United and a comprehensive 6-1 win over Barnsley, we spent the whole of August sitting at the top of the table believing that this really could be our year.

A day after my 28th birthday, on 26 September, we would be on Sky for the third time already that season. It would be fantasy stuff these days to be playing Manchester City in a league match at all. Beating them live on TV is another matter altogether. That is exactly what we did that night.

The visitors had two future Ipswich players in their ranks as both Kevin Horlock and Mark Kennedy started for Joe Royle's side. David Johnson gave Town the lead two minutes before the interval and when Shaun Goater equalised for City five minutes into the second half, one could be forgiven for believing that these two heavyweights of the division would cancel one another out.

But nobody had the foresight of expecting full-back Gary Croft to produce a winner midway through the half on what was his Ipswich debut. We were to end September in second place in the league.

It would be the beginning of December before we would appear on TV again, by which time we had slipped to fourth place. A visit to Nottingham Forest came at a suitable time for us as they were on a run of five defeats in six games and were with just three wins in 16.

A close encounter was settled by Matt Holland's 79th-minute winner when he swept home from close range after veteran goalkeeper Dave Beasant, 40, had saved David Johnson's header.

In the Forest line-up that day was striker Stern John who would later go on to play for Town.

A break from league action saw Town's next live game feature a third round FA Cup tie when we hosted Premier League Southampton in an unusual third round slot in mid-December.

One goal was enough to see Southampton advance through to round four courtesy of a 40th-minute header from Dean Richards. With cup competitions now out of the way before the turn of the year, Town really could throw everything at the old 'concentrate on the league' mantra.

It would be over two months before we saw Ipswich on TV once more. A visit to St Andrew's, and Birmingham City on a Sunday afternoon being Sky's preferred option for the weekend.

By now, Ipswich were on a run of 17 league games unbeaten that included ten wins which saw us sitting in second place.

This would be a difficult game, I recall, given that Birmingham were also in the top six. Our cause was not helped when Tony Mowbray dived full-length to header an own goal after 17 minutes, but David Johnson equalised on the stroke of half-time and 1-1 is how the game finished.

The extension to 18 games unbeaten was the best record in the country at the time and only league leaders Charlton Athletic were in better current form.

If such a run was getting us carried away, finally believing that this would be our year, then we should have known better. The result at Birmingham sparked a sequence of five games without a win including defeats at home to Portsmouth and Norwich and a loss at Wolves. Despite this, we had only slipped one place to third going into April with just over a month and seven games remaining.

An away game at West Bromwich Albion on 4 April, would be our next appearance on Sky. After getting the season back on track with wins over Tranmere Rovers away and Fulham at home, a win at struggling Albion seemed a good opportunity to cement ourselves in the leading pack further.

We fell behind to a goal by Lee Hughes in the 43rd minute before Matt Holland brought us level on 68 minutes and the final whistle came with no further scoring. A chance to reclaim second spot had gone begging. In fact, we were now down to fourth. Another major concern for Town fans was that the goals had dried up for David Johnson.

Yes, he was our leading marksman at this stage with 17 goals, but only three of those were scored in his last 17 appearances.

Three weeks after that game at West Brom, the Sky cameras were back at Portman Road as we welcomed Crystal Palace on Tuesday, 25 April.

Prior to this game, the worries over Johnson's goalscoring form had evaporated. He had scored in two of the games sandwiched between that game at The Hawthorns and the visit of Palace. And once again, he was on target to score the only goal of the game in the 26th minute to see off a resolute Eagles outfit.

The win saw us close the gap on second placed Manchester City to two points with two games to play.

Unlike the previous season, there was no television showdown in either the penultimate or final games of the season. Quite bizarre really when you think about what was riding on the final game after Town had won their last game of the season 3-1 at champions Charlton Athletic.

For the second season in a row, we went into the final game knowing that a victory coupled with a result elsewhere would see us automatically promoted.

We had to beat Walsall, which we did, 3-0, while Manchester City had to fail to win at Blackburn Rovers. And just like a year before, momentarily, results were going our way and we occupied the second automatic promotion spot.

But alas, City turned their game around to clinch promotion, Walsall were relegated due to our win over them, and it is fair to say that there was not one of the 21,908 fans at Portman Road who would have left the ground happy.

For the fourth year in a row we had to settle for the play-offs, and for the second year in a row the opposition would be Bolton Wanderers. By now, the familiarity of the lottery that is the play-offs had no doubt bred contempt among us Ipswich fans. The feeling was to treat the upcoming two games against Bolton with total disdain.

In my introduction of this book, I mentioned some regrets along the way of supporting Ipswich Town and one has lived with me ever since – the first leg at the Reebok Stadium.

The summer of 2000 was a horrible time in my personal life. I had no desire to go to any of the play-off games. And by not being present to watch our Marcus Stewart-inspired comeback from two goals down in that first leg, I am forever feeling haunted.

I chose instead to play for my Sunday morning football team in a run-of-the-mill league game. When we congregated at what was our usual Sunday drinking hole after our matches, I had made it just in time for the 1pm kick-off where the match was being shown on a giant screen.

I did not feel entirely comfortable watching the game at all, let alone in a pub full of people who were not Ipswich fans. I have never been one to watch football in pubs if I can help it, especially for big tournaments like the World Cup.

My team-mates were mostly West Ham fans, and they hated Ipswich. By the time Bolton were 2-0 up after the 26th minute they had boundless joy in mocking me and telling me how Ipswich had bottled the play-offs again.

My frazzled mental state could not take any more and I just got out of the place. This of course meant that I went on to miss two incredible Stewart goals that dragged us back into the tie. I was guessing later that day, that those team-mates of mine were no longer laughing.

They were the first live TV goals that Stewart would score for Ipswich in his third on-screen appearance for us. What an incredible player he was. He was just so clever and was one of the best strikers of his generation.

Manuel Thétis played his last game for the club in this game while David Johnson sustained a neck injury that we all thought that it might have made him a doubt for the return leg (he made it in the end). Tony Mowbray was another to leave the field through injury, but like Johnson, Mogga was fit for Portman Road three days later. To get out with a 2-2 draw gave us all hope for the return leg at Portman Road and Stewart's goals were a fitting way to mark Town's 50th live TV game.

It is just as well that the second leg was not live on TV and therefore a feature for this book. I could have written a whole chapter on that game alone. But suffice to say, we finally came through and at last, after three previous seasons of failure, we were going to Wembley – or as it became commonly known at the time, WemBurley.

My continued poor state of mind meant that I did not want to go to that second leg against Bolton. I was in a right state mid-afternoon about not wanting to be there. But I forced myself to go. At least by being there, I had no need to add further regret to the list. I was certainly in a happy place on the pitch after the game joining in with the 'que sera, sera' songs.

It took a meeting of the Clacton branch of Ipswich supporters to work out how we were going to get our tickets for the final and ensuring that we could sit with as many of our friends and relatives as possible.

I do regret to a degree not going independently on the train and taking in even more of the atmosphere, but I had my brother Shaun with me on the coach and we can remember this day together forever.

Our coach journey down the A12 was a calm affair and everyone seemed in a relaxed mood. That was how I remained right up until kick-off. Even these days, I am a nervous fan at times. A standard league game can get my nerves wrangled. I certainly cannot listen to matches on the radio and prefer keeping up to date via Twitter when I am not present.

But this was a remarkable day in many ways. The walk down Wembley Way was just a sea of red and blue. Fans of both Ipswich and Barnsley mingled and enjoyed the occasion for what it was. I do not remember how early I made my way to my seat, but it was just the most incredible sight and atmosphere.

Ipswich fans were at the same end of that famous old stadium from when we won the FA Cup there some 22 years earlier. Among the group I was standing with were Don, Kevin, Pat, and Jill. I thought how they had been in that very end (if they were of course) to watch us win the FA Cup. The memories this day must have evoked for them, unbelievable. I wanted some memories of the incredible kind too.

When the players finally emerged from the tunnel, I had never heard a noise like it. The official attendance for that day was given as 73,427. I believe that over 40,000 were Ipswich fans. I had never stood with so many before or since in one place, with exception of the civic receptions at the town hall on the Cornhill in Ipswich following this final win and after winning the 1991/92 Division Two championship.

The beauty for me was that I was right in the middle behind the goal, 20,000 Town fans to my right, 20,000 Town fans to my left (plus those in front of and behind me of course).

When referee Terry Heilbron blew the first whistle, from out of nowhere, my nerves well and truly kicked in. I cannot explain the feeling that encapsulated me at that moment. How amazing would it be if we finally made it back to the Premier League? What if we lost? Could I handle that? Within 90 minutes, I could be about to experience either one of the most precious moments of my life or one of the absolute cruellest.

Six minutes in, and with Barnsley attacking the goal down our end, Craig Hignett tried a speculative effort from about 30 yards which cannoned off the crossbar, struck the diving Richard Wright's shoulder, and rebounded in for an own goal. Our end fell to a deafening silence that was punctured seconds later when the cacophony of noise from the Barnsley end had found its way to us.

Here we go again, I thought. After suffering nine semi-final heartaches, I suppose I was going to have to suffer the worst of all – a final heartache. I was shot to pieces and the game had only just started!

Then the moment we had all been waiting for – celebrating an Ipswich goal at Wembley and in my case, for the first time.

First-team coach Tony Mowbray was not involved with the playing squad at the start of the season. The semi-retired 35-year-old had stated that he would only play in an emergency. But after we had lost 4-1 at home to QPR in mid-October, he answered George Burley's SOS call to come in and shore up our defence. We went on to lose only five of the 35 league games in which he started for the rest of the season.

When he rose to head home Jim Magilton's cross at the far past to draw Town level after 28 minutes (just Mogga's second goal of the season), mayhem ensued among the delirious supporters. Bodies were all over the show. I was grabbed by friends, strangers, and my inner self. What a moment, the most raucous of goal celebrations I had ever experienced in my life. Now we were level, I wanted more.

But before I could even think about going through all those emotions again, Barnsley were awarded a soft penalty as Wright caught Hignett after the Barnsley man had knocked the ball past him and was already in dive mode. Hignett had played for the penalty – and won it. But Wright then became our latest hero, diving to his right to save Darren Barnard's effort and we went into the break on level terms.

Half-time is so often a hindrance at games. But boy, did I need this one. As I suspect the thousands around me and watching on TV at home all needed to take a breath and draw on some reserve energies. We had another 45 minutes of this to go – at least.

Then, my next Ipswich Town regret was to rear its ugly head and it is just the biggest one that still lives with me today.

I had been desperate to visit the loo at the break and figured I should wait until the queues had died down. I left it until around five minutes before the second half began thinking they would be empty. Wrong!

I joined a queue in the hope that it would not take too long to get back to my seat. Little did I realise that while waiting, the second half had restarted. And while in the toilets, Town would score again.

The roar of the noise that came down the stairwell, through the concourse and into the toilets was akin to a low-flying jet. It was a beautiful sound to hear but also, a sound that had me instantaneously thinking what I had done.

Upon coming out of the toilets, I saw two policemen and wandered over to them asking to be arrested. They laughed and asked why. I simply told them that I had just committed the biggest crime of my life, I had missed Ipswich score at Wembley.

I turned and walked back up to the top of the steps and just stood there admiring the bodies that were once again, falling over the top of one another. This was proper 'limbs' stuff.

Why is that when we are under the stand and miss a goal, the first thing people will tell you when you get back to your seat is 'we scored'? That is what I got upon my return. Yes! I know we scored. Make me feel worse why don't you!

I was of course delighted that we were now in front but I was also gutted to have missed Richard Naylor's goal, hey-ho.

Fortunately, I only had six minutes to dwell on the matter as Town scored a third, Marcus Stewart heading home Jamie Clapham's cross from the left. What emotions that were still left came to the fore once more and all the feelings of joy that emerged simply replicated what poured out of me for Mowbray's goal. Two headers I had seen us score and now, the Premier League dream was well and truly alive.

Stewart's goal was to later cost Ipswich £250,000. That was the sum owed to Huddersfield Town if we won promotion as part of the deal to sign him for £2.75m. At least Stewart had made a personal contribution to that add-on fee.

Just when we thought we might be cruising to victory, the final 15 minutes became the worst I have endured at a match.

Barnsley started to get back into the game and on 77 minutes, Mowbray's flailing arm caught Geoff Thomas and they were awarded a second penalty. This time, Hignett made no mistake from the spot to make it 3-2. Suddenly it was all Barnsley. Our end started to quieten. Nerves were getting the better of all of us

Then came a moment that stopped a beat or two in my heart. In the 83rd minute substitute Georgi Hristov met Thomas's cross, and the Macedonian's header seemed all but certain to go in from close range. As it was down the far end to us, it all happened in slow motion.

Then from a point-blank position, Wright pulled off a remarkable save to keep the ball out. I no longer wanted to be there at that point. I could not handle what was unfolding.

I wanted to be at home, in the kitchen making a cup of tea, or just doing anything else other than watching this game. My nerves were by now, simply gone. Could we hold on?

And then the most beautiful moment occurred in stoppage time. A substitute of our own became a hero for life for every Ipswich fan. Martijn Reuser had only been on the field for seven minutes when he latched on to Naylor's pass on the halfway line. As he ran directly towards us, he took an age to arrive on the edge of the area. We were roaring him on, could this be the moment to seal victory? When I saw him pull the trigger some 20 yards from goal, I thought no, why haven't you come forward a bit more? The next thing I saw was the net bulge. Oh lord, the hairs on my arm are standing up right now as I write this.

This was our moment. After three years of failed play-off bids, we were finally going up. I cannot remember who the first person I embraced was, but I held on to them for dear life. My physical energy had been drained and mental exhaustion momentarily kicked in. The relief was immense. I was metaphorically shedding all the tears of joy that one could release.

The final whistle sounded with equal relief but by then, the job had been done. The proudest moment of my Ipswich life was watching Matt Holland lift that trophy. As a captain, he deserved that moment. As did the whole squad. To a man, they will always be legends of Ipswich Town.

At this point, I can only write nothing but praise for the Barnsley fans. The majority had stayed behind and not only to show their appreciation to their beaten heroes, but also to afford applause to our own when doing our lap of honour. What a credit they were to their club, and I will always have a soft spot for them now.

The Wembley Stadium PA did a fantastic job in keeping the after-party going. M-People's 'Moving on Up', and Queen's 'We Are the Champions' got us all singing again. Reuser then came back out on to the pitch and was having the time of his life lapping all the adoration up.

We had been in the stadium long after the final whistle and when we eventually found the energy to make our way out back to the coach, I remember how surreal the atmosphere was outside. It was, in the main, quiet. None of us had anything left to give. The coach journey home was one of euphoria and full of conversation about being back in the big time. Bridges on the A12 had Town fans waving scarves and flags. I was having a small dose of what it must have been like for the fans and players coming back from Wembley in 1978.

That evening, I went to a local pub to celebrate with my good mates Don and Chris. Don had his boys Luke and Jordan with him too. It was yet another great moment.

Upon returning home, I then found myself sitting on my own and had gone from being around so many joyous people to being alone. I was sad to be alone, everything suddenly seemed so empty. I just stuck the TV on and watched ITV highlights of the game, imagining what those at home that afternoon had gone through watching the entire game on Sky Sports.

Just like those immortal FA Cup Final words by Peter Jones that I referred to earlier in the book, ITV commentator Peter Brackley had two of his own, 'Reuserrrrr; Premiership!'

We were back in football's promised land after a five-year absence. None of us really knew how we would fare in our first season back. Those three years of play-off defeats before finally winning through had set the grounding for George Burley's troops to go on and have a good season.

By the time we got to our first live TV game of 2000/01, I would say we were doing very well indeed. Six wins from our opening 13 league games saw us head into a Monday night clash at Coventry City sitting in sixth place.

At this point, my personal life had taken a turn for the better as five weeks before this game, I met Pegga who would in less than two years become my wife.

When I was 18 years old, I had designed an Ipswich Town-related tattoo. I always wanted to have it done but my phobia of needles put me off. Pegga has a tattoo and when I first saw it, I suppose it gave me the inspiration to finally get it done after 11 years of putting it off. And you know how it is when you first meet someone, it is the best time to show a bit of bravery and conquer your fears.

I took Pegga along with me to the tattoo shop, acted as brave as I could and now have the Suffolk Punch horse engraved on my leg with the wording 'Ipswich Town FC' above it and 'Ad Vitam Aeternam' below the horse. That translates to 'to life's eternity' or 'forever' if you like.

Then, feeling like a brave hero, I met up with two work colleagues at one of their houses to settle down and watch Ipswich hopefully round the day off with a win at Highfield Road.

In what was a poor game, I remember saying to my colleagues around five minutes from time that it was games like that which made me wish I had not got an Ipswich tattoo done.

And then in the 90th minute, Dutch duo Martijn Reuser and Fabian Wilnis combined for the latter to score a winner. I punched the air and screamed 'that is why I got my tattoo!' We found ourselves at the dizzy heights of fifth after that win.

A month later and in the period in between Christmas and new year, the Sky cameras came to Portman Road for the first time that season with Tottenham being the visitors.

We were in confident mood outside the ground before kick-off as Town fans were singing the 'Walking in a Stewart Wonderland' song. We were still in the top five and the season was going far better than anyone had dared to dream of.

To say that we had torn Tottenham apart is an understatement. A 3-0 win for us totally flattered them. Stewart got the ball rolling in the ninth minute when an exquisite cross from Matt Holland looked set for Stewart to blast home. But instead, it seemed to bounce off him and past a despairing Neil Sullivan.

Chances came and went, and we were really toying with Tottenham's beleaguered defence. But it would not be until the 62nd minute that we doubled our lead through the recently signed Alun Armstrong after strike partner Stewart had created the opportunity.

The icing on the cake came in the 88th minute. David Johnson, playing his final game for Town, passed to Jamie Clapham, who had only been on the pitch for three minutes, to fire home the third.

We were to end a simply impressive calendar year in third place of the Premier League. Life had gotten better ten-fold.

Two weeks later, we were live on Sky again as we were now becoming a team that were making those outside of the Ipswich bubble, sit up and take notice. How far could we push this fairytale of a season? The answer in short was – a lot further!

That said, a 2-0 win over Leicester City came in among a mini slump where we had lost 4-1 at Sunderland, and we were to lose our next game at Chelsea, again 4-1, before going down narrowly to Leeds United and Arsenal.

We left it late to see off Leicester. With ten minutes remaining and no goals scored, we feared that we would have to settle for a point. But Marcus Stewart was his consummate self to put us ahead and James Scowcroft made sure of the three points in injury time to preserve fourth place.

New England boss Sven-Göran Eriksson was at Portman Road and how Stewart never went on to play for for the national team remains a mystery to many Town fans. Remember, he was to end the 2000/01 season as the highest English goalscorer in the Premier League.

A further seven weeks would pass before Bradford City visited Portman Road for our next live game, on Sunday, 4 March. Since that win over Tottenham, we had lost in the fourth round of the FA Cup 1-0 away at Sunderland and lost a two-legged League Cup semi-final against Birmingham City for my tenth semi-final loss in my time as an Ipswich fan.

But unlike those play-off defeats, getting knocked out at the same stage in the League Cup did not seem to hurt as much. I was still disappointed of course but our league situation was intriguing to say the least. A place in Europe in the following season was now growing into a very distinct possibility.

When we had previously faced Bradford on 21 October, we came away from Valley Parade on the back of a 2-0 win which had sent us into the top six for the first time and here we were almost six months later, having not fallen outside that position all season. In fact, we were mostly fluctuating between fifth and third. This was a remarkable achievement for a newly promoted team.

Once again, we were to run out winners by a two-goal margin, this time 3-1. Benito Carbone had given the Bantams a first-half lead when netting after 27 minutes. Two goals from Martijn Reuser on 59 and 72 minutes edged us in front and victory was sealed when Mark Burchill scored on 75.

The game will be remembered for Hermann Hreidarsson's dive into the crowd. This happened on the other side of the North Stand goal to where my season ticket seat is, but I had a magnificent view of the Icelander's launch into the crowd. Somehow he managed to escape a yellow card from referee Andy D'Urso, but he did have the misfortune of having what he thought was his goal credited to Burchill.

The win moved us up to third, a position we were to hold for the next seven games until the last three matches of the season.

We only had to wait a further four weeks until our next live appearance. This time, it was away at Southampton for a Monday night fixture in what was the last game to be played under floodlights at The Dell. The date was 2 April 2001, and this was the first day of a special week in my life. I would be setting off on this date for a break at Center Parcs in Elveden with Pegga and her family.

Before we left home, I had my first phone call with Kevin Beattie, often cited as Ipswich's greatest ever player. The purpose of the call was to arrange to interview Beat for a forthcoming edition of the fanzine *Those Were The Days*. I was terribly excited to be speaking to such a legend. We fixed a date, and I was one happy chap leaving for our break.

When we arrived at our Center Parcs villa, I was delighted to find that we had Sky Sports available on our TV. That meant I could settle down in front of the box with my father-in-law-to-be Allen that night and watch Ipswich. What a cracking start to the holiday.

The game is remembered as the Marcus Stewart show as he scored Ipswich's first hat-trick live on TV in an enthralling 3-0 win. His first saw him latch on to a superb pass that split the Saints' defence for a tap home. Martijn Reuser came so close to adding a second when his audacious effort from 50 yards hit the crossbar.

Then a moment of Hermann Hreidarsson magic saw him burst down the wing, beat three defenders in the process, before crossing for Stewart to flick into the top corner for his and Ipswich's second.

Then when Matt Holland was adjudged to have been pushed in the area to earn Town a penalty, up stepped Stewart to score for his hat-trick and in the process became the Premier League's highest goalscorer to date that season.

My break had seen the perfect start. The following day it was Pegga's birthday, but I had to wait one more day for the exciting moment when I got on one knee and asked her to marry me. She said yes and the rest as they say is history. What a week that was. Town win on the box, Marcus Stewart scored a hat-trick, and I got engaged.

It was another four weeks before we were seen live on TV once more when we visited Charlton Athletic for a Monday night game on the last day of April.

We still occupied third place with three games to go and not only was the European dream now a real possibility, there were also hopes of qualification for the Champions League. Looking back at that today, it is incredible to think of what we achieved that season.

Charlton included Mark Fish in their starting line-up, the centre-back who would later play a half for Town before never being seen again. Another future Ipswich player, Kevin Lisbie, was among their substitutes and came on.

Charlton finished the season in a credible ninth place, so we knew that we had a strong task on our hands if we were to come away from The Valley with a victory.

Mathias Svensson gave the Addicks a 12th-minute lead that was to last for only eight minutes before Martin Reuser drew us level. Excitement levels rose among the watching Town fans and we continued to dare to dream.

But Richard Rufus put Charlton back in front on 57 minutes before Mark Burchill came off the bench to replace Stewart for what was to be the last of his seven Ipswich appearances.

The game was to finish 2-1 and results elsewhere over the weekend prior to this game meant that we were now down to fourth.

Two games to go and just one week later, the Sky cameras were back at Portman Road as we appeared live on TV in successive matches.

If you are of a youthful age reading this, what happened that night would seem incomprehensible now. We beat Manchester City to relegate them to Division One.

Just over 25,000 packed into Portman Road and for the last time, I took up my usual position at my season ticket seat in the old North Stand.

I had stood in this place from the mid-1980s until it became all-seated in 1992. I have been there ever since. But the old single-tier North Stand holds so many memories for all of us that experienced it. It was a sad moment when they knocked that down.

City, still under the guidance of Joe Royle, were to throw everything they could at us knowing that they needed to win both of their last games and hope results elsewhere would go their way to survive.

Shaun Goater, who had replaced Tony Grant as a half-time substitute, put City ahead with just 16 minutes remaining. While doing everything they could to save themselves, they were seriously trying to dent hopes of our own in our quest to qualify for the Champions League.

It took just four minutes for Matt Holland to equalise, and with five minutes remaining Martijn Reuser scored a winner. How we taunted the City fans with songs of 'going down' and such like while at the same time, rejoicing in the fact that whatever competition we were to qualify for, our European dream was achieved.

The final whistle saw huge celebrations in the North Stand and beyond and in a moment of romanticism, many Ipswich fans started to break their seats up for a keepsake to remind them of their second home. This included Jason and I doing the same.

We took our usual route down Portman Road after the game where an eagle-eyed policeman had spotted us walking along with square chests. When he asked what we had stuffed inside our jackets, I put on my best perplexed face and politely told him nothing. His quick search found us in possession of two seats (just the bit you sit on I will add), and he thought that we might be using them as a weapon rather than a memento so confiscated them.

Not to be denied, we were that summer afforded the opportunity by the club to purchase a seat, which I did. At least on this occasion I could obtain the full set of a seat including the frame which I could screw into the ground if I should choose to do so when I got it home. I never did and it has since been dumped. Should that be a further regret?

As the season ended, we drew 1-1 away at Derby County in our final game of the season and finished fifth. We had qualified for the UEFA Cup after finishing three points behind third-placed Liverpool with third being the lowest position that a team could finish in those days to qualify for the Champions League third qualifying round. For the record, Manchester United won the league and finished ten points above Arsenal. The gap between the Gunners and us was a mere four points. That is how close we came to finishing in the top two.

Leeds United were fourth, two points ahead of us and in another thought to stun the youngsters of today, we finished five points ahead of Chelsea.

That remarkable season ended with Marcus Stewart being the leading English Premier League goalscorer with his 19 league goals. Only Chelsea's Jimmy Floyd Hasselbaink scored more with 23.

The crowning moment of the season came when George Burley was announced as the Manager of the Year despite the achievements of Sir Alex Ferguson and Gérard Houllier. Burley guided our newly promoted side, who were tipped as relegation candidates, to that astonishing finish with a haul of 66 points – the highest total in Premier League history for a promoted team since the switch to a 20-team format.

A year after my first experience of seeing Ipswich win at Wembley, I now had the pleasure of watching Ipswich involved in European competition for the first time.

Between my first game in August 1978 and the last time that Ipswich had played in a European tie against AS Roma at Portman Road on Wednesday, 29 September 1982, I was of an age where I could only go to games when my dad took me.

It was always with a tinge of sadness that I had never witnessed a European match in person. Dad had taken me to a few night games during that time, but not to any of the games that we played against AZ Alkmaar (twice), SW Innsbruck, Barcelona, Norwegians Skeid of Oslo, Grasshoppers of Zürich, Aris Salonika, Bohemians Prague, Widzew Łódź, Saint-Étienne, FC Cologne, Aberdeen or AS Roma at Portman Road.

Approaching the age of 30 and always dreaming of attending such a game, I honestly felt that the time would never come in my life. But the chance to do so was to come soon. But before Europe, our first live TV game of the new season was a Premier League affair at home to Blackburn Rovers on Sunday, 16 September 2001.

Our opening four league games had returned just the one victory with two Finidi George goals inspiring us to a 3-1 home win over Derby County.

We went into the Blackburn game in front of the Sky cameras in mid-table.

Town took the lead on 15 minutes through Alun Armstrong who was well-placed to tuck home a rebound after George had seen an effort rebound off the crossbar.

Then a set of events conspired against Town as Blackburn drew level. Firstly, Corrado Grabbi clattered into Chris Makin and while we all expected Graham Poll to blow for a free kick, he allowed play to go on and Matt Jansen lobbed the out-rushing Matteo Sereni to score.

We then lost Armstrong to concussion after a collision with future Ipswich loanee Alan Mahon. Titus Bramble had missed a header in front of an almost open goal, and Richard Naylor failed to convert a one-on-one opportunity. When Pablo Couñago entered the field, Town looked more dangerous. We thought we had then scored a winner. Couñago held off a challenge from Henning Berg and laid the ball off to Marcus Stewart who fired over Brad Friedel. As the stadium erupted, Poll indicated that Couñago had pushed Berg and disallowed the goal. We knew at this point that it was simply not going to be our day and the game finished 1-1.

Four days later, and on the Thursday evening, came the moment I had waited over 23 years for – watching Town in Europe. It was not just me of course; thousands of others were in the same position and the cameras for this game ensured many others back home could settle down in front of BBC One to share the occasion too.

Torpedo Moscow were to be the first European opposition that I would see Town play against in the UEFA Cup, and we went into this game with an unbeaten home record in Europe stretching 25 games. So imagine how I felt when Town were losing 1-0 with five minutes to go. I thought typical, I wait all these years to see such a game and our record goes.

Torpedo scored their goal after 14 minutes, having capitalised on a Titus Bramble mistake. We had an excellent opportunity to equalise ten minutes before half-time when Pablo Couñago was adjudged to have been fouled inside the area and Town were awarded a penalty. The ever-reliable Marcus Stewart took the kick and one assumed he would score. Unbelievably, his penalty went wide of the goal. Just before the break, a Couñago header hit the bar and once more left us wondering if this was another night that would not go our way.

Relief all round was to find us when we equalised, and Bramble redeemed himself to become the hero of the night. Jamie Clapham's cross from the left was perfect for Bramble to make no mistake when sweeping home. There was enough time for both Richard Naylor and Clapham to hit the woodwork before the final whistle brought the curtain down on my first taste of European action and our home record was preserved. The second leg in Moscow would be just a week away.

It was Channel 5's turn to put the live spotlight on Town – the first time that we appeared on this channel. It was also two days after my 30th birthday and I was hoping for a lovely birthday run of extending our European tour.

Our first problem was to nullify Torpedo's away goal that they had scored in the first leg. And they seemed content to sit back on that goal with their apparent focus on defending resolutely rather than penetrate in attack.

Their ploy to hit us on the break almost paid off when two gilt-edged chances were missed. Firstly, with the Town defence expecting a flag to go up for offside. Matteo Sereni found himself in a two v one situation in favour of the Russians. Dmitri Vyazmikin hit the bar when it looked easier to score. And moments later, Vyazmikin found himself in space but shot into the side netting. Town were off the hook and went into the beak with the game still at 0-0.

George Burley made a tactical switch at half-time by pushing Finidi George further forward and this paid instant dividends two minutes after the restart.

A corner from Mark Venus was not cleared and George was on hand to fire home inside the six-yard box. Town were now in the ascendency and had an away goal of their own.

Seven minutes later, the Town fans in both Moscow and back home watching on TV were celebrating when Marcus Stewart added a second.

Vyazmikin pulled a goal back when he looked more than suspiciously offside on 65 minutes, and we were then indebted to Sereni who pulled off two excellent saves in the final 20 minutes.

Tommy Miller came off the bench with four minutes remaining for his Ipswich debut and then the sound of the final whistle sent fans into euro ecstasy as our run in Europe would be stretching into at least another round.

Three days later, we were live on TV once again, as the Sky cameras returned to Portman Road for the visit of Leeds United.

That earlier win over Derby remained as the only league victory up to this point, and with six games having been played by now, we were languishing in the bottom four of the Premier League table.

Leeds on the other hand were riding high and would pose a difficult challenge, especially as we had only arrived back from Moscow just 48 hours earlier.

For much of this game, Ipswich more than held their own and took the lead in the 22nd minute with yet another goal from Marcus Stewart.

The lead was held until the 70th minute when Robbie Keane equalised for Leeds and the hope among us all watching on would be to secure a draw.

Four minutes from time, an own goal from the unfortunate Mark Venus gave Leeds a win and the league form was now starting to become a concern having finished in the dizzy heights of fifth the season before.

On 18 October 2001, European football returned to Portman Road once more, and again, we were afforded the national TV limelight with the BBC One cameras present for coverage as we welcomed Helsingborgs IF. The evening started with a firework display to commemorate the opening of the new South Stand. Sadly, the players were unable to produce their own fireworks on the pitch.

The game was to finish 0-0 on a night of pure frustration. Turgid football was the order of the day, with the Swedes content to soak up any pressure and hit us whenever possible on the break.

No goals and a game of very few chances to be had. One could argue that we came out of this tie in a healthier position than we had after the first leg against Torpedo Moscow. At least Helsingborgs had no away goal to protect on home soil.

One point of interest that did occur in this game was that when Sixto Peralta came off the bench in the 58th minute to replace Jim Magilton, he became the 100th Ipswich player to appear live on TV.

Before our return leg in Sweden, it was back to the pressing matter of our struggles in the league. After that home defeat to Leeds, we had drawn at 0-0 home to Everton and 1-1 at Fulham, then a 3-3 draw at Southampton saw me in attendance and a stunning long-range goal from Mark Venus. This meant that going into our next televised game, we were still hovering one place above the relegation zone in 17th place.

West Ham were the visitors to Portman Road on Sunday, 28 October, and a five-goal thriller would have made good viewing for the West Ham fans and the neutrals, but sadly, not for us Ipswich fans.

Thomas Gaardsøe lined up in defence for his Ipswich debut. For what seemed to be the norm by this stage of the season saw Town start well but fall a goal behind when Paolo Di Canio put the Hammers in front on 22 minutes. They held the lead until the break where George Burley reshuffled his side. On came Sixto Peralta for Jamie Clapham and Town had a much better half. We got our reward with an equaliser from Hermann Hreidarsson on 63 minutes when he headed home a Mark Venus free kick.

We got right behind the team at this point with the Ipswich fans in full voice, urging the team to go on and find a winner. But nine minutes after Hreidarsson's goal, the Hammers were back in front in fortuitous fashion.

Frédéric Kanouté miss-hit a shot on goal, but the ball deflected off Hreidarsson and bobbled over a stranded Matteo Sereni.

Jermain Defoe replaced Di Canio on 88 minutes, and it took him just two minutes to find the back of the net for West Ham's third.

The ground was now rapidly emptying when Ipswich pulled a goal back with a stunning drive from Matt Holland.

But the damage had been done and we lost 3-2 to remain 17th.

Four days later, on the Thursday, we were back in European action, and this was the break we needed to get away from our wretched league form.

A few paragraphs ago, I talked about a regret that my dad never took me to a European game at Portman Road. And now, I had the pleasure of watching both Torpedo Moscow and Helsingborgs IF in home first leg ties. OK, they may not have been Barcelona, Real Madrid, Saint-Étienne, or any of the other big guns of Europe that came to Suffolk in the years gone by. Nevertheless, I could now say that I had witnessed UEFA Cup football in person.

Our seventh live TV game already of the season was upon us as BBC Two were to show our return leg on Thursday, 1 November 2001.

I never dreamt of watching Ipswich play a European tie in Europe itself. But a conversation was had between my friends Don and Jason, and we decided that we would make the trip to Sweden. This was mesmerising for me and no doubt Jason too. Don was a veteran of watching Ipswich abroad. Not only was he at the UEFA Cup Final in 1981, but he had been to many other countries too, including the trip to Moscow in the previous round. He was the experienced travel rep to hopefully keep Jason and myself in check.

Having agreed to part with what was a huge sum back in those days for a day trip nine days earlier, every day in between was excruciating as I could not wait. I was like a kid on Christmas Eve for each of those nine evenings.

I thought the trip had cost me in the region of £400. But having dug out the receipt that I still treasure, the actual cost of the whole package which included flight, transfer from Malmö airport to Helsingborg and match ticket, cost the royal sum of £618! When I see that price, I am gobsmacked really. That would have paid for a week on a beach somewhere in those days. And if you are not too fussy where you go, it would comfortably do so these days too!

A couple of days before the big day arrived, we had a fourth person wanting to join us in the form of another friend of many years and a great Ipswich fan, Colin Love.

Colin had taken over the booking of Jill (of the Clacton supporters' branch) as she could no longer make the trip. The only problem here was that Colin's flight was to Copenhagen.

When I left my flat, the clock on the wall showed exactly 4am on that Thursday. I picked Don and Jason up and then it was Colin to collect, and we were then on our way to Stansted airport. Here in my car were four teenagers inside men's bodies. The excitement was off the scale.

The first thing we had to do when arriving at the airport was to check in and then we could go and grab some breakfast. Within a matter of minutes we saw a queue checking in which was full of Ipswich fans and assumed that would at least be for our desk to check in or, at worst, the one Colin required. It turned out to be for neither of us. This is how it went on for the first few lines of fans we spotted.

I do not know how many flights collectively transported our supporters to all manner of places in Sweden and Denmark that day, but it's safe to say there were several hundred of us leaving Stansted throughout the morning, all for the one same place. This all added to the excitement even further.

Once safely checked in, we made our way to one of the airport restaurants and even though it was still not 6am, the only fluid I could see being consumed by Ipswich fans was of the alcoholic variety. I am not a great drinker at all now and was not in 2001 either. I think I must have been the only fan sipping on tea while those around me were downing pints and unbelievably, shorts.

At this point, we also planned where we would meet Colin. Remember, he was flying to Copenhagen, while Malmö was our destination. Helsingborg is the centre of the northern part of western Scania and Sweden's closest point to Denmark. From here, you can catch a ferry over to Helsingør which takes about 30 minutes and then catch a train to Copenhagen which takes about 45 minutes. We figured that as we had around ten hours to pass before the game, we would find a lot more to do in Copenhagen than we would in Helsingborg. And so, we agreed to meet Colin there.

Other than the surreal feeling of flying to watch an Ipswich game, the flight and transfer passed without much of note. When we arrived at the stadium, we decided to head to the nearest pub. The first we came across had some rough-looking fellas in it. Fearful of stumbling upon Helsingborg ultras, we decided not to hang around. But on the way out we noticed that they were in fact Ipswich fans. We still left, not wanting to cramp their style and all that.

As we walked down the road, we spotted a St George's flag hanging out of a hotel window. We could clearly see the lettering ITFC in the corners, but not the place name going through the middle of the flag.

When we got nearer, we were astounded to note that the place name was of our very own town – Clacton-on-Sea. It is a small world, although as Don would say, 'But you would not want to paint it!' We wondered who else had travelled from Clacton which was to be revealed later.

After a walk through a shopping mall, we noticed a fast-food outlet near the port and decided to get something to eat before heading over to Denmark. To this day, I still have no idea why we did not turn left to catch a ferry and instead, we crossed the road to discover Harry's Bar. The place was already filling up with Ipswich fans and we decided we would have a drink there.

The problem was, one drink led to two, two led to four and so on. What a fantastic day we spent in there. Any fan reading this who was there that day will know exactly how great it was. The venue was like a Wetherspoon if you like but without the cheap prices. I think the price of a pint was about £5 to £6. There was music too and by mid-afternoon with the place rammed, DJ Otzi's song 'Hey Baby' reverberated around the place. This led to us blasting out the lyrics 'heyyyyyyy, Martijn ROOSAHHHH'. What a sound and what a sight.

Every picture frame, wall light, hook, plant, or anything else fixed on the wall had Ipswich flags draped depicting places from all corners of the UK. This was like what you would see at an England away game, but all were Ipswich flags.

I remember at one point and after about five ciders, I went to the front door to get some air. There was a queue of Ipswich fans waiting to get in that must have been about 20 deep. I got talking to the doorman and he looked a bit agitated. I asked him if he was OK and he said that he was worried about the sheer number of English fans inside one place. He said to me, 'Too many hooligans – I am on my own here!' I promised him that he would have nothing to worry about.

An hour or so later, Town chairman David Sheepshanks came into the bar and got the welcome of a hero – mostly from a load of drunken blokes. He loved it though and I managed to get a photo with him. What a lovely touch that was from him to come and see us.

After around eight pints, I am not sure how I left the place in a straight line. I would need my stomach pumped now if I drank that much. But upon leaving, I came across the doorman once more and he was laughing. I asked him again if everything was OK. He told me that my promise was worth every word, and that he was having the best working day of his life. He could not believe he was getting paid for having so much fun. 'That is Ipswich fans for you,' I told him.

It was only when we were walking to the ground that we suddenly remembered poor Colin, stranded on his own in Copenhagen. All we could do was to apologise and blame it on the drink.

We found him outside the ground and of course, he asked where we had got to. But I think Colin had as much fun as us in Denmark's capital city with other Ipswich fans. All was good, thankfully.

The only regret that I have of the stadium is that our seats were up in the top tier of a side stand. When I looked down to my right, the packed away end behind the goal looked like the place to be. There was a lot of fun being had in there that night – mostly involving inflatables!

As for the game, Matteo Sereni made a horrendous error when the ball squirmed through his arms and into the net after just seven minutes. Hans Eklund could hardly believe his luck.

Over an hour then passed without further goals and our European run was seemingly ending. That was until Hermann Hreidarsson brought us level on 69 minutes and then two more outstanding Marcus Stewart goals on 81 and 88 minutes saw us home 3-1 on both the night and on aggregate. Seventeen-year-old Darren Bent had also come off the bench to make his Ipswich debut.

We were warned not to miss our coach after the game at the stated departure time as it would not wait and therefore, we would miss our flight. Due to the consumption of alcohol as much as anything else, we had no idea as to where we had been dropped off. We asked some Helsingborgs fans who directed us accordingly but wanted to stop and chat with us about how good Ipswich were. We simply did not have the time to do this.

We broke into a run to where we had been told our coach would be waiting. Our relief at finding parked coaches soon turned to despair. The coaches were numbered, and while I do not remember what number our coach was that day, I know that the coach with our number displayed had turned from a single decker to a double decker!

It turned out that we were at the wrong end of the ground. So, we had to sprint back to the other end. By now my head was banging and the cider in my stomach was swirling. I do not know how, but we found our coach just in time.

When we took our seats on the plane, it was gone midnight local time. I placed the passenger headphones over my ears and was pleased to hear the Lightning Seeds' 'The Life of Riley' being played at that moment in time.

I had certainly lived the life of Riley that day and will never forget it. By the time I returned to my flat, the kitchen clock still showed 4am. At first, I thought the batteries had stopped. Then I realised that I had departed that room exactly 24 hours beforehand. I had had the best 24 hours as an Ipswich fan ever.

Town drew Inter Milan in the next round, and I had spent all my savings on that trip to Helsingborg so could not afford to go to the San Siro. Don went and I remember him saying that I had gone to the best game as we were free to roam around in Sweden whereas his experiences of Russia and Italy were good, but very much controlled by the local police forces.

We were, by now, appearing live on TV almost on a fortnightly basis thanks to our wins in Europe. When we returned in front of the Sky cameras on Sunday, 18 November for the visit of Bolton Wanderers, this was the 50th live TV game of George Burley's reign and he remains the only Ipswich manager to achieve this number.

Our last league game had seen us lose 2-1 at Chelsea and we were now sitting in the relegation zone.

Gudni Bergsson scored as early as the sixth minute to put Bolton in front and when Michael Ricketts doubled the lead on 25 minutes, it was game over. The mere mention of Ricketts did not go down well with Town fans at the time. He had received an England call-up while Marcus Stewart continued to be overlooked.

Matt Holland pulled a goal back in first-half injury time, but with no further goals, our winless league run now stood at 11 games with that sole victory still being the one over Derby back in August.

This game saw Ulrich Le pen come off the bench for his Ipswich debut.

While league football continued to be our enemy, we had very much found a friend in European affairs.

Four days later, on 22 November, we welcomed Italian giants Inter Milan and once more our slot on national TV belonged on BBC Two. In terms of the opposition, this was the biggest night of my Ipswich life.

Although the lower tier of the new North Stand opened that night to allow a reduced number of fans to sit there, we were still ensconced high up in the Churchmans (sorry, Sir Alf Ramsey Stand), where North Standers had been relocated by the club while our new 'home' was being constructed.

For the first time, and just over a year after we had first met, Pegga decided that she would like to come to a first team game with me. I think it was more to do with eyeing up several Italians than the football itself. I told her that in the away end, there would only be about 50 local waiters present and was proved about right.

The only time Pegga had been to a game with me previously was an FA Youth Cup sixth round tie at Portman Road eight months earlier when we hosted the youths of Nottingham Forest. They had Jermaine Jenas in their line-up that night and whenever we see him on BBC's *The One Show* now, I always tell her that she saw him play at Portman Road once. I only keep telling her because she never listens to this fact. But I digress.

Just over 24,500 fans at the ground and thousands more at home witnessed a great Ipswich performance that night. Town won it 1-0 via an Alun Armstrong header in the

81st minute, just four minutes after replacing Richard Naylor. The added joy for me was that in those days, I always had a bet on the first goal of the game to be scored between the 80th and 90th minute. I had won enough money to pay for Pegga's ticket!

That was a night we will never forget, and it set up the return leg at the San Siro perfectly.

Our fourth and last live game of November 2001 alone, on the 27th, saw us in cup action of a different kind. It was the first and only time that we would appear live on the brand-new ITV Sport channel. A League Cup fourth round tie at Newcastle United lay in wait for us.

What a disastrous night that proved to be; 4-0 down after 40 minutes was totally demoralising. Goals from Laurent Robert (18), Shola Ameobi (26) and Alan Shearer (37 and 40) left us with only pride to play for in the second half.

And pride I suppose you could say was gained as we 'won' the half 1-0. Darren Bent came off the bench in the 71st minute to replace Armstrong and scored his first goal for Ipswich six minutes later after being put through on goal by Jamie Clapham.

The first Thursday of December saw us back on Channel 5 for the UEFA Cup third round second leg at the San Siro. The Nerazzurri (black and blues) were clearly a worried outfit after their defeat at Portman Road.

Into their squad came the big guns. Christian Vieri started and proceeded to score a hat-trick, before being replaced by Brazilian superstar Ronaldo on 79 minutes – eight minutes after his third goal. Mohamed Kallon had also scored a minute into the second half to put Inter 4-0 up on the night.

But the moment of the game came seconds before Ronaldo's introduction when Town scored a penalty through first-leg hero Armstrong. The penalty was awarded after Matt Holland's shot struck the arm of Javier Zanetti.

Over 10,000 Ipswich fans made up the 25,358 of those in attendance that night and it was in front of them that Armstrong scored from the spot.

We may have lost the tie 4-2 on aggregate, but we left the competition with our heads held high in the knowledge that we had given a European giant a run for their money, including that famous 1-0 win at home.

We now had to find a way of converting our football in Europe into league games to edge our way out of the relegation zone.

With Christmas fast approaching, and with a draw and two defeats since that loss to Bolton behind us, we were now bottom of the FA Premier League. How had we gone from finishing fifth last season to this position now?

Was our foray into Europe really to blame for our attentions being elsewhere? Was it the introduction of fresh players that had unsettled our strong squad that George Burley had built over a four-year period? It was a job to put a finger on exactly what was wrong, but there were huge concerns among the fans.

A Monday night game at Villa Park on 17 December was up next for the Sky cameras and we somehow needed to bring an end to a 14-game winless run which now included eight defeats.

I was on a work Christmas do that night, but my only thoughts were to find an establishment that was screening the game. A group of us broke away from our main party and headed for the Roaring Donkey, a pub that sits in Holland-on-Sea. One of my colleagues insisted on playing pool for money. I was not interested as watching Ipswich was my only concern. He was a Leeds fan who had been in my brother's year at school. He had finished a few drinks at this point and while I was a tad concerned at being bullied into playing pool, I still refused as my desire to see Town win was greater.

When Finidi George put us ahead on 18 minutes, I thought that this might just be a game we could win and turn our season around.

Juan Pablo Ángel had other ideas though and scored in the final minute of the first half, and then added another on 70 minutes as Aston Villa won 2-1. Not the early Christmas present that we had hoped for.

Bottom of the table, one league victory all season, 15 games without a win and three defeats on the spin. What was happening?

Incredibly, the spark that we had been seeking for so long to get our season going ignited in the very next game just three days before Christmas. And surprisingly, it came at Tottenham where we won 2-1. We then followed up this success with two more wins followed by a 3-2 defeat at Charlton after we had been 2-0 up.

Two more wins then came our way in January when we completed a remarkable double over Tottenham, and then we did the same to Derby. By the time our next live game came around, we had gotten ourselves out of the relegation zone.

That match, however, was an FA Cup fourth round tie at home to Manchester City.

City were playing a level below us and were considered the underdogs. But they were in fine form that season and won the Division One championship at a canter, finishing ten points ahead of West Bromwich Albion on 99 points after scoring 108 league goals. Although it was still January, we knew that it would not be easy, even though we were now in much better form.

What followed was an inferior performance and for the fourth time that season, we conceded four goals.

City held a slender half-time lead with Eyal Berkovic scoring on 43 minutes. Shaun Goater added a second on 65 minutes and just when we thought we were out of the game, Marcus Bent pulled a goal back seven minutes from the end with a spectacular effort from 30 yards. But City still found the space and time to add two more through Goater again and in injury time, Darren Huckerby scored.

This had been our fifth game shown live on BBC One and the only win remained that very first one, the 1978 FA Cup Final. It was fast becoming a poisoned chalice of a channel for us to be shown live on. We really could now concentrate on the league, and boy, did we have to.

When we returned to league action, we followed up a home win over Fulham at the end of January with a fine 2-1 victory at Everton on the first weekend in February. We had now won seven in eight and climbed to the lofty position of 12th. After that single win in our first 17 games, we had managed to pull ourselves out of trouble and I recall that we were 8/1 with most bookmakers to get relegated at that stage of the season.

In the back of my mind, I kept the fact that our final game of the season would be away at Liverpool, our penultimate one would be at home to Manchester United and a visit to Arsenal was on the cards four games from the end. We simply had to get the points on the board by the time we visited Highbury, which just happened to be our next live TV game on 21 April.

Following that win at Everton, in the next nine games leading up to Arsenal we were back in the dreadful form of the first half of the season as we lost six and drew three.

Even now I look back and wonder how we could be poor for 17 games, excellent for eight, and then capitulate for the remainder of the season. We were back in the bottom three ahead of this game.

It is true to say that we gave a good account of ourselves at Arsenal, and watching the game on Sky Sports I thought that at least we were showing the fight to avoid relegation. But a brace from Freddie Ljungberg (68 and 78) condemned us to a 2-0 defeat. Darren Ambrose got his first taste of action in an Ipswich shirt in this game when replacing Martijn Reuser on 85 minutes.

A 1-0 win over Middlesbrough in our next game gave us all some hope. We were 18th but now only two points behind Sunderland with two to play.

The problem was the opponents in those final two. Sunderland meanwhile had to play at Charlton, who had nothing to play for, and at home to Derby, who by now were already relegated. I held next to no hope to be honest, and both games were to be shown live on Sky Sports.

As we head into the penultimate match of the season, at home to Manchester United on Saturday, 27 April, we did so in the knowledge that Sunderland had only drawn at Charlton. Win this and we would get ourselves out of the relegation zone with one game to play.

What then occurred still annoys me when writing about it some 20 years on. After an excellent battling display from Ipswich throughout the whole first half, two minutes into stoppage time came a decision that I still cannot fathom. Ruud Van Nistelrooy slipped inside the penalty area. Nobody had touched him, he slipped. Unbelievably, a penalty was awarded, and Van Nistelrooy picked himself up to score from the spot for the only goal of the game.

As much as I and many others were aware that inevitable relegation could and should not be blamed on this one incident of the whole season, it certainly took away any lingering hope that we may have survived. It was a sad final game for Sixto Peralta, a wonderful player that brought happy memories for many Ipswich fans.

We went into that last-day fixture at Liverpool needing more than a miracle. For a start, we needed to win and then hoped that Sunderland would lose at home to Derby.

We knew it would be a tall order and by half-time, all hope had evaporated. John Arne Riise scored twice, and it was, game over. Michael Owen added a third a minute into the second period and 11 minutes later, Vladimir Šmicer added a fourth. Two minutes from time, Nicolas Anelka, who had only just come off the bench, netted and Liverpool ran out comfortable 5-0 winners. It was our seventh live TV defeat in a row to end a season that brought us so much joy in the UEFA Cup, but much more misery in the league.

Titus Bramble played his last Ipswich game in this match.

Sunderland made certain of safety with a 1-1 draw against Derby and Town were relegated a year after finishing fifth. I felt so low that night, one of my worst moments as an Ipswich fan.

We had been live on TV no fewer than 16 times in the 2001/02 season, winning just those three UEFA Cup games. To be screened live on so many occasions for a club of our size shows how magic that era was. At the time of writing, 11 May 2002 remains the last time that we played a Premier League match.

To put those 17 live fixtures into context, and the magnitude of where we were as a club, our return to Division One saw us feature live on TV on only four occasions in the 2002/03 season, which included our very first game of the season, away at Walsall.

Having endured three seasons of losing in the play-offs before finally winning them in 2000, I remember that it seemed a massive chore to have to try and do it all over again. Would it take another three or four years to achieve? Would we win them again at all? We had climbed the ladder of achievement but having reached the top row, we were now sliding back to where we started, feeling lower than a snake's belly.

We were one of the pre-season favourites with most bookmakers for promotion and with no disrespect to Walsall, it was a game that we expected to win, which we duly did 2-0. A goal in each half, scored by Darren Ambrose (37) and Marcus Bent (62), at least got our season up and running at the first time of asking. Bent's effort was our 100th live TV goal.

Five days later, I was off to Europe once more with my good mate Paul Love (brother of Colin, who came to Helsingborg with me) for the UEFA Cup qualifying round first leg in Luxembourg as Town took on Avenir Beggen. We laboured to a late 1-0 win before winning the return leg 8-1.

Despite being relegated from the Premier League the season before, Town had qualified for the UEFA Cup via the unorthodox route of the Fair Play League.

Along with SK Sigma Olomouc of the Czech Republic, we were the two teams drawn from the 17 national associations in the Fair Play League.

The following month, and back in Division One, on 15 September we were to renew our rivalry with Norwich, and naturally, it was a game screened live. After winning our first two matches of the season, we went in on the back of two draws and a defeat and sat in 12th place. Apathy had started to return to Portman Road and already, concerns were brewing for the season ahead. Those heady days of the Premier League seemed long gone.

Over 29,000 packed into Portman Road and the latest East Anglian derby was a tense affair with a controversial climax.

With 11 minutes remaining, Norwich went ahead through Malky Mackay and a defeat to that lot up the road looked on the cards. Five minutes into injury time, Portman Road erupted into a frenzy when Town were awarded a penalty after Adam Drury handled a Pablo Couñago cross.

With the roof ready to be lifted, Darren Bent hit his spot-kick against the post. Darren Ambrose then saw the rebound saved by Robert Green and not once but twice, we had come close to celebrating in a heightened, ecstatic fashion. But in the same moment, as our feelings were being torn apart, Couñago smashed home the second rebound from two yards to send us crazy. Bodies were once again falling over each other in the North Stand. Shins were bruised, arms were pulled, caps and hats were flying off, but nobody cared. We had equalised in dramatic fashion against our arch enemies and emotions took over as fans spilled on to the pitch. What a moment.

In the grand scheme of things however, a point did little to improve our league position as we had now dropped to 14th. Defeats followed at Stoke City and at home to Derby County, two games that were encompassed by cup ties against Brighton and Hove Albion in the League Cup, and a two-legged UEFA Cup tie against FK Sartid. Unlike the season before, none of our UEFA Cup ties were to be screened live on TV in 2002/03.

After a 3-0 defeat at Grimsby Town on 8 October 2002, George Burley was sacked and that dramatic draw against Norwich was to be his last live TV game as manager of Ipswich, bringing an end to a record run of 60 screened matches.

CHAPTER 3: THE 'NEARLY' MEN

The Joe Royle era (25 games)

Joe Royle had taken charge of Ipswich for 14 games by the time he was to manage his troops for the first time on TV, a Boxing Day 2002 visit to Leicester City.

I chose to watch this game with my dad at his house which has been a rare thing to do in all these years. It was a chance to see him over the festive period and watch the match at the same time as in those days, I did not subscribe to Sky Sports. I took Pegga with me, much to her delight because, as I have already said, she hates football.

Leicester included in their line-up both a former and a future Ipswich player in James Scowcroft and Matt Elliott. The game was not one of the best and staying truly captivated was difficult.

Leicester scored a penalty through Paul Dickov on 55 minutes after Hermann Hreidarsson had pushed Matt Heath. I remember that with ten minutes remaining, I said something like my Christmas being ruined by a suspected defeat. Pegga told me not to worry as we would win 2-1. Now, under the circumstances, I thought that she was just trying to cheer me up and as she did not know what Ipswich could be like, I took her words with little merit.

When Thomas Gaardsøe equalised on 84 minutes after heading home a free kick from Darren Ambrose, I wondered if she would be right.

Then two minutes from time the game turned on its head when Ambrose turned from provider to scorer when hooking the ball home from close-range. Pegga was right and it was a happy Christmas. Joe Royle won his first live game in charge thus becoming only the second Ipswich manager to do so after Sir Bobby Robson.

It would be 18 April before we were to appear live on TV again for a Good Friday fixture at home to already promoted Portsmouth. While they were sitting on top of the league, we had found ourselves stuck in seventh place for over a month and through an eight-game period where we just could not find a place in the elusive top six and yet another play-off battle.

In those days, pre-match drinks were often had in Brannigan's situated on Ipswich's Cardinal Park, where DOUGH&co now resides.

The pre-game atmosphere there could be electric at times and was the place to be. On that day, I was joined by my brother Shaun and our dad. Shaun had been there many times with me, but this was a first for dad. I had hoped that the pre-match songs would act as a good warm-up for his experience in the lower tier in the North Stand.

Over 29,000 were once again present and the atmosphere was as electric as I hoped it would be. Portsmouth fans were playing their part too, no doubt highly charged in their emotions at being promoted to the Premier League.

Whether Portsmouth were suffering from a promotion hangover or whether we were just simply too good on the day, I have no idea. But I would like to think that it was the latter.

Martijn Reuser gave us the perfect start on 11 minutes when latching on to Arjan de Zeeuw's loose pass across the edge of his own area. We then doubled our lead on 27 minutes through Tommy Miller. Portsmouth had failed to clear a cross from the left by Matt Richards and Miller smashed the ball past Shaka Hislop.

To cap a perfect first half-hour, we wrapped the game up with a fine third goal from Pablo Couñago. The Spaniard turned de Zeeuw inside out and his expertly struck shot soared into the roof of the net.

Matt Holland became the first player to play in 50 live TV games and this also proved to be his last live appearance for the club too. What a wonderful servant he had been and a pivotal player in firstly George Burley's, and then in Joe Royle's engine rooms alongside Jim Magilton for the most part.

The result saw us remain in seventh place and following a defeat at Rotherham United and a 5-1 hammering at home to MK Dons, our final game saw us win 4-1 at Derby and we had missed out on the play-offs by one place and four points. That visit to Derby brought the curtain down on Holland's Ipswich career (as well as those of Andy Marshall and Thomas Gaardsøe) and the overall feeling going into the summer of 2003 was one of sadness and disappointment that we did not bounce back at the first attempt.

Joe Royle's first full season in charge in 2003/04 got off to a poor start and four defeats and two draws in our first six games saw us rooted to the bottom of the league by mid-September.

But six wins in the next seven saw us up to seventh by the time we were to feature live on TV for the first time that season as we welcomed Stoke City and the Sky cameras to Portman Road for a tea-time kick-off on Saturday, 18 October.

Pablo Couñago had the ball in the net in the fifth minute but was clearly offside and then Town lost loanee Alan Mahon to injury as early as the 12th minute.

With Couñago and Jermaine Wright squandering further chances, the game looked as if it would be goalless going into half-time. But two minutes before the break we scored through the most unlikely of sources.

A cross from the right was headed back across goal by Jim Magilton and Matt Richards blasted a shot high into the net for his first senior goal.

Town were wasteful in the second period as Couñago and then Tommy Miller spurned excellent chances and Stoke goalkeeper Neil Cutler then made smart saves to deny Shefki Kuqi and Miller. Georges Santos saw a header cleared off the line and anxiety began to grow around me in the North Stand as failure to kill the game off led to worrying thoughts of Stoke snatching an equaliser. With two minutes to go, our fears almost came to fruition.

Former Norwich player Darel Russell crossed to future Town player Keith Andrews, who saw his side-footed effort strike both posts before rebounding into the grateful arms of Kelvin Davis.

Much to the relief of all watching both at the game and back home, we held on for a 1-0 win and broke into the top six for the first time that season.

By the time that we were next to appear live, the season had progressed through to 7 February, and a Saturday afternoon visit from Paul Jewell's Wigan Athletic. We were still in the top six with just two defeats from the previous 12 games. Our last game at Portman Road prior to this fixture was a crazy 6-4 win over Crewe Alexandra. We had hoped for another goal feast and victory to show the watching nation that we were fair value for money and serious promotion contenders once again.

Alan Mahon, who had previously been on loan at Ipswich, was now with Wigan and they also had Jimmy Bullard who would years later be voted as Ipswich supporters' player of the year. Their dangerous strike duo of Jason Roberts and Nathan Ellington (Ellington would also later play for Ipswich) were the danger men that we needed to keep a close eye on. And at the back, Jason de Vos, who would leave Wigan to join Ipswich less than six months later, showed just why the visitors were also among the promotion hopefuls.

A goal apiece by Roberts (18), and Ellington (33) sent the Latics into the break with a two-goal lead and the writing was on the wall for us fans as far as this game was concerned.

Gary Teale added a third on 53 minutes and despite Shefki Kuqi grabbing a goal back seven minutes later followed by the dismissal of Leighton Baines, Wigan held on for the three points to leapfrog Town and into third place.

Then 20 March became well-remembered by both Dean Bowditch and those of us who watched the game.

Bowditch became only the second Ipswich player to score a hat-trick in a live TV game and aged just 17, he remains the only teenager to score three goals in a live game for Ipswich.

Watford were the opposition and for their goalkeeper Lenny Pidgeley, it was an afternoon to forget. The first goal had a touch of Bryan Gunn about it. Pidgeley gifted the England youth international the opener as early as the fifth minute. As he went to clear Sean Dyche's back-pass, the ball bobbled off his standing foot, leaving Bowditch with a simple finish. This was right in front of us standing in the North Stand too and of course, we gave Pidgeley the bird for the rest of the half.

Bowditch had previously scored only one goal for the first XI in a Carling Cup victory over Kidderminster Harriers. Now he had scored his first league goal and there was more to come as on 24 minutes, he showed composure beyond his years to slot home his second.

It was not all one-way traffic however, and Scott Fitzgerald brought the Hornets back into the game with a goal in first-half injury time.

In the 61st minute, Bowditch completed his hat-trick after yet another Pidgeley error. Bowditch took advantage of the on-loan Chelsea goalkeeper's hesitation and calmly slotted home.

Jermaine Wright completed the rout in the 90th minute and Town stormed to a 4-1 win to edge back up to seventh place.

Two weeks later, and with the race for a play-off place heating up, Town were back on Sky once more for a Sunday afternoon visit of West Bromwich Albion.

We had followed up that win over Watford with a 2-1 win away at MK Dons but found ourselves back down to eighth place. West Bromwich Albion were battling with Norwich for both the title and automatic promotion. This was a big game for both teams. Over 24,500 in the ground, and many more in living rooms back home, anticipated an intriguing match-up. It would be a good test of our credentials at this stage of the season.

On my way to this game, I recalled how West Brom were one of my favourite teams to watch Ipswich play against. We just never seemed to lose against the Baggies. It probably stemmed back to the 1978 FA Cup semi-final at Highbury when we beat them 3-1. My brother Shaun and I felt that we always beat them by that score. We would comment of standing near the back of the old North Stand watching us win 3-1 with views of the trains arriving and departing at Ipswich Station which in those days could be seen above the single-tiered Churchmans – if of course you stood far enough back in the North Stand.

On checking the records, we had won 3-1 at home to West Brom in my time as a fan in 1989, 1990 and 1999. So, I guess we had a point with that scoreline. I also recall being present when we hammered them 5-0 in January 1997.

My personal record of games watched between Ipswich and West Brom prior to this encounter stood at ten games, with eight wins and two draws in our favour.

West Brom were also the opposition that I was to see both the 600th and 650th goals in games that I had attended. You can see why I liked them.

Three minutes before the interval, Tommy Miller put us in front and the hope obviously was that yet another win against West Brom would be witnessed.

A crazy final 20 minutes saw four goals, but an Ipswich defeat.

Jason Koumas, a half-time substitute for the visitors, equalised on 71 minutes, and two minutes later another substitute, Lloyd Dyer, put them in front. He had only been on the field for six minutes.

Five minutes after falling behind, Town were back on level terms thanks to Darren Bent and just as it looked as if the game would finish in an entertaining 2-2 draw, Albion found a winner.

Geoff Horsfield was initially in an offside position when Albion broke forward four minutes into injury time but deemed inactive. Lee Hughes sent over a low cross and Horsfield was on hand to sweep home much to our gasps of despair.

It was Albion's fifth successive win and the end of our three-game winning run. Those involved in the race for the play-offs were now closing in on one another. We were down to ninth but a single point from fourth.

This was the Joe Royle era of going all out in attack, but to the detriment of defence. At this stage we were the leading scorers in the division but had conceded more than any other team outside of the bottom five. It was a joy to watch but frustrating in equal measure too.

On the last day of April, we made the trip to Sheffield United for a Friday night fixture, once again on Sky. Having won the next three games after that defeat to West Brom, followed up by a defeat at Nottingham Forest, we went into the last two games of the season, both live on Sky, with a play-off place yet to be confirmed.

Neil Warnock's United were also desperate for the three points to reach the play-offs themselves.

When Andrew Gray put the hosts in front on 64 minutes, there was a sense of fear that we were about to repeat the previous season's achievement and miss out on the top six again. But seven minutes later, Ian Westlake scored for Town after shooting through goalkeeper Paddy Kenny's legs. The point was more valuable to Town as Warnock's side would ultimately miss out on a play-off place by two points.

The play-off finals in that era were being played at the Millennium Stadium in Cardiff while Wembley was being redeveloped. And it was Cardiff who provided the opposition for the final game of the season, at Portman Road on Sunday, 9 May.

There were the usual nerves associated with last-day results that we had experienced many times in recent seasons, and a whole permutation of results could see us finish anywhere between fourth and eighth.

Shefki Kuqi scored on 26 minutes to ease many nerves and momentarily, we were fourth. But Lee Bullock equalised for Cardiff on 41 minutes and with no further scoring, it was eyes elsewhere to see where we would finish.

In the end our final position was fifth, above Crystal Palace on goal difference, and two points ahead of both Wigan Athletic and Sheffield United who had missed out altogether. This had been an ending too close to call and we breathed a collective sigh at finally having yet another crack on promotion.

Cardiff's goal was the 72nd we had conceded in the 2003/04 season. Only 19th-placed Burnley (77) and rock-bottom Wimbledon (89) had conceded more. Yet we finished the season as the leading goalscorers in the division with 84 goals. A combined 156 goals over 46 games at 3.39 per game epitomised Joe Royle's cavalier and exciting approach to our campaign. Nine of our games that season saw five or more goals scored. Our matches were certainly excellent value for money.

Had we beaten Cardiff, we would have finished fourth and held the advantage of playing the second leg of the semi-final at home. Instead, we took on West Ham at lunchtime on Saturday, 15 May at Portman Road, looking for a decent lead to take to what would no doubt be a highly charged Upton Park.

Over 28,000 fans were present at Portman Road, and thousands more were watching on television. We were back to a situation that we had become accustomed to on four occasions between 1997 and 2000.

This was the 13th semi-final of my time supporting Ipswich and winning this one meant so much to me.

Throughout my life, the biggest rivalry I have had is with fans of West Ham. At school, both primary and secondary, at work, within my Sunday morning football team, and with some friends in general, it was always arguments/banter with West Ham fans.

The Essex coastal town of Clacton-on-Sea, where I live, has a large population of ex-east Londoners and with that brings the Hammers. I simply never had any rivalry with a Norwich fan growing up. I do not know what it is like to live in say Lowestoft, Diss, Needham Market, Bury St Edmunds, or any other location close to the Suffolk/Norfolk border where I am sure that the Ipswich/Norwich rivalry is rife.

I never came across a Norwich fan at school or work and to this day, I know of only about three who live in Clacton. As a child growing up in Kirby-le-Soken, close to the better-known places of Frinton-on-Sea and Walton-on-the-Naze, an old boy who lived next door to my home called Jack was a Norwich fan. But he never said anything to me while we were winning the FA Cup and UEFA Cup and were regarded as one of the best teams in Europe. I am glad I moved away from him before the Canaries had their time over us though.

So, I dislike West Ham more than Norwich if that is possible. I certainly want them to both lose every game, but when they play one another and if a draw cannot be the result, it is the only time that I am not overly bothered should Norwich win.

To put it simply, I was desperate to win this play-off semi-final more than all those that we had featured in previously.

Portman Road was buzzing that day. The North Stand was rocking, and I had a hoarse voice by the time the game had kicked-off.

John McGreal was to play his final game for the club, as was Chris Bart-Williams who came off the bench to replace Jim Magilton.

The game flowed from end to end and had its fair share of near misses and disallowed goals, and then in the 57th minute the only goal was scored, sending the Blue Army delirious.

When a Richard Naylor effort cannoned back off the bar, for a split second the moment looked like it had gone. But there was Darren Bent to head home the rebound. You only need to look back at the celebrations in the North Stand as Bent ran across the front of it to take in the hysteria of a frenzied crowd. I was in among that and other than Paul Anderson's goal against Norwich in the 2014/15 play-offs, I do not believe that I have celebrated a Portman Road goal more vociferously. Breathless and with my heart beating off the scale is how I remember feeling by the time I had stopped throwing myself around.

We won 1-0 and while there was doubt that it would be enough to see the game off three days later, we were in the ascendency in the knowledge that a draw at Upton Park would see us through to the final in Cardiff.

Despite my thoughts of West Ham, I must concede that Upton Park was a special place on special nights like that second leg. The atmosphere that old ground held was second to none of about every other ground I have visited. If I was a West Ham fan going to Upton Park on a regular basis, I think I would have hated the move to the London Stadium. Having all that history, all those memories and 'home' being in the heart of the East End taken away would have hurt me. As Ipswich have not yet played at West Ham's new home ground, I have yet to visit there. But I do imagine that it is less atmospheric and not as intimidating as Upton Park.

For the fourth successive game, we were once more live on TV and that second leg was massive in so many ways. I needed this win to take back to my West Ham mates. A loss would be a moment that I would never hear the end of.

Half-time came with no goals and we were 45 minutes away from the final. Had Darren Bent scored a glorious chance after just two minutes instead of dragging a shot across the face of the goal, our situation would have looked even better. How we rued that miss.

Matthew Etherington scored to level the tie on 51 minutes and when Christian Dailly scored a second goal for West Ham on 71 minutes, it was game over. We could not force our way back and for the 11th time in those 13 semi-finals, a defeat was yet again having to be dealt with.

This game was also the last time we would see Matt Elliott, Jermaine Wright, Alun Armstrong, and Martijn Reuser in an Ipswich shirt. Those latter three players had been part of momentous occasions for the club and were players that to say farewell to, was sad.

The final kick in the teeth came on the way home when I put the radio on and heard the game still being talked about. Never mind my teeth, I wanted to kick the radio in when I heard one of the presenters on Radio 5 Live state that it was no more than what West Ham fans had deserved! What about us Ipswich fans? Did we not deserve it too? That comment riled me. It still does. I was already hurt but now I was in a bad mood. All I can say is that it was a good job then that I was not to know that I would have to go through it all again a year later. West Ham lost the final 1-0 to Crystal Palace.

As the 2004/05 season started, there was a sense of same old, same old being an Ipswich fan. Feel optimistic for the new season, flirt with automatic promotion, reach the play-offs or narrowly miss out instead, get the hopes up for promotion when reaching the play-offs, lose in them, press the reset button, and go through the same motions again the following season.

The past eight seasons had seen five of them end like this and 2004/05 would become the sixth to put us through the same emotions once more.

Our first live TV appearance of the season came seven league games in when we hosted Millwall on Sunday, 12 September, for a 1pm kick-off, in front of the Sky cameras. We had made a good start to the season with four wins, and a draw to our name and were sitting in the top three.

The game was a scrappy affair with two late goals sealing victory for Town. Darren Bent marked his 100th Ipswich appearance with our first on 83 minutes. Pablo Couñago flicked on a long clearance which Bent latched on to after a slip by Darren Ward and the Town striker fired past Graham Stack in the Millwall goal.

Couñago then made sure of all three points in the final minute, turning in a cross from the left by Bent. The win sent us to the top of the league, a point ahead of Wigan.

Three weeks later, we appeared on the same channel again for another Sunday lunchtime fixture for our latest TV clash with Coventry City. After Norwich (24 times), our next most-faced opponents in live TV games are the Sky Blues with seven matches screened so far. I have never really understood why such a fixture should prove so popular for TV coverage.

Our results post-Millwall took a slight dip with only one victory in four games seeing us drop to third.

We went on to secure a deserved but fortunate victory in this encounter to record our second away win of the season in the league. This saw us go level on top with Wigan who had a slightly better goal difference.

A scoreless first half saw an entertaining battle with both sides creating plenty of chances. Darren Bent had the ball in the net for Town but was ruled offside.

Coventry had a perfect opportunity to open the scoring when Tim Sherwood was fouled inside the area by Drissa Diallo. Stern John, who would become an Ipswich player later in his career, saw his spot-kick well saved by Lewis Price.

Dean Bowditch saw an effort hit the crossbar and it seemed only a matter of time before a goal would be scored.

Ipswich started to dominate the second period but squandered several chances to keep us frustrated at our wastefulness in front of goal. But with 20 minutes remaining, we finally got the goal that we deserved.

Bowditch was in the right place at the far post to finish an excellent cross from Bent. However, the lead was to last only seven minutes as Coventry dug deep to grab an equaliser against the run of play.

Bjarni Gudjonsson played in substitute Patrick Suffo who lobbed Price for an excellent finish just four minutes after coming off the bench.

Just when it looked like all three points would not be gained, Coventry defender Matt Mills mis-kicked a back-pass to onrushing goalkeeper Luke Steele to find an open goal to hand Ipswich the win we thoroughly deserved, and we were now back up to second place in the table.

While Coventry are our second most-faced opponents live on TV, Sunderland are only a further game behind, level with Sheffield United on six.

Our fourth TV clash with the Wearsiders would be our next live game on Sunday, 21 November. This fixture would be a difficult one to watch as for the first time on TV, we were up against the legendary Marcus Stewart.

It was horrible seeing him line up for Sunderland that day. It just did not feel right, and I would like to thank Marcus for not scoring against us to prevent us from feeling any worse. Sunderland, though, would still go on to win 2-0.

We went in on an excellent run of form. We were unbeaten in 11 and were on a four-game winning run and a victory at the Stadium of Light would send us to the summit of the league. Sunderland were also in fine form though and Mick McCarthy's side would go on to win the league that season. They were just too strong on the day.

Goals from Stephen Elliott (60) and substitute Chris Brown (75) succumbed Town not only to defeat, but for the first time that season, we failed to score in a league game too. Darryl Knights came off the bench for Ipswich to replace Shefki Kuqi in the 80th minute for his one and only Ipswich appearance.

Exactly one month later, and four days before Christmas Day, our top-of-the-table clash with Wigan Athletic was the Tuesday night choice by Sky for their live game. We were the division's top two teams at the time. It was a game that had a tremendous ending, and one that I should have not been attending.

Two months prior to this fixture, I fell awkwardly in a Sunday morning match. The injury was to end my career at the ripe old age of 32. I had been at my club for 12 years and was gutted that my time ended in such a fashion.

A few days before the Wigan game, I had my knee operated on and was still heavily strapped and on crutches when it came around. Over 28,000 were present and I simply wanted to be one of them and had a long unbeaten run of home games attended to maintain.

Thank heavens the North Stand remained standing that night. It was far more comfortable leaning on my crutches rather than trying to sit with an outstretched leg.

Wigan once again had the dangerous duo of Jason Roberts and Nathan Ellington up front – both had scored in a previous TV encounter against Town and would need careful attention once more. Roberts spurned three excellent chances in the first 11 minutes. Was this a sign of things to come?

To date, we had an unbeaten home record to preserve and once we found our groove, we were giving the visitors as good as anything they could throw at us, with Darren Currie, making his full Ipswich debut, instrumental in much of our play.

However, it would be Wigan who would take the lead in the 56th minute with one of the best goals Portman Road has ever seen. Leighton Baines hit a stunning effort from at least 35 yards that gave Kelvin Davis no chance. It was a goal worthy of winning a match between two sides at the top going toe to toe in an epic battle. But it was of course not for us to hope that would be how the game should be won.

And ten minutes later we got ourselves back on level terms. After Ian Westlake had been fouled, Currie's free kick found Richard Naylor who headed the ball past the reach of John Filan for his fourth goal of the season.

Then a minute from time came the most ecstatic moment of the season Portman Road was to see.

Tommy Miller hit a long, hopeful pass forward and when Shefki Kuqi challenged Ian Breckin, the ball ran loose into the area, where Darren Bent nipped in ahead of Matt Jackson and looped it over Filan and into the net to spark pandemonium in the stands.

It was as much as I could do to hop around on one leg, both crutches high in the air in celebratory mode and Christmas had come early for us all. We would be the Christmas number one outside of the Premier League, a position that we would retain until the last week of February.

Before then, we would feature twice on Sky, including a week after that excellent win over Wigan for an unusual Tuesday lunchtime fixture against Stoke City which was our 50th Portman Road game screened on live TV.

Millwall had beaten us 3-1 at the New Den on Boxing Day, so it was imperative for us to get back to winning ways quickly to maintain our place at the top.

Given our position, I recall the atmosphere being subdued, even though there were more than 26,000 fans present. Perhaps the kick-off time had something to do with it, but it was the opposite of that night against Wigan.

Shefki Kuqi's goal on 34 minutes, after a neat one-two with Ian Westlake, was enough to win 1-0 and extended our lead at the top to five points.

Four wins in our next six maintained our place in pole position as we head into our next live match away at Preston North End for a Friday night game on 18 February.

We were up against David Nugent who throughout his career enjoyed scoring against Ipswich, especially at Portman Road. On this evening, 19-year-old Nugent marked his first Preston start by scoring on 36 minutes, the first of what would become one of many goals against Town.

Fortunately, Tommy Miller popped up with his eighth goal of the season in the 69th minute as goalkeeper Gavin Ward had failed to hold his first effort.

Ward was then forced off after a collision with Ian Westlake and youngster Chris Neal took over in goal. He was to make a point-blank save to prevent Darren Bent from scoring a late winner.

The draw put us six points clear at the top going into the Saturday fixtures, but this was to be the first of a four-game winless run as we lost our next three to slip to third, including a much-damaging 1-0 defeat at promotion rivals Wigan.

But a 6-0 victory over Nottingham Forest sparked a revival where we won four and drew one of our next five games before we were covered live again by Sky.

A Monday night visit to Wolves on 11 April came after we had moved back up to second with a 4-3 home win over Rotherham United the week before.

We were now heading into the last five matches of the season dreaming once more of automatic promotion.

Glenn Hoddle's side came out of the blocks firing on all cylinders and within the first quarter of the game, they were two goals ahead.

Colin Cameron scored after five minutes with his effort going in off the underside of the bar and we were all at sea.

Watching on, I could not believe how the game was unfolding with what was at stake. Wolves could have been five up by the time Carl Cort added a second with only 22 minutes on the clock. Only Kelvin Davis was preventing an even worse scoreline.

Ian Westlake was later to hit the bar and Shefki Kuqi clipped a post. But in truth, we did not deserve anything out of the game. With Wigan winning at the weekend, we now dropped back into third place with four to go.

Our next game, on the following Sunday, was also screened live and once again saw Sunderland as the opposition.

A crowd of 29,230 fans packed into Portman Road to witness an epic battle between two of the top three. Again, Marcus Stewart lined up for the visitors and just as had happened in the reverse fixture earlier in the season on live TV, Stewart kept his scoring boots at home. He even had the misfortune of missing a penalty at 0-0, rolling the ball wide, to keep our legendary view of him intact.

Sunderland were strong at the back and dangerous on the counter attack and only a combination of poor finishing and a fine save by Kelvin Davis saw half-time arrive with the score at 0-0.

Sunderland then hit the bar before Ipswich undeservedly took the lead in the 66th minute. A corner exposed the inexperience of visiting goalkeeper Michael Ingham who punched the ball towards his own net and Richard Naylor was on hand to force it over the line. Somehow, from nowhere, we were in front and were in full voice behind the North Stand goal.

Three minutes after our goal, Stewart was substituted and received a heart-rendering round of applause from both sets of supporters, the striker reciprocating by acknowledging all four stands with his hands clapping high above his head.

His replacement, Stephen Elliott, took less than two minutes to draw his side level.

Later, Davis made an excellent save to deny Dean Whitehead but was powerless to stop Carl Robinson from scoring in the 84th minute to give Sunderland the lead.

With a minute remaining, it was the Ipswich fans who were to be frenetically celebrating once more as Darren Bent equalised. Pablo Couñago latched on to Shefki Kuqi's header and set up Bent for an excellent finish. Kuqi almost won the game for Town in injury time, but Ingham denied him, saving with his chest.

The draw kept Sunderland's lead at the top of the table to five points over us in third place, with Wigan sandwiched in between.

Our next and final game of the regular season away at Brighton and Hove Albion was screened live by Sky, as was Wigan's home clash with Reading. It would be another afternoon of keeping an eye on Town and an ear on what was going on elsewhere to see if we could once again claim automatic promotion. Both went into this deciding day level on 84 points but with Wigan holding an advantage of 13 on goal difference.

I have mentioned my good friend Jason previously and it was his flat where we settled to watch this game with a mixture of hope, nerves and tensions shrouding our thoughts. This was either going to be another momentous occasion to share with one another or one that would have us wallowing in our self-pity.

Back then, Brighton still played at the Withdean Stadium and a small crowd of just 6,848 were crammed into their ground. Thousands of Ipswich fans would be glued to their TV sets, just as we were.

Having been promoted to the Championship the season before, Brighton desperately needed something out of the game too to avoid suffering immediate relegation. The tension was engrained into their fans as much as ours, as they too were interested in results elsewhere at Crewe and Gillingham.

The omen that I clung on to was that we had relegated Brighton in 1992 with a victory at Portman Road on the final day, so could we do it again?

The game sparked into life from the outset and Shefki Kuqi put us ahead in the fourth minute to increase our hopes that we could be on to something special.

But before we could get ahead of ourselves, Brighton levelled six minutes later through Adam Virgo.

News then filtered through after 18 minutes that Wigan had gone ahead against Reading. Worse still was that just three minutes later, they scored a second.

The Bennett residence was suddenly quiet, and a déjà vu sense of reality started to kick in.

How we were not awarded a penalty after Darren Bent was clumsily fouled by Charlie Oatway, I will never know.

With no further scoring in our game, our automatic promotion dream was over, again. Wigan claimed a 3-1 win and were promoted along with Sunderland to give Paul Jewell his second promotion to the Premier League in six years.

The point was enough for Brighton to stay up. Had they lost, they would have joined Nottingham Forest and Rotherham United in going down to League One. Instead it was Gillingham who went down with Crewe surviving by virtue of a better goal difference of one goal. We were once again faced with the play-offs for the sixth times in nine seasons. And just like the year before, our league games in that season had plenty of goals. With 85 scored, we were once again to finish as the division's top scorers. We had managed to shore things up a little at the back with only 56 conceded – the joint third best in the top six.

Barely a word was being spoken between me and Jason when he switched on Radio Suffolk to listen to the phone-in. As supporters phoned in with their thoughts and comments, the presenter of the day asked for people to call with thoughts on the play-offs.

I decided that I would try and get through to say my piece and lo and behold, I was the next caller on.

I know that emotions were high, and they were not of the happy kind, but I declared to the presenter that I did not think that we would win the play-offs. Firstly, because we had the disappointment of finishing third and teams historically that just missed out on automatic promotion rarely won through in the lottery of such games.

And my other considered reason was simply because of our awful record in the play-offs. I was not being negative, just realistic. It is how I write my column today all these years on. Realism comes with moments of celebrating the good and bemoaning the bad.

The response from the presenter staggered me if I am honest. I will not name him, but he had a go back at me for my negative thoughts. He wanted my opinion, and I took the time to give it, yet he did not like it. Without giving me the courtesy of time to respond, he cut me off and moved on to the next caller. Fair enough but what happened next was out of order.

He asked the next caller if they thought we could win the play-offs or, and I quote, 'Are you going to be like that last idiot and think we will lose in them?'

So, I was an idiot for having an opinion that he courted but could not agree with!

A year or two later, I attended a supporters' function. A friend pointed out to me that this presenter was also there. My friend walked over to the guy, said hello, and followed up with, 'My mate Karl is here, the one you called an idiot on the radio. Would you like to have a chat with him?'

Of course, he was not prepared to speak to me face to face. I am not a confrontational person at all. I would have just liked the opportunity for him to apologise to me though for labelling me as such on air. But he did not have the nerve to speak to me.

At the time of writing, I have almost completed ten years of writing my *East Anglian Daily Times* column. Not bad for an idiot whose opinion that day was apparently worthless.

So here we were again, in about the same position as one year earlier – a two-legged semi-final against West Ham once more. The only difference this time was that the first game was to take place at Upton Park.

What had we learnt from a year ago? How would we nullify the enthusiastic fans at Upton Park? If the previous year's win really was no more than what West Ham fans had deserved according to one radio commentator, then surely this year, victory over the two legs would be no more than Ipswich fans deserved, right?

On Saturday, 14 May, live on Sky Sports 1 and with a 12.15pm kick-off, the Town fans present at the ground were in fine voice. We knew that we had to play our part too.

It took just 13 minutes to silence us and have us cursing once again. Former Town loanee Marlon Harewood scored in the seventh minute. Our tormentor of a year before, Matthew Etherington, was at it once more, teeing up a cross for Harewood to steer home and then six minutes later, Etherington again made a run before sending a cross over which took a deflection off Jason de Vos into the path of Bobby Zamora who slammed home.

West Ham went on to dominate the first half and could have been out of sight but failed to add to those two goals. In fact, just as fans were disappearing under the stands for a half-time break, it was Ipswich who pulled a goal back, much to the annoyance of the West Ham faithful.

Referee Uriah Rennie awarded a free kick to Town that saw Hammers Czech defender Tomáš Řepka remonstrating, pleading his innocence. His dissent saw him receive a yellow card and Rennie advanced Town's free kick ten yards further forward. This all happened in front of the Sir Bobby Moore Stand from where a chorus of boos rang out. Town were to seize the moment.

Tommy Miller struck the resultant free kick against the left-hand post only for it to rebound off the diving Jimmy Walker's back and into the net. Walker would later join Ipswich as goalkeeper coach in Paul Lambert's days in charge.

We had gotten the lifeline we needed and so incensed were the home fans, Rennie had to be escorted off the pitch.

Jim Magilton, playing in his 50th live TV game and equalling Matt Holland's record, had been barking at his team-mates throughout a poor first half. We hoped and prayed that the second half would be better. I remember thinking that this could be Bolton all over again from 2000. There was a similar pattern brewing. We were 2-0 down early on, we had reached the interval only 2-1 behind, so could we match that game and find an equaliser in the second period?

Joe Royle made a double substitution at half-time with Matt Richards replacing the out-of-sorts Drissa Diallo who was never to be seen in an Ipswich shirt again, and Darren Currie took over from Kevin Horlock.

It was Currie's introduction that proved to be pivotal. In the 74th minute he floated a diagonal ball into the area for Darren Bent to send towards goal. His shot was blocked, looped up and when Anton Ferdinand and Walker challenged each other, the ball dropped for Shefki Kuqi to gleefully poke home and we had completed an unlikely comeback. How we celebrated that goal and one felt that we were now in the driving seat, just as we had been at Bolton five years earlier.

The second leg on the following Wednesday saw a massive Portman Road crowd of 30,010, to take the combined attendance for the two games to nearly 64,000. Thousands more would be watching on Sky Sports too.

This game would see one party continue with the dreaded play-off curse. Ipswich had lost on five previous occasions while West Ham boss Alan Pardew saw his side lose in the final the year before, as well as having two failed play-off campaigns with Reading.

It was West Ham who made most of the running in the first half, but Jimmy Walker was deceived by a swerving shot from Darren Currie that slipped out of his grasp, although fortunately for him the ball went wide.

Tension and anxiety started to creep into the game for both sides after the break. I was in the North Stand looking up to the heavens above, praying for my no doubt watching grandad to send some help our way. I was a nervous wreck. All I was asking for was a repeat of the 1-0 win in the home leg a year previously.

But in the 61st minute West Ham scored. Harewood received a ball from Carl Fletcher, sprinted powerfully to the byline and delivered into the box where Bobby Zamora was left with a simple tap-in for his first of the night, and his third of the tie overall.

A little over ten minutes later, it was game over as Zamora scored again, volleying home yet another Harewood cross after having all the space and time he required to pick his spot past Kelvin Davis, who was playing his last game for Town – as was striker Darren Bent.

It was incredulous to have to suffer defeat to West Ham again. It was even more inexplicable that once more, and for the 12th time, I was suffering play-off heartbreak. I just stood there at the final whistle staring into the abyss. Yet again, I was down and this time, the kicks just reigned in even harder. How much more of this could any football fan take?

I did not want to hear if West Ham fans deserved it again. I just looked at the stadium emptying feeling the pain of every single Ipswich supporter who was departing with shattered dreams again.

The end of this season also marked my 11th successive campaign without missing a home game, a run of 303 games. Some 44 of those were screened live on TV. We won 21 and drew nine of those games which, given our overall record on TV, was not a bad return I suppose.

By the time the 2005/06 season came around, and the reset button was yet again pressed, Ipswich fans had been victims of many emotional battles in recent years and were geared up to go through yet another one.

My thoughts had turned back to those four play-off semi-finals at the end of the 1990s. Would Joe Royle need the same number of attempts as George Burley to succeed in them? Or could he do it in a year less and get promotion this season? One thing was for sure, if we were to gain a play-off place, we would not have to face West Ham once again as they had won the final this time.

But the start of this season saw an Ipswich squad with several changes with six of the 2004/05 group having departed. It did not feel like the Burley era that built up a head of steam based on a consistent squad with the odd introduction of additional quality when it mattered.

On the opening day of the season alone, we saw five new debutants play in a 1-0 win over Cardiff City.

Our first live game of the new season came on Bank Holiday Monday at the end of August. Preston North End, with David Nugent in the starting line-up, were the visitors to Portman Road.

I took my sons Karl and Craig and took up an unusual position in the ground with them in the lower tier of the Pioneer Stand. Our opening five games had seen us already sitting in the top six. We had won both of our home games so far, against Cardiff and Sheffield Wednesday, and the sun was beating down. I hoped that the boys would see a win and a performance that would have them begging for more. I was looking to introduce fans of the future, which is something so many of us parents love to do.

What followed was everything that I did not want to see, and I am surprised that Karl and Craig ever wanted to go to another game.

I should have known that with Nugent present, things would not go to plan. After half an hour without any goals, the Lilywhites scored three by half-time.

Nugent scored the first two (31 and 34) and David Jones added the third in stoppage time. Talk about shell-shocked. That had been a disastrous 15 minutes and there would be no way back.

It was not until the 85th minute that Preston added a fourth through substitute Patrick Agyemang, just three minutes after he came off the bench to replace Danny Dichio. Once again, we lost in front of the Sky cameras after completely wilting in the sun.

It would not be until 16 October that we would appear on Sky once more. This was for a Sunday lunchtime kick-off at Reading. Since that heavy defeat to Preston, we won just two of the next six games. We had at one point dropped to 13th but clawed our way back to eighth. Reading on the other hand were flying and were sitting second in the table, three points behind leaders Sheffield United.

Joe Royle sent us into this game with a new-look 3-5-2 formation which proved to be a tactical disaster.

Kevin Doyle was Reading's man of the match, and Jason de Vos was lucky to escape a red card when hauling the Irishman down with just two minutes on the clock.

On 18 minutes, Doyle created Reading's first goal. He exploited Fabian Wilnis's lapse in concentration to send the ball across the face of goal where Richard Naylor slid in and could only find the back of his own net when attempting to clear.

Royle realised the need to change the formation at the break and sent on Adam Proudlock for his Ipswich debut at the expense of de Vos.

But just 120 seconds after the restart, Reading had a second. Glen Little crossed from the right, and Doyle rose above Sito at the far post to head home.

Thereafter, Leroy Lita hit a post, Doyle then sent the rebound against the bar and Bobby Convey had a goal disallowed for offside.

Monday, 28 November 2005, away at Cardiff City, was a milestone live TV game in Ipswich's history.

Firstly, this was our 100th to be screened. Secondly, Jim Magilton played his 54th and final live game for Ipswich which currently stands as a record. But for

both club and player, the occasion would not be celebrated with a victory.

There was a concern building among the fans as we were plummeting down the table. We had won just one in the eight leading up to this game, a sequence which started and ended with defeats to Reading, who would go on to win the league at a canter, finishing with 106 points, 16 ahead of second-placed Sheffield United. The Royals lost only twice in the league all season.

Michael Ricketts had an excellent opportunity to put City in front in the first half when they were awarded a 13th-minute penalty. Cameron Jerome was brought down by Fabian Wilnis and the Dutchman was harshly sent off to become the second Ipswich player to be awarded a red card in a live TV game. Lewis Price then saved Ricketts' weak spot-kick.

Royle felt that Town were hard done by over the awarding of the penalty. Justice was done by Price's save, but the loss of Wilnis for the remainder of the game was a heavy punishment to swallow. Even Bluebirds boss David Jones suggested that a yellow card would have been sufficient punishment.

Ricketts would make amends however when he fired past Price on the half-hour to give Cardiff a lead they held until four minutes from time.

Billy Clarke came off the bench to replace Jim Magilton on 65 minutes for his Ipswich debut and we had witnessed Magilton's last TV cameo as an Ipswich player.

Jimmy Juan scored his first live TV goal for the club when hammering home an excellent free kick to give us hope of securing a draw.

Two minutes later, Alan Lee, who would join Town less than two months later, replaced Ricketts, and Jason Koumas slammed home an injury time winner for the hosts to ensure that we left our centenary TV game with no points to shout about. We had now dropped to 15th.

Our next live game would not be until 5 February, which proved to be our last live outing of the season. How we had fallen. We were no longer an interesting proposition for live coverage.

This was mostly because since the last TV match, at Cardiff, three wins in ten saw us drop to 16th. Had it not been for the fact that this was to renew a battle with Norwich, our first game against them on TV for over three years, perhaps we would not have been screened live at all in the second half of that season.

This was the 11th East Anglian derby to be shown live, and at this stage, Norwich held the upper hand in the head-to-head stakes with five wins over Ipswich's four and the sole draw being that last live game played between the two in September 2002.

I have missed very few live Ipswich matches, whether in the ground or watching on TV, and my latest Ipswich regret at the time found its way to me following this game.

I had been poorly overnight with little sleep, and was in bed all day on this day. With around a couple of hours before the 11.15am kick-off to go, I figured that I could get some sleep then watch the game upon waking up.

I was to sleep until just after the final whistle. You know when you wake up in such circumstances you struggle for a few seconds to think what day it is, never mind the time? Yes, that. I needed a couple of seconds to work out exactly what the time was.

As soon as I saw that on the bedside clock, I gasped in horror that I must have missed the game. Hoping I had not missed a tremendous victory, I panicked for a few seconds until I got into my phone to check the score. We had won 2-1.

My first instinct was to punch the air and scream get in. But then I realised I had missed us beating Norwich. Is there a worse feeling?

When I later saw the highlights, I had a wry smile when I saw the style in how we had scored our winner two minutes from time. The result certainly worked better than any medication I was on that day I can tell you.

I later learnt that Norwich's expensively assembled side had been outplayed by our young side. Jason de Vos and Richard Naylor were solid at the back, and 18-year-olds Owen Garvan and Danny Haynes caught the eye for Town.

We dominated the first period with Matt Richards the closest to scoring when he saw an effort hit the post. And then against the run of play, Norwich went ahead.

Youssef Safri lifted a hopeful long ball into the Ipswich half and for the first and only time in the game, our offside trap failed to snare a Canary.

This allowed Jonatan Johansson to run on and lift the ball neatly over Lewis Price.

The chirps of the Norwich fans though were to last only five minutes as Ipswich were soon back on level terms. Jimmy Juan struck a free kick from 25 yards out and with Robert Green looking to have the effort covered, he saw the ball take a wicked deflection off Johansson and nestle into the back of the net. Juan claimed the goal and rightly so.

Half-time saw Norwich boss Nigel Worthington send on Carl Robinson and Darren Huckerby to halt the constant Ipswich pressure, but nothing changed.

Danny Haynes, the scourge of Norwich, had come on as a 25th-minute substitute for the injured Gavin Williams. He proved to be a constant menace and went close to putting Ipswich in front in the second period when he reached Garvan's long punt forward before the on-rushing Green could get there and headed towards goal. Just when it looked like the ball might cross the line, Norwich's Zesh Rehman cleared.

Haynes might have followed up himself had Green not flattened him, but referee Keith Stroud saw nothing wrong. The official also waved Ipswich appeals for a penalty away two minutes later when Gary Doherty fouled Alan Lee. Joe Royle described both appeals as 'blatant penalties' after the game.

Just when Norwich thought they might get away with a draw, up popped Haynes to score an 88th-minute winner.

Matt Richards crossed from the left, Lee headed across the goal and Haynes flung himself forward to bundle the ball over the line.

Norwich claimed that he had scored with his arm. After the game, Haynes himself admitted that he did not know which part of him the ball had hit. But he was right when he also said that Town were the better side and deserved the victory.

With this win, Town went up four places to 12th and won their next two games to climb into the top ten. But two wins in our final dozen matches saw us end up in a disappointing 15th place – our lowest league finish since 1966.

That win at Norwich proved to be Joe Royle's last live TV game as manager of Ipswich – not a bad way to bow out, I guess. And the season's ending marked the end of Royle's three-and-a-half-year spell altogether.

We will always look back on his time where he had to cut the wage bill significantly but kept us competitive throughout most of his time in charge. We were always excellent value for goals in our games – at both ends – and those two play-off semi-final defeats to West Ham will always have us remembering Royle's side as the 'nearly' men.

CHAPTER 4: IT STARTS AND ENDS AT QPR

Jim Magilton (14 games)

On 5 June 2006, and to the surprise of many Town fans, Jim Magilton was named as the new Ipswich manager. The Irishman had been a hero as a player and held legendary status for his hat-trick against Bolton Wanderers in that play-off semi-final victory in 2000.

In the main, he was a popular choice albeit with some trepidation as to whether he could be equally as successful in his first managerial role.

By the time we reached Magilton's first televised game at the end of August, we had lost our first three league matches, followed by a 0-0 draw at home to Hull City. We were already concerned as we sat in 22nd place.

Loftus Road would be the venue on Friday, 25 August, as Queens Park Rangers looked to defend their unbeaten home league record after a draw against Leeds United and a win over Southend United.

This was always one of my favourite away grounds to visit. The Springbok pub near the ground was a good place for away fans to be and I recall that before a game in December 1998, I found myself talking to the sister of Lee Hodges. That name may not ring too many bells with younger Ipswich fans, but Lee made four substitute appearances during November and December 1998 when on loan from West Ham. He came off the bench that night to replace Adam Tanner. Lee's sister was buzzing with excitement prior to the game that night.

Despite Billy Clarke rattling the crossbar, an otherwise drab, goalless first half left us in the School End wondering where our first win under Magilton might come from. It certainly did not look like being on that night.

Our fears increased when Kevin Gallen scored to put the Hoops in front, and I was concerned as to where and how we might turn things around. Little did I realise that the question would be answered in less than five minutes.

When things are not going your way as a team or an individual, you just need a bit of luck to change your fortunes. Town needed the luck, and it is hard to argue that the penalty we were awarded was not with its degree of controversy.

When Gavin Williams broke into the QPR penalty area, he took the slightest of touches from Damion Stewart and fell to the ground easily. Referee Lee Mason initially looked as if he was allowing play to continue before changing his mind and pointing to the spot.

Simon Walton stepped up to strike the ball low under the body of Paul Jones and draw Ipswich level.

Town had been on the ropes for much of the game, but that moment of good fortune reinvigorated them.

Walton came close to adding his second goal of the night when hitting a post with a volley from the right of the area, and then Town took the lead.

Mark Noble, on loan from West Ham, swung a corner over which was met by Alan Lee who flicked the ball on to the far post where Jason de Vos bundled home. Our tails were now well and truly up.

Four minutes from time, Williams broke down the left and produced a cross which rebounded to substitute Dean Bowditch who coolly sent a header past Jones to give us a 3-1 win. We were now much happier in that away end and sung our way to the final whistle.

As a result of this victory, Magilton followed Sir Bobby Robson and Joe Royle in becoming the third Ipswich manager to win his first televised game.

Magilton's second TV outing came at the end of September for yet another Friday night date on Sky and a visit to Layer Road, home of Colchester United.

For so long, the U's were my second favourite team. My dad and grandad would often take Shaun and I to Layer Road for Friday night games in the late 1970s and early 1980s. Some of my favourite early football memories were created by those nights.

Nowadays, I put them into the Norwich and West Ham bracket, purely down to how some of their fans react about anything Ipswich-related. I know we took their dreams away in 1956/57 when we pipped them to the Division Three South title by a point and they did not go on to the illustrious history that then came our way, but that is a long old time to bear a grudge.

The Championship in 2006/07 was littered with East Anglian clubs with Colchester, Norwich, Southend, and Luton joining us.

Following that win at QPR, we were now in good form having won three and drawn one of the following four games and had worked our way up to eighth place. Colchester were also going well having climbed from the bottom after four matches to sit just one place below us.

This was our first league clash with Colchester in 49 years and we were expecting a tight encounter, which was how it turned out in terms of the narrow margin of victory secured by the hosts.

Former Ipswich midfielder Geraint Williams was by now in charge at Colchester and came into this game on a six-game unbeaten run which saw him being tipped for the Manager of the Month award.

A sell-out crowd of 6,065 saw the only goal of the game arrive after just nine minutes when Lewis Price saw Jamie Cureton's effort late and pushed the ball out to Karl Duguid to score his first league goal for three years.

Some Colchester fans have said to me in the past that they remember Duguid's goal ever so well. I reply with 'so do I' – when we beat them 3-2 later in the season at Portman Road.

That defeat sparked a three-game run of losses to send us back down to 18th before two more local derbies were to be played. A 3-1 win at Southend was followed by our next live game at home to Luton on 29 October, exactly one month since Colchester.

We would go on to win this game 5-0 for our biggest victory on live TV, both at the time and still standing at the time of writing.

Barely two weeks had passed since we had conceded five at home to West Bromwich Albion and in between, Luton had scored five past Leeds at Kenilworth Road. So it is fair to say that nobody saw this result coming.

Even before we scored, Billy Clarke blazed over from six yards, Dan Harding dragged a shot just wide, and Alex Bruce saw a header tipped on to the woodwork. From the resultant corner, we finally got the breakthrough that we had thoroughly deserved.

Sylvain Legwinski met a Matt Richards corner on 20 minutes to angle a precise header into the net.

Luton thought they had equalised moments after the half-time interval when Rowan Vine slotted into an unguarded net following clever work by future Ipswich man Carlos Edwards. However, Vine was flagged for offside, a position he was deemed to have been in at the start of the move but clearly was not when he scored.

This decision only served to spur Ipswich on. Seven minutes after this incident, Harding's cross was headed down by Alan Lee for Jaime Peters to turn the ball home for the first goal of his professional career.

Thereafter, the game became all about Lee. On 66 minutes he latched on to Legwinski's through ball to drive home his first of the afternoon. Ten minutes later, following yet another corner from Richards, Danny Haynes saw his effort saved by Luton's goalkeeper Marlon Beresford who could only palm into the path of Lee to score his second.

In the dying seconds, another Luton player who would later feature for Ipswich, Kevin Foley, fouled Gary Roberts inside the area and up stepped Lee to score the resultant penalty for his hat-trick. It was his first for the club and took his tally to eight goals in seven games.

Lee became the third Ipswich player after Marcus Stewart and Dean Bowditch to score a hat-trick in a live TV game and is currently the last player to achieve such a feat.

The win, coupled with the inconsistent nature of many teams in the Championship, meant that having started the day only five points above the relegation zone, we were now only six points off an automatic promotion place.

Three weeks later, we were once again on Sky for a customary clash with Norwich.

The season by now was one of frustrating inconsistency. Having thrashed Luton, we then drew at Plymouth, lost at Burnley, and lost again at home to Sheffield Wednesday. We were down to 17th on the back of this run.

Danny Haynes, scorer of that dubious winning goal at Carrow Road in the previous season, which was later officially credited to him, came off the bench in the 76th minute, replacing Billy Clarke, to add to his cult hero status among Ipswich fans.

Norwich would have been sick of the sight of him – even before this game. The Canaries had once rejected Haynes as a youngster and how he would go on and make them pay. He had scored multiple goals against them at both youth and reserve levels and was now doing so in senior football.

No fewer than eight Town players were making their East Anglian derby debuts, including four on loan. Goalkeeper Mike Pollitt was one of those players and in fact, this was to be the only game that he would feature in for Ipswich. Defender Matthew Bates was also playing his first game for the club.

Town tore into Norwich from the start and fully deserved victory in this encounter. But it would be the visitors who opened the scoring on 26 minutes through Luke Chadwick, capitalising on a sliced clearance by Matt Richards.

Bates was later to put a crunching tackle in on Chadwick that saw the Norwich man fall awkwardly and taken to hospital with a shoulder injury.

Five minutes before the break, Ipswich were back on level terms. Sylvain Legwinski put in a strong tackle to break up a Norwich attack. The ball was played out to Gary Roberts who in turn fed Billy Clarke. He then fed the ball back to Legwinski who with an astute finish, rounded off the move he had started.

While Ipswich were dominating the second half, the elusive second goal would not come until the introduction of Haynes.

Jim Magilton said after the game that with a sapping pitch, he noticed that Norwich's back four were starting to tire and knew it was the right time to send Haynes on. A minute after replacing Clarke, and with just his third touch, Haynes was once more causing Norwich fans heartache. He met a cross perfectly from Roberts and powered the ball home past the despairing Paul Gallacher.

In the 90th minute, Haynes scored again. Richards laid the ball off to Haynes who curled home from the edge of the area to seal a 3-1 win. How we celebrated yet another win in the stands against Norwich.

Following this game, and despite the campaign only being in November, Town were not to feature live on TV again for the rest of the season. A sign of how we were no longer a viable option for Sky or indeed, any other broadcaster.

Our final position in 2006/07 was 14th. The days of reaching the play-offs every season were now long gone.

Although Jim Magilton's first season was very underwhelming, he was bucking a trend as far as live TV games would go. A win rate of 75 per cent from his first four was good going and this figure climbed as high as 83 per cent when he was to oversee Town go on to win their first two live matches of 2007/08.

First up was our third game of the season, and the second at home, as Crystal Palace were the visitors for a Bank Holiday Sunday lunchtime kick-off on 26 August in front of the Sky cameras.

In the Palace line-up were former Ipswich players Mark Kennedy, and James Scowcroft, while Shefki Kuqi was later to come off the bench to replace Stuart Green and received a warm reception from the Ipswich fans when entering the field of play.

Town had beaten Sheffield Wednesday 4-1 on the opening day of the season and followed that up with a 1-1 draw at Plymouth to sit in fourth place.

Palace were lucky not to lose goalkeeper Julian Speroni to a red card in the first half after a deliberate handball outside his area.

Town had taken control after goalkeeper Neil Alexander saved a free kick by Stuart Green, which was the closest that Palace came to scoring all game.

The only goal came on 72 minutes when Jon Walters scored his first live TV goal for Ipswich when he headed home a pinpoint cross from Gary Roberts.

This victory moved Town to the top of the table, but two defeats in the next two games sent us tumbling all the way down to 15th before the Sky Sports camera returned to Portman Road on 22 September.

I was not at Portman Road and neither did I get to see it on TV. It is one of the very few live games that I have missed altogether.

However, I would like to think that I had a justifiable excuse. A year earlier, my twin daughters Lola and Angel were born, and this day was all about celebrating their first birthday. I did of course keep an eye on my phone like any good multitasking dad would do.

Coventry City were once again our opponents, and it was a bittersweet moment for me as we went on to record a 4-1 victory. I was disappointed to have missed such a fine win, but of course, was delighted all the same.

Both Leon Best and Jay Tabb, future Ipswich players, were in the Coventry starting XI.

In a one-sided affair, the deadlock was opened after ten minutes when Jason de Vos rose above Arjan de Zeeuw at the far post to head in an Owen Garvan free kick.

Best should have done better with a header that failed to trouble Neil Alexander and when Alan Lee went close in the 18th minute, it was only a matter of time before Town would score again.

On 24 minutes, Pablo Couñago showed excellent composure to beat two Coventry defenders before sliding the ball past Dimi Konstantopoulos.

Moments before half-time, the late afternoon got even better for Town as Jon Walters made it 3-0 to head in a Gary Roberts cross.

Couñago headed a Garvan cross into an empty net on 57 minutes for 4-0 and Town threatened to run riot. Their scoring though had ended, and Stephen Hughes pulled one back for Coventry on 69 minutes.

Town saw the game out comfortably to win 4-1 and inflict upon City their first away defeat of the season.

By the time that Town were next live, we had made our way back up into the top four. This after three wins and two draws had backed up that win against Coventry.

On 4 November Town headed to Norwich for the latest instalment of the East Anglian derby and Jim Magilton on a run of four successive live TV victories.

This game marked the 50th live TV appearance for Fabian Wilnis in an Ipswich shirt, becoming only the third player to achieve this feat after Matt Holland and Magilton. For Norwich, Glenn Roeder was taking charge of his first game.

By half-time we were feeling incredibly happy with how the game had progressed after putting ourselves into a two-goal lead. An opening goal for Town almost happened after just 20 seconds, but Billy Clarke narrowly failed to connect with a cross by Jon Walters.

It was not just Town though who were carving out openings. Neil Alexander made a stunning save in the seventh minute to deny Dion Dublin from point-blank range. Dublin then headed a good chance wide before Ipswich took the lead.

Alan Lee flicked on a goal kick to Couñago and as the Irishman turned his marker, the Spaniard played an inch-perfect ball back to Lee who calmly rolled the ball past David Marshall and into the far corner for his eighth goal of the season on 27 minutes. This was Ipswich's 150th goal in live TV games.

Jason Shackell then thumped a header from Darren Huckerby's free kick against the base of the post as Norwich looked to get back on level terms.

Four minutes before half-time, Couñago doubled the lead. Lee's poor free kick deflected to Clarke who saw his effort brilliantly saved by Marshall before Clarke was able to prevent the ball from going out of play and sent it back across the six-yard box where Couñago had an open goal at his mercy.

Norwich reduced the arrears in the 56th minute when Martin Taylor headed Simon Lappin's in-swinging delivery off Owen Garvan for an unfortunate own goal.

Eleven minutes later, Norwich were level. Cureton latched on to John Hartson's flick-on and lifted the ball over Alexander for 2-2.

The introduction from the bench of Danny Haynes in the 75th minute failed to have the desired effect for once, and Norwich fans were relieved that he was not to score on this occasion.

In stoppage time, Huckerby was shown a straight red card for a high challenge on Walters.

No doubt that the Norwich camp was happier with the draw after coming from two goals down, and we left Carrow Road feeling like we had lost and bemoaning the throwing away of such a lead.

The point though was enough for us to maintain our place in the top four.

I have already mentioned that after Norwich, our most faced opponents in live TV games are Coventry. And sure enough, our next live game, on 29 December, would be against Coventry at the Ricoh Arena, for what would be our 50th screened match away from home.

Our previous televised game at Coventry had seen us win 2-1. A repeat of that result would have made for an excellent belated Christmas present for Town fans, but we went on to witness a reversal of that score.

At this stage of the season, Town's home form alone was maintaining our push for a play-off place with ten wins and two draws from our dozen games at Portman Road played to date.

Away from home, it was a different Ipswich team altogether, with eight defeats and four draws.

Jim Magilton blasted his side after the game for the sloppy defending that allowed Coventry to take all three points.

Julian Gray had given the Sky Blues an 11th-minute lead, but it was Town who would be the better side for the remainder of the half. Danny Haynes levelled matters three minutes from the interval when heading home a rebound after David Wright's effort had rattled the underside of the crossbar.

The second half saw a less-than-convincing performance and Dele Adebola scored Coventry's winner on 64 minutes.

Tommy Miller became the third Ipswich player to be sent off in a live TV game when he received what looked like a harsh red card.

We had now dropped down to eighth and with the January 2008 transfer window just around the corner, it was reported that Magilton had a transfer war chest of £12m to spend after the recent acquisition of the club by Marcus Evans for a reported £44m. On the evidence of the season to date, Magilton certainly needed to strengthen areas to start getting the results away from home to match those gained at Portman Road.

We were to feature in only one further live game that season, on the final day, at home to Hull City on Sunday, 4 May.

Hull were already in the play-offs with a third-placed finish guaranteed. As for Ipswich, we were back to the good old days of the late 1990s, where we could go into a tense last day needing a win and results going our way elsewhere to achieve a particular desired outcome. How we had missed those days.

On this occasion, we needed to beat Hull and hope that both Watford and Wolves slipped up in their games to reach the play-offs.

Our home form throughout the season had remained excellent. Fourteen wins, seven draws and one defeat was our record going into this final home encounter. One more win when it mattered most is what we craved.

How we won this game only 1-0 I will never know. We battered Hull who clearly had their heads turned to their forthcoming play-off ties. We needed to make the running and our intensity ensured that we achieved our target. For much of the game, the goal we deserved looked like it might not arrive.

Pablo Couñago hit a post and when Shefki Kuqi tucked home the rebound our celebrations were shortlived after the offside flag was then raised.

Tommy Miller then saw his effort hit the upright and excellent chances went begging as Couñago, Alan Quinn, and Jason de Vos all spurned their opportunities.

As the game entered the final 20 minutes, and our nerves shredding by the second, enter Alan Lee off the bench to replace Quinn. A minute later, we were celebrating wildly as our hopes were raised – as was the North Stand roof by our crescendo of noise.

Jon Walters headed a ball back across the goal and Lee rose to power a header into the corner of the net. The final whistle blew, and we had our 15th home win of the season.

The players celebrated momentarily, but then eyes and ears were on what had happened elsewhere. But it was negative responses all round as Watford drew at Blackpool and Wolves won 1-0 at home to Plymouth. They finished level on 70 points, but it was Watford who claimed the coveted sixth place by virtue of a better goal difference of just one goal.

We finished one point further behind in eighth and with a better goal difference than both Watford and Wolves.

Once again, there was disappointment for fans watching both at the game and back home as our season had been ended by the thinnest of margins.

The total sum of just three away victories all season proved to be our downfall and Magilton would have to pick his side up again over the summer. But he would do so without Stephen Bywater, Danny Simpson, Jason de Vos and Shefki Kuqi at least, who all played their last games for the club in that win over Hull.

The first three games of the 2008/09 season saw a reverse of Town's home versus away problems of the season before, as we lost our first two home matches but won 3-0 at Burnley in between.

Our fourth game was televised at Vicarage Road, home of Watford.

The Hornets were by now considered very much a bogey side for Ipswich. They were unbeaten against us in seven games which included a run of six successive wins going into this one.

Defender Moritz Volz made his Ipswich debut after joining on loan from Fulham. Watford's line-up included Tamás Priskin who would later join Ipswich in a £1m move.

We got off to a dream start when Pablo Couñago scored with just two minutes on the clock. Watford goalkeeper Mart Poom gifted the opportunity when clearing straight to the Spaniard who slotted home after holding off a challenge from Leigh Bromby.

From this moment, Town were on top and looked to add a second. Gareth McAuley found himself in the opposition area and totally unmarked, but saw his shot deflected out.

Kevin Lisbie then evaded the offside trap but chipped wide when he should have squared to Couñago for a simple tap-in.

Watford felt that they should have had a penalty when McAuley brought Priskin down with the goal gaping and then Jon Harley hit a Town post.

The hosts drew level in the 58th minute when John Eustace headed home Lee Williamson's corner.

Chances came and went at both ends and just when we thought we could leave with a deserved point, Watford scored a winner.

Richard Wright failed to hold a shot by Jobi McAnuff and the ball fell nicely for substitute John-Joe O'Toole to nod home from close range.

I left the game thinking that when it came to Watford we were cursed. This was their seventh win and that cursed run extended as they went another seven against us unbeaten including five more wins on the trot.

Jordan Rhodes had come off the bench in this game and little did we know at that time, this would be the last we would see of the young striker in an Ipswich shirt.

A month later, a Saturday teatime game on 27 September saw the Sky cameras back at Portman Road as we hosted Crystal Palace. With just two wins in our opening seven games, we were down to 16th and the excitement of the end of the previous season was long since forgotten.

Palace were also experiencing struggles of their own and came into this game in the bottom three.

Richard Wright was being kept busy in the Ipswich goal, but it would be Town who would take the lead in the 23rd minute through Jon Stead who scored his 50th career goal.

However, the lead would last only two minutes. Victor Moses was denied by a brilliant save by Wright but was on hand to head home the resultant corner.

Shefki Kuqi would later come off the bench for Palace, but with no further scoring, Jim Magilton's 100th league game in charge ended in a draw, and Town had managed just one win in their first four home matches of the season.

It would be mid-November by the time we saw Town on our TV screens again as we visited Doncaster Rovers for yet another early Saturday evening kick-off.

We had picked ourselves up since that draw with Crystal Palace with four wins, three draws and one defeat lifting us to eighth. Bottom side Rovers had not won in the league for 12 games and had not scored at home since August. This felt like an opportunity for Magilton to get his first live TV win of the season.

Richard Naylor had hit the bar on 20 minutes, and then David Norris wasted a good opportunity when scuffing wide. Town paid the price for their wastefulness when defender Shelton Martis scored the only goal of the game three minutes before half-time.

After the break, Darren Ambrose came off the bench for his second debut having returned on loan from Charlton Athletic and striker Jon Stead was also introduced from the bench as Ipswich searched for an equaliser.

Ambrose almost made an immediate impact as his brilliant volley was acrobatically tipped over the bar by Neil Sullivan. Doncaster held on for the win.

Three weeks later, our fourth live game of the season was back at Carrow Road. We were clinging on to a place in the top ten when this game was upon us, and it felt that we could just not get going this season.

Richard Naylor became the fourth and last player to make his 50th live TV appearance in an Ipswich shirt.

Too many Town players were off form on that day as Jim Magilton was to taste a derby defeat for the first time.

In the process, Town suffered their third successive away defeat and Norwich claimed their first win against us in six attempts.

If Jon Walters had scored in the 50th minute to put us in front, it could have been a different story.

Walters broke clear from his own half to beat the offside trap and as he was bearing through on goal, it was a Martijn Reuser Wembley moment where everything happened in slow motion, and it would only be a matter of time before our man in blue would score.

But David Marshall stood firm until the last moment to turn away the effort.

Ten minutes later, Norwich made Town pay for that miss and took the lead through Lee Croft whose effort from 22 yards swerved spectacularly into the top corner.

That goal led to Magilton bringing Danny Haynes off the bench for Ambrose in the hope that Haynes could rekindle some of his own derby magic. Haynes almost obliged but saw his header produce an instinctive save by Marshall from close range.

With Gareth McAuley off the pitch in the 82nd minute having a head wound tended to, Norwich capitalised on Town being temporarily down to ten men. David Bell swung over a free kick and Stead could only head the ball against Matty Pattison who, from close range, smashed it into the net off the underside of the bar to give Norwich a 2-0 win.

Yet again, we had been poor in front of the live cameras, as this stretched the winless run for the season of four live games. This was a fact noted by Magilton in his post-match press conference when he declared, 'We've saved all our worst performances for the cameras.'

Our last live game of the 2008/09 season came as early as Saturday, 21 February with another trip to QPR.

Our inconsistencies saw us still in tenth place and we were just struggling to find a significant run to break into the top six – a position that ultimately, we would not find all season.

At the fifth attempt of the season, we would finally win a game live on Sky, and what an excellent shift by the lads to secure the victory.

Leading up to this game, there were growing calls by some Ipswich fans for Jim Magilton to be sacked. This result would quieten those fans – for the time being.

Nobody could have seen this win coming though when we fell behind in the third minute thanks to a goal by Samuel Di Carmine who netted a Wayne Routledge cross at the near post.

Eleven minutes later, Town levelled through Jon Stead who turned in a weak and deflected effort by David Norris.

Town should have scored again just before the break. Gavin Mahon attempted an ambitious header back to his goalkeeper Lee Camp, but the ball was intercepted by Pablo

Couñago. With his back to goal, he laid the ball off to Jon Stead who somehow managed to fire wide of the unguarded net.

We were not to be denied however, when in the second half, we turned on the style and took the lead just after the hour mark.

Couñago won the ball off the dithering Mahon, brushed off another couple of challenges and found the time and space to fire past Camp.

Before QPR could restart the game, Jon Walters came off the bench to replace Luciano Civelli and nine minutes later it was Walters who capped a fine night by scoring Town's third.

He took a sublime 50-yard ball from Alan Quinn in his stride and with his second touch, he fired his shot home.

This victory saw Town close the gap to the play-off places to just two points and owner Marcus Evans gave Magilton a heartfelt vote of confidence.

That vote of confidence turned out to be the dreaded vote, as so often happens in football. Magilton remained in charge for just a further ten games after that win at QPR, in which time he would only see his side win twice more.

The second of those wins came in his final game in charge, a magnificent 3-2 victory at home to Norwich which unusually for such a fixture, was not screened live. Nearly 29,000 would witness Magilton's last stand.

Having seen Ipswich up to ninth on the back of a memorable victory, it came as a bit of a surprise to see him sacked just three days later.

Only five Ipswich Town managers have been in charge for ten or more live TV games and of them all, Magilton has the best win percentage which sits at exactly 50 per cent.

His live TV games ended where they started – with a 3-1 win away at Queens Park Rangers.

CHAPTER 5: FROM ARSENAL JOY TO POSH WOES

Roy Keane, Ian McParland, Paul Jewell (15 games)

After the sacking of Jim Magilton, Marcus Evans made a decision that would throw the club into an intense media spotlight for the next 18 months or so with the appointment of former Manchester United and Ireland captain Roy Keane.

This was a statement of intent and many supporters felt this would be a sign of the club moving up a level and on to much better times.

Keane was in place to take charge of the final two games of the 2008/09 season, which were both won, 3-0 at Cardiff City and 2-1 at home to Coventry City on the final day. We finished ninth and some eight points off the play-offs but with plenty of optimism going into the summer and with excitement in looking forward to 2009/10.

Keane's appointment drew a lot of media attention, and it was normal to come home from work, switch the television on to Sky Sports news and see him in an Ipswich training top. But he was not necessarily talking about Ipswich-related matters.

Sky would jump straight on to the Keane bandwagon by making their first live Championship fixture of 2009/10 our visit to Coventry, which would of course make it successive games against the Sky Blues under Keane's guidance. A repeat of the 2-1 win in the previous fixture would get the season off to a great start and heighten our expectations further. Sadly, it did not work out that way.

Pre-season was a sign of Keane's strict regime that was to come as he talked of taking Town players out of their comfort zones. This included a training camp with the Paratroop Regiment.

This opening day game saw Ipswich debuts for Damien Delaney, Lee Martin and from the bench, Tamás Priskin.

Within 25 minutes, Town were 2-0 down. Coventry's opening goal on ten minutes was proper route-one stuff. Their goalkeeper Keiren Westwood launched a long ball forward that saw his opposite number Richard Wright leave his line to claim.

But the ball had found its way to Clinton Morrison who swivelled and sent a high shot over Wright and into the net. It was a good finish, but question marks were left over Town's defending.

Morrison then scored his and Coventry's second after sending a diving header into the corner of the net. We looked on stunned that already, we were two behind and this was supposed to be a glorious new era.

Five minutes later, we were able to shed some of those fears when Jon Walters ran on to a diagonal pass from Jon Stead and scored with a first-touch finish.

That is how the scoring had finished and we fell to a 2-1 defeat. While we were licking our wounds and dissecting the defeat, Coventry boss Chris Coleman commented on how strong we looked and there would not be many better teams to face than us. That was a bold statement to make so soon, but one of course that we were hoping would be proved right.

Two home games saw a draw and a defeat against Leicester City and Crystal Palace respectively and if we thought that the season had gotten off to a bad start, this was just the beginning. Matters got much worse.

Sky were of course more than interested to give Keane ample viewing and in just the third week of August, they showed us live for a second time as we visited West Bromwich Albion.

Just like at Coventry, we went behind in the tenth minute as Albion's new summer signing from Paris Saint-Germain, Youssouf Mulumbu, beat Wright with a low drive to open his account for the season.

And to extend the replication of events at Coventry further, Albion were two up in the first half through Robert Koren. The Slovenian started and finished the move after playing a one-two with teenager Chris Wood (who later joined Town on loan), to then beat Wright with a rising close-range drive at the near post.

Town went on to lose 2-0, and but for Wright the result would have been far greater. He capped his performance by saving Luke Moore's 74th-minute penalty.

Ipswich fans leaving The Hawthorns were sounding concerned in their discussions as to how things could change around quickly. We were by now just one place above the foot of the table.

The day after my 38th birthday in September 2009, Town were afforded a primetime television slot as BBC Two hosted our home clash with high-flying Newcastle United. Eight league games had been played up to this point and we were still without a win and still languishing in the bottom two. We had also been dumped out of the League Cup by Peterborough United.

The chances of turning the tide seemed remote even to the most optimistic of Town fans. Ipswich and Newcastle are identified closely with the link to Sir Bobby Robson. It was appropriate that this game came at the end of the week that had begun with a memorial service to him at Durham Cathedral. Fans of both clubs would sing 'there's only one Bobby Robson' prior to kick-off – an action that always brings a lump to my throat.

Some 40 ex-Ipswich players from the Robson era were introduced to the crowd and Laura Wright from the All Angels operatic group sang 'Abide With Me' and 'My Way', two of Sir Bobby's favourite songs.

At half-time, Lady Elsie Robson cut a ribbon to rename the North Stand the Sir Bobby Robson Stand. This was an emotional day of the highest order.

On the pitch, Town were simply outplayed once more.

With 30 minutes on the clock, and with the score still at 0-0, we were at least thankful that we were not losing. Four minutes later, we found ourselves 3-0 down. Kevin Nolan scored two goals in two minutes, and Ryan Taylor then scored a third with Town's defence all at sea.

That was a devastating spell in the game from Newcastle and there was no looking back from those four minutes onwards.

Six minutes after the break, Nolan completed his hat-trick and Newcastle won 4-0.

A further five games followed this with Roy Keane still in search of his first win of the season. Fourteen league games played had seen six defeats and eight draws. Town would spend the whole of October sitting rock-bottom.

All the hope, goodwill, excitement, and clamour to be on the glory-hunting trail had dissipated. We were in fact at our lowest point for many years under our highest-profile manager.

By the time that we were next shown live, we had finally gained our first win of the season thanks to a 1-0 victory at home to Derby but followed this up with another draw, 1-1, away at Reading.

The BBC once again opted to put us in front of the watching nation and this time promoted us from BBC Two to BBC One. Sheffield Wednesday were our visitors on 21 November.

Wednesday, without a win themselves in five games were indebted to goalkeeper Lee Grant for a string of fine saves to earn his side a point in a 0-0 draw. As Town threatened to make it successive home wins for the first time in 2009/10, Grant stood firm and repelled everything that was thrown at him.

At the other end, Asmir Begović was playing his final game in goal for Town after joining on loan from Portsmouth. Begović would later in the season join Stoke for a fee of just over £3.2m before moving on five years later to Chelsea for £8m and then Bournemouth two years later for £10m. He certainly showed all that potential in the month that he was with Town.

Despite Keane's presence at the helm, our lowly position was sending us into the background as far as televised games were concerned.

We appeared live only once more that season with a return of the Sky cameras broadcasting our game away at Leicester City on 10 January.

Our form had picked up a little in the next six games after that game with Sheffield Wednesday. Three wins, two defeats and a draw saw us climb out of the bottom three, but we were still not clear of the possibility of getting involved in a relegation fight. The second half of the season needed to be one with many improvements.

There were three players in the Leicester squad with Ipswich connections as both Wayne Brown and Richie Wellens started, and Martyn Waghorn came off the bench for the last 20 minutes.

This game was the last time that defender Alex Bruce would be seen in an Ipswich shirt.

With just 20 seconds on the clock, Town caught Leicester cold and took the lead through David Norris. Jon Walters sent Jack Colback away down the left, and his cross went in off a combination of Norris and City defender Ryan McGivern. What a start for Town who had in fact scored inside the first five minutes for a fourth successive game.

Leicester though had scored in 11 consecutive games and would add to that on 38 minutes when Steve Howard made the most of some poor Ipswich defending to fire low past Arran Lee-Barrett and into the corner of the net.

Tempers flared in the second half as Norris and Matty Fryatt clashed which sparked a melee, and with both sides having good chances to score the 1-1 result was about fair. Leicester remained fifth in the table while Town moved up to 18th.

With no further games shown live in 2009/10, it was just as well as we limped to a 15th-place finish in a season that did not live long in the memory of Ipswich fans.

It would not be until the end of November that we saw our next live game and the first of the 2010/11 season.

We had made a decent start to the new campaign and after the first week of November, we were sat nicely in the top six. But we then went on a six-game losing run, in the middle of which, came a score and performance on BBC One that was to upset us all, as we fell to a heavy defeat at Norwich.

At the very beginning of this book, I commented on how the lack of live TV back in the day prevented our achievements under Sir Bobby Robson from being regularly showcased. The BBC had Norwich's Jeremy Goss as a guest and of course showed his goal at Bayern Munich a few times. That for me set the tone of how I would just grow more discontented as the afternoon developed.

Town had Gianni Zuiverloon making his debut and Rory Fallon would come off the bench for his debut too. It would be one for both the Dutchman and New Zealander to forget as Ipswich would suffer their heaviest league defeat at the time to the Canaries.

A crowd of 26,532, the highest since Carrow Road became an all-seater stadium, would see Norwich dominate and ease to a 4-1 win.

Grant Holt scored his first of the afternoon on 13 minutes and despite being on the back foot, Town levelled through Damian Delaney on 29 minutes. Holt scored a second moments later and then Delaney went from hero to villain when he was sent off for pulling the striker back.

Holt completed his hat-trick 14 minutes from time and substitute Wes Hoolahan added a fourth two minutes later to compound a miserable afternoon for us watching in the stands, in the pubs and back home. What a horrible way to see Ipswich's 50th live TV defeat.

Less than a week later, Town had an immediate opportunity to banish the TV blues from the previous Sunday – a hair of the dog moment, as Swansea City came to Portman Road for a Saturday lunchtime encounter.

In between these games, we had beaten Premier League West Brom 1-0 at Portman Road to reach the League Cup semi-finals where we would face Arsenal.

But back in the Championship, Town were in freefall in the table and needed to get the supporters back on side at the first attempt following that defeat at Norwich.

But if we were looking for any comfort from this game, then we were to end disappointed once more. With no goals before the break, Andros Townsend scored five minutes after the restart to give us some hope of better times ahead.

But that notion evaporated as Craig Beattie and then Joe Allen put the Swans in front with 20 minutes remaining.

Town had good shouts for a penalty at 2-1 in the 88th minute when Carlos Edwards appeared to be tripped inside the area. Referee Andy D'Urso turned away our appeals and 30 seconds later, it was game over. Beattie scored his second of the game with a stunning goal. It condemned us to our eighth defeat in ten Championship fixtures.

Before those two Arsenal semi-finals, Sky had us back on a week before Christmas 2010. Leicester City were the visitors for a Saturday evening game that will be remembered mostly for one thing – snow!

Roy Keane's live TV record up to that point was not good. In the seven matches screened, he had overseen five defeats and two draws.

Six successive defeats had seen us back in trouble and the signs did not look good for the visit of Sven-Göran Eriksson's outfit.

At the time, it was debatable as to whether the game would even go ahead. Conditions were not good and a blizzard was covering the surface as well as those in the lower regions of the terraces.

The fact that referee Stuart Attwell allowed the match to take place at all was to bring strong criticism from Eriksson after the game.

It was Town who weighed in with an avalanche of their own as no fewer than three goals were scored in an incredible first half.

David Norris opened the scoring inside six minutes and then a double strike from Jason Scotland (27 and 39) saw us well-placed for a rare win.

But half-time brought more snow and real doubt as to whether the game could continue. Typical of our luck, we were thinking, just as we had got ourselves into a winning position.

The ground staff worked frantically to clear the snow around the lines on the pitch and while Eriksson was pleading for the game to be abandoned, we kept our fingers crossed.

When Attwell took the teams off for ten minutes in the second half, it looked all but certain that the match would be called off, and our three-goal lead would also be gone too.

The ground staff did an excellent job to clear the lines once more and the players came back out and continued with the use of an orange ball.

I recall Shane O'Connor having his best game in an Ipswich shirt and he received warm applause when substituted for Carlos Edwards 13 minutes from time.

Miraculously, the game would reach its natural conclusion, with Attwell even playing on for another minute beyond the announced three minutes of additional time.

Gianni Zuiverloon made his last appearance for the club in this match and Roy Keane had also managed his Ipswich team for the last time in a live TV game. Three weeks later, and after a 1-0 home defeat to Nottingham Forest, he was sacked by Marcus Evans. His one victory in eight live TV games gave him a win rate of just 13 per cent, which was the lowest at the time by any manager who would oversee Town in live TV action for eight games or more. He would not get to manage Ipswich against Arsenal in the League Cup semi-final.

Ian McParland was to lead Town on a temporary basis for two games following Keane's sacking. And they would not come much harder than cup games against two of the Premier League's heavyweights.

First up was an FA Cup tie at Stamford Bridge which saw Chelsea run out comfortable 7-0 winners, and then McParland had to pick his side up for one of the biggest nights that Portman Road would see in years – the League Cup semi-final, first leg, and live on Sky Sports 2, on Wednesday, 12 January.

With over 29,000 packed in the crowd, thousands more would be watching on TV screens around the globe. This was a massive stage for Ipswich to somehow see off Arsenal – the biggest cup clash between the two since the 1978 FA Cup Final. And the scene of my next and biggest regret of all my time in supporting Ipswich so far.

To put it simply, I did not get a ticket for this game. Season ticket holders, as in most seasons, had to claim their seat during a particular priority timeframe. I did not achieve this and by the time I thought about getting a ticket, all those remaining on general sale had gone and Portman Road had its first sell-out since December 2003. I only had myself to blame.

As I sat and watched the game at home, I could not believe that I had missed out on such an occasion. Of everything I had previously been to and of all the matches to miss – here I was feeling right sorry for myself. And what a performance and result I was not present for.

I do not know anyone who had given us any chance whatsoever on the night. But McParland made some tactical changes from the heavy defeat at Chelsea, one seeing Tamás Priskin playing a lone role up front and Connor Wickham moving out to the left.

From the outset, our work rate was phenomenal and in McParland's subtle changes, our midfield had enough bodies to break up Arsenal's intricate passing.

Priskin came close to giving Ipswich an early lead when shooting narrowly wide of Wojciech Szczęsny's right-hand post. Then Wickham saw a shot deflect wide and Gareth McAuley headed a Carlos Edwards corner narrowly over. This was much better from our boys.

Dangerman Priskin had the ball in the net just before half-time but was well offside. The interval brought rapturous applause – and that was just me in my lounge! So far, this had been a performance to enthuse about. Arsène Wenger might have started to regret leaving the likes of Robin van Persie, Samir Nasri, and Gaël Clichy at home, but he was still able to field a strong line-up. Yet his side did not carve out a single chance in that first half.

If we expected Arsenal to come out for the second period fired up and with improvement on their first 45 minutes, then we were pleasantly surprised.

Priskin continued to be Ipswich's main threat and was causing Arsenal's centre-backs Laurent Koscielny and Johan Djourou all kinds of problems.

Town fans could be heard loudly singing 'we're gonna score in a minute' and despite a couple of half chances created by Arsenal, they were not wrong.

When Town beat Arsenal 1-0 in the FA Cup Final in 1978, Roger Osborne had scored in the 77th minute. And at almost the very same moment Priskin scored the goal that Town had deserved.

Arsenal's defence once again failed to deal with a simple through ball and Priskin got in behind Djourou. He kept his composure to direct the ball inside Szczęsny's post. Cue delirium in the stands and at home.

Furthermore, Town held on to a famous 1-0 victory over the Gunners – just like they had over 32 years earlier. The only downside on this occasion was that this was only the first leg. A battle had been won, but the tie was not over.

The players celebrated with the fans at the final whistle. Yes, there was that next leg to come, but this night deserved to be celebrated and for Ian McParland, he became the fourth and at the time of writing, the last Ipswich manager to win his first live TV game. He also joined an illustrious list with Sir Bobby Robson to have won their only live game for Ipswich, both 1-0 against Arsenal.

Before that victory, Paul Jewell had been announced as the new boss following Roy Keane's sacking. However, he had chosen to watch the Arsenal game from the stands to allow McParland to take the reins.

Therefore, his first game in charge was in the Championship at Millwall which Town lost 2-1, but they followed that up with a 3-2 win over Doncaster Rovers. A day short of two weeks since beating Arsenal, the return leg was upon us at the Emirates Stadium for Jewell's first live TV match.

After missing that first leg, I had to do everything possible to be at the return to hopefully see Ipswich win, or at least draw and hold on to their slender advantage to seal a place in the League Cup Final at Wembley for the first time. I could not bear the thought of having to watch another leg at home, this time on BBC Two.

Despite Town's allocation of around 9,000 tickets, I still could not get one. But I knew a man who could.

At the time, I worked with one of the nicest guys I have ever met, Jamie Cater. Jamie is a Liverpool fan but was watching a lot of Ipswich games as he was dating the sister of a Town player at that time.

In our office a week or so leading up to the game, we had made a pact that if one of us could get a pair of tickets, then we would take the other with us. My chances of getting even one ticket were next to none. But I had relied on Jamie not having any problems as he could tap into his girlfriend's brother who had been in the squad for the first leg.

As one could imagine, players must get inundated with requests for tickets, especially for an occasion such as this. And sure enough, Jamie delivered the unwelcome news that his request had been refused. The tickets allocated to the player in question had been snapped up by other family members. It looked like I would miss out on the second leg too.

I then remembered an old acquaintance within my social media contacts who I thought might just be worth contacting.

Back in 2002, a set of circumstances led to the then owner of Clacton Town, Jeff Dewing, inviting me to write a column for his award-winning matchday programme. He said, 'We can call it "The Fuller Flavour".' I agreed and my writing and the name has stuck with me ever since including in the *East Anglian Daily Times* and *Ipswich Star*.

Although at the time of this game I was not in regular touch with Jeff, I had seen through his social media account that he worked for a company that had Arsenal season tickets. So, I thought, why not ask Jeff – which I did.

It was one of those occasions that felt a bit cheeky to ask, especially of someone I had not really spoken to for a few years, but Jeff replied within less than five minutes.

'Karl, two tickets have your name on them mate,' was his response. Wow, just like that, I had two tickets. OK, I was going to have to sit among Arsenal fans but at least I would be at the Emirates. I was just typing a message to Jamie when Jeff sent me a further text message. 'Dress smart, as they are hospitality tickets.'

I really did not know how to respond to that. I had never had hospitality at a match, and this was an amazing gesture. I let Jamie know that we were going, and I doubt he could believe it until I explained more to him at work the next day. Unbelievable Jeff, indeed.

It had then dawned on me that being the world's fussiest eater, hospitality would be wasted on me. But I would deal with that when the time came.

Jamie and I travelled on the train from Clacton to London with my good mate Paul and a couple of his friends. Paul adores his football. If he is not watching Ipswich home or away, he can be found watching Liverpool at Anfield. Otherwise, he will be watching England at home or abroad and all the time he takes his son Alfie. What a great education he is getting, by the way. He should be top of the class in Geography.

Paul and his friends went to a particular establishment frequently before England games at Wembley. They took Jamie and I as we had a couple of hours to kill before we were expected at the Emirates Stadium. It was certainly an eye-opener of a place, but we had to leave before we had too much fun.

When we arrived in one of the Emirates' many hospitality suites, I had never seen anything like it. I thought I was in a hotel. There were staff walking around with carpet sweepers.

Here I am with Ipswich Town's first-ever live TV goalscorer Roger Osborne in 2012 at Rushmere Sports Club where Roger worked. Who will ever forget his goal in the 1-0 win over Arsenal in the 1978 FA Cup Final?

My first-ever photo taken with an Ipswich Town player! Paul Cooper, who played in goal for Ipswich in the club's first full live TV game, the 1978 FA Cup Final, visited my primary school, Kirby Cross, in 1981.

Kevin Beattie, who played in only one live Ipswich game – the 1978 FA Cup Final – is with me above, having just been presented with an award from the East Anglian Daily Times *after 'The Beat' was voted the 'Greatest Ipswich Town Player' of all-time by their readers.*

George Burley took charge of the club in 60 'live TV' games – more than any other manager for Ipswich Town. Below, I grabbed a photo with George at a players' awards evening in the late 1990s.

Jim Magilton (with a bottle in his hand) has played in the most live TV games for Ipswich (54 apps). He is pictured above with Clacton Branch of supporters Secretary Pat Edwards (right) and her Niece Carly Mitchell (left) at the 1999/2000 Players' Awards evening. John McGreal (29 apps) is also in the picture.

And here I am pictured with Jim Magilton in the late 1990s...

Matt Holland (right) was the first Ipswich player to play in 50 live TV games. I am nicely in the middle of two ITFC legends, with Terry Butcher on the left. I had the pleasure of meeting Matt and Terry at a legends evening at the Ipswich Corn Exchange in March 2022.

Fabian Wilnis has made the second highest live TV appearances for Ipswich (51 apps) and is pictured below with me on the left and my good mate Paul Love back in the late 1990s.

Richard Naylor (left) is one of only four Ipswich players to play in 50 live TV games (50 apps). Clacton Branch of supporters Secretary Pat Edwards (middle) and Wayne Brown (right, eight apps) share a photo with Bam Bam at the 2002 Players' Awards evening.

Marcus Stewart has scored the most live TV goals for Ipswich (12 goals). He was happy to pose for a photo below with myself and my two sons, Karl (standing) and Craig.

And here I am again with Marcus at the Playford Road training ground in 2001 after an interview for the Ipswich fanzine, Those Were The Days.

L to r: Don Welsh, myself and Jason Bennett in Harry's bar, Helsingborg, where we spent most of the day prior to our UEFA Cup tie with Helsingborg IF.

One of Ipswich's greatest 'live TV' games was the 2000 play-off final at Wembley. Here is my match ticket signed by the four Ipswich goalscorers, after we beat Barnsley 4-2 to clinch promotion to the Premier League.

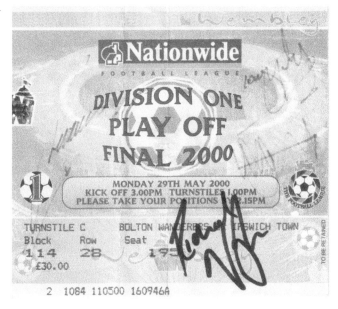

I do not recall what the food was but got through that before we took our seats. What a view, what a stadium. The Emirates is hands down the best ground in this country that I have been to, although a recent trip to Anfield, the home of Liverpool, does come close.

There was one obvious problem for me though. Our seats were level with the edge of the penalty area, and we were in the very end hospitality box. Immediately to my left, and below was the beginning of 9,000 Ipswich fans that snaked round to the other side of the ground directly opposite me.

As the only Ipswich fan in our box, it was difficult for me not to join in with the singing. It was unusual to be so close to my fellow fans but not in with them. It gave me an outsider's view but with an insider's knowledge. I knew they would be loud and proud, and they met my expectations. They were superb that night.

At half-time there had been no goals scored and we still held that lead from the first leg. We were now 45 minutes away from a Wembley final. But Arsenal had made most of the running before the break and it did have a sense of how much longer we would hold on.

I decided to take it in nine blocks of five minutes at a time, and as of those blocks of time passed, both my levels of excitement and nerves rose. This worked until the 61st minute when Arsenal finally scored through Nicklas Bendtner. We were still level overall and all was OK, I thought. Three minutes later that thought was gone. Arsenal scored again through Laurent Koscielny. They added a third on 77 minutes when Cesc Fàbregas scored and won the game 3-0. Another semi-final defeat, my 13th, and again we had come so close.

I never expected us to get that close when the draw was made, I will add. But over the two games we did ourselves proud.

My last memory of the night was after the game, and we were queuing outside the underground station waiting to be let in. Ipswich fans were singing and looked the happier.

Next to us in the queue was a family of Arsenal supporters. I told them to cheer up, they had just reached a Wembley final. I do not think they appreciated me saying that, but they did look a tad miserable.

The older guy in the family group then remarked that it was only the League Cup, what was there to be happy about?

It remains one of the most incredulous and ungrateful comments I have ever heard from a fellow football fan. I get that the League Cup would have been low down on Arsenal's priorities, but it was still a Wembley final after all.

I could only respond with that they should have let us win then. Ipswich fans would have been over the moon to have made the final and would certainly have appreciated it.

I was glad when Birmingham went on to beat Arsenal in the final. I would not have wanted Arsenal fans to have been upset at the thought of them seeing their team winning 'just' the League Cup.

By the time that Jewell's first live league game hit our screens, our form had shown little sign of improvement and we were stagnating just below mid-table when we visited Cardiff City on 5 March.

Cardiff were in the hunt for a play-off place, which they would go on to achieve by finishing fourth. Few Ipswich fans had given us much hope of getting anything out of this game, but few had banked on a star performance by Jimmy Bullard.

Town had goalkeeper Márton Fülöp to thank for keeping Cardiff at bay in the initial stages. He had single-handedly denied the hosts with some great saves to thwart future Ipswich player Jay Emmanuel-Thomas on no fewer than three occasions and to also prevent another player who would later join Town, Michael Chopra, from finding the back of the net. When Peter Whittingham hit the crossbar, one could sense that it might not be Cardiff's day and we could snatch something ourselves.

And with the game still lacking goals in the 67th minute, that was precisely what we would do. Bullard latched on to a loose ball after some excellent closing down by Town striker Jason Scotland and hit a low effort past the helpless Stephen Bywater, who was previously an Ipswich player.

Four minutes from time it was 2-0, and once again Bullard was on target. His super strike from outside the area appeared to take a deflection and once more, Bywater was well beaten. Only a good save by Bywater then prevented Bullard from scoring a hat-trick when he tried his luck with an effort from 18 yards. This was Town's fifth consecutive victory over the Bluebirds.

Bullard, who only joined the club in February on loan from Hull City, would go on to score a total of five goals in 16 appearances in 2010/11 and his efforts were recognised by Town fans as he went on to with the supporters' player of the year award.

Town were not to feature live on TV again that season and finished in a disappointing 13th place.

Our first televised match of the 2011/12 season will go down in Ipswich history as being one of the worst and most embarrassing moments we will probably ever see in a live Ipswich game.

The Sky cameras were in place at London Road, home of Peterborough United, on Saturday, 20 August for an early evening kick-off.

The season started well with an opening-day 3-0 win away at Bristol City, but this was followed up with a 1-0 home defeat to Hull and more worryingly, a 5-2 defeat at home to Southampton.

Those five goals conceded against the Saints saw our defence torn to shreds and the hope was that there had been plenty of work going on at the training ground and we would be much tighter in defence at Peterborough.

When Keith Andrews put Town ahead after 23 minutes with a 30-yard blockbuster, nobody watching at the ground, or indeed at home, could have seen what was coming next from the half-hour mark onwards.

Paul Taylor, who would join Ipswich from Peterborough for a fee of £1.5m a year later, scored an equaliser from 15 yards on 30 minutes.

Just eight minutes later, Posh went ahead thanks to Lee Tomlin. Before we could even take stock of the situation, which had dramatically altered the context of the game, Taylor scored again two minutes later to put Peterborough 3-1 ahead. The hopes at this stage would be to get to the half-time break and work out how we would pull two goals back.

Incredibly, just a further two minutes on, Tomlin then added his second for 4-1 and there was still time for Lee Martin to get himself sent off for serious foul play to leave us with ten men. The half-time whistle blew, and we were simply stunned.

We had totally imploded, and defeat was now more than inevitable. There were two mountains stacked on top of one another to climb.

I have no idea what was said in our dressing room during the break, but suffice to say, it did not work. Within a minute of the restart Tommy Smith was sent off for denying an obvious goalscoring opportunity and we were down to nine men.

Two minutes after that red card, Grant McCann scored his first of the afternoon, and when he scored his second after 56 minutes we were 6-1 down. What on earth was going on? This was jaw-dropping stuff.

How our nine men then held out until the 90th minute before conceding again was a minor miracle. Tomlin completed his hat-trick and in good old vidiprinter style, the final score was Peterborough United 7 (seven) Ipswich Town 1.

I suppose the only other time until this game that I had been equally shell-shocked was when I was at Old Trafford to watch Manchester United thump us 9-0. This defeat hurt. Jewell was equally as ashamed as we were in his post-match interview, and rightly so.

A month later, we were back on Sky once more with a Monday night home fixture against Coventry City to look forward to. When I say look forward to, after two wins in our opening six games and with four defeats already in the bank, we were sat in 17th place and in all honesty, not looking forward to too much at all. But die-hard football fans will dust themselves down and hope that the next game will be the one where everything falls into place. Just like what dogs are to their owners, our love is so often unconditional. That heavy defeat at Peterborough would have to be forgiven, even if it could not be forgotten.

And this time, it would be Town who would be asking all the questions – and two goals to the good after just 15 minutes.

With just six minutes gone, Aaron Cresswell's cross from the left was headed into his own net by Coventry's Martin Crainie, and then Keith Andrews played a one-two with Michael Chopra and cracked a rising shot past Joe Murphy from just inside the area.

With Coventry all at sea, Town should have scored at least one more before the break, with both Chopra and Jimmy Bullard going close.

Jason Scotland sealed the three points on 67 minutes after sliding in to finish off another assist by Chopra. Town moved up to 13th, three points off the play-off zone while Coventry remained out of the bottom three on goal difference.

Our next live game would also be our last one of 2011/12 and came as early as Saturday, 10 December.

The previous weekend, we had played at home to Watford. My friend Jamie, who I mentioned going to the Arsenal game with, had asked me at work on the Friday before the match for any betting tips over that weekend. I told him to put whatever money he had on a Watford win as that was an almost guaranteed result.

He asked me to go into the bet with him and put my money where my mouth was. I was not comfortable doing that of course but found a betting site that was offering a free bet when an account was opened with them. The upshot was around £70 had been won on Watford's standard victory.

Rather than cashing out and entertaining the idea of handling blood money, I suggested to Jamie to put the winnings on a Barnsley win in the next live fixture. My reasoning was that quite often, Ipswich lost games up north when the game is shown live. So that is what happened – the money all went on a Barnsley win.

When Barnsley led 2-0 at half-time, I had a phone call with Jamie congratulating him on the money won and what should happen to it next. My betting app today would pay out early for a two-goal lead – but not back then.

Less than five minutes after the restart, Town were level thanks to Keith Andrews with a volley and a header accounting for his goals.

I was smiling of course seeing Town get back on terms but did spare a thought for Jamie. Midway through the second half, Town scored twice again in a two-minute spell.

First, defender Danny Collins scored with a header. Then, Michael Chopra finished clinically for 4-2.

Jason Scotland added a fifth with seven minutes to go, before Craig Davies scored in the last minute for Barnsley and the game ended in a 5-3 win to Town.

'You win some, you lose some,' is all I could say to Jamie. This game saw the last appearances for Ipswich for both David Stockdale and Reece Wabara.

The season petered out into one that would be slightly worse than the year before as we finished 15th. The calls were growing larger for Paul Jewell's head, but he survived the axe over the summer and was still in the hotseat for the start of 2012/13.

Over the years leading up to the start of that season, I had built up a great friendship with the legendary Ipswich Town journalist Dave Allard. Dave used to write the match reports and stories for the *East Anglian Daily Times*, *Ipswich Star*, the *Green 'Un* and some of the nationals. I remember Dave taking me to the ground on a non-matchday and he walked me along the corridor on the middle floor below the Pioneer Stand. All the way along were framed newspaper match reports, all written by Dave.

He was always good for a Town story of the Sir Bobby Robson era and was just someone I truly admired. He was always encouraging me with my writing too and would give me the nudge when I needed it most.

I told him that I wanted to approach the *East Anglian Daily Times* about writing a column. He told me who to write to and chance my arm. I did exactly that and was so pleased to be offered an interview by *EADT* sports editor Mark Heath.

Looking back, I did not have a professional portfolio. Instead, I went armed with press cuttings of my previous work that had been published. I was offered a position as a weekly columnist, and at the time of writing I am still penning my thoughts for the *EADT* almost ten years on. Dave was my inspiration that I will never forget, and Mark has been so good to me in having me back each season. They are both true legends in my eyes.

My column debut came five weeks into the 2012/13 season and less than a week after that meeting with Mark. Paul Jewell was still not having an enjoyable time of it. One win and four defeats in our opening seven games saw us sitting just one place off the foot of the table.

My very first column, after a 1-0 defeat at home to Charlton Athletic, was themed around a lack of patience among the supporters. My words of displeasure were scribed on my very first day in the office.

Saturday, 6 October proved to be the only time that Town would appear live on TV in the whole of the 2012/13 season. A home game against Cardiff City and Jewell desperately needed a win to halt that run of one win in now the last nine games.

Jewell handed starting debuts to Richie Wellens and DJ Campbell, while Bilel Mohsni would come off the bench for his debut and Massimo Luongo also came on for his final game for Ipswich.

It would be Town who went into half-time ahead thanks to Campbell's debut goal in stoppage time. The goal had some controversy surrounding it as Campbell had used his hands to turn Lee Martin's cross into the net. It was a surprise to us all that the incident was missed by the match officials.

Just after the hour mark, Cardiff drew level through Heidar Helguson who capitalised on an error by Scott Loach after he had dropped the ball, and then the Icelandic striker won the game for the Bluebirds in the 87th minute.

The North Stand booed at the final whistle and Jewell looked a beaten man.

Two more defeats followed for Jewell, and after the second – 2-1 at home to Derby County – he was sacked after one win in the opening dozen games.

He had watched from the stands as the joy of beating Arsenal at Portman Road would see him slide into the hotseat with the club on such a high but he would later never really recover from the woes of that horrendous defeat at Peterborough. Once more, Town were in search of a new manager.

CHAPTER 6: THE NOT SO FAMOUS FIVE

Mick McCarthy (29 games)

When the appointment of Mick McCarthy as manager of Ipswich Town was confirmed on 1 November 2012, I was happy. He was my first choice at the time, and I had also seen an early betting market where he was a generous 12/1 to be our next boss.

I cannot recall the other names on that list, but there was nobody lower than those odds who appealed to me. My gut instinct was to bet on McCarthy which of course paid off.

With one win in the opening 13 games and with Ipswich sitting at the bottom of the table, McCarthy won his very first match in charge – 1-0 at Birmingham City. We did not appear in a single live game for the rest of that season, and McCarthy guided us to safety and a 14th-place finish.

It would not be until his first anniversary in charge of Town before he would oversee a live TV game, when on Friday, 1 November 2013, Sky covered the visit of his hometown club, Barnsley.

The Tykes had lost every away game in the league that they had played to that date, while Town had won four of their first six home matches of the season. The odds looked good for an Ipswich win.

At half-time Town looked on course for that win thanks to Daryl Murphy's first live TV goal for the club when he scored from an Aaron Cresswell corner.

The second half saw a different Barnsley outfit who had missed a couple of good chances before they eventually scored with 20 minutes remaining. Jim O'Brien, who had come off the bench just before the interval, steered home Paddy McCourt's cross past the despairing dive of Dean Gerken.

As the match entered injury time, Town nearly won it, but Frank Nouble was inches away from connecting with a Jay Tabb shot.

There was still time for Aaron Cresswell to be the seventh Ipswich player to be awarded a red card in a live game when he was sent off for foul and abusive language. So late was the card, I never even saw it at the time. I only learnt of it on the radio when I was back at my car.

Our only other live game of 2013/14 came in our final away trip of the season, at Burnley. Thanks to a Saturday 12.15pm kick-off, travelling Town fans would have had to leave incredibly early. I had been to Burnley at the end of the season before on the train, and that was one heck of a trek.

We were back in familiar territory of seasons gone by where we entered still with an outside chance of reaching the play-offs. We needed to win both of our final matches and hope for results elsewhere to go our way. Burnley were already promoted as runners-up to Leicester. We had hoped that they would be taking their foot off the gas.

However, less than ten minutes after the start of the second half, Michael Kightly put Burnley ahead with his third goal in as many weeks, and his strike proved to be enough to give the hosts a 1-0 win.

Burnley had further chances to add to their lead, while only a fine save by their goalkeeper Tom Heaton prevented Paul Taylor's free kick from going into the top corner in the 80th minute.

Town would end the season in a much-improved ninth place and four points outside the top six. McCarthy had our team back into a decent and competitive outfit.

On the back of that much-improved season, television companies, and mostly Sky, were once again interested in the value of screening Ipswich games and no fewer than 13 in 2014/15 were to be shown live. Only 16 in 2001/02 saw us shown live on TV more in a single season.

The first live game was also the opening day, at home to Fulham, who had just been relegated from the Premier League after a 13-year stay, with the kick-off being moved to 5.15pm. Town gave a debut to Bálint Bajner, and Kevin Bru would also come off the bench later in the game for his bow.

Fulham, meanwhile, had in their line-up Cameron Burgess who would later join Ipswich from Accrington Stanley.

Town put in an impressive display and were much more determined in their tackles than the Londoners and would go on to claim a deserved win, even if we were hanging on a little by the end.

Daryl Murphy scored our first goal of the season in the 32nd minute. He was played in by Luke Hyam, sped past Shaun Hutchinson and finished emphatically past Jesse Joronen. This goal was Ipswich's 100th live TV goal scored at Portman Road.

Bajner had found his first game in England challenging and was replaced just before half-time by Davin McGoldrick. It would be the substitute who would stretch Town's lead just after the hour mark. The ball broke to McGoldrick from Murphy's cross, and he drove firmly home for 2-0.

Fulham pulled a goal back four minutes from time through Tim Hoogland and nearly snatched an equaliser in the last moments.

Town held on and were excellent value for their win and McCarthy was able to celebrate his first live TV victory on the back of having just signed a new three-year deal.

Two weeks later, a Saturday lunchtime fixture saw yet another encounter with Norwich City at Portman Road and once again, it was the Canaries who showed the superior quality.

One goal was enough to win them the game as Lewis Grabban scored a controversial one in the 23rd minute.

A Norwich corner from the right was headed clear by David McGoldrick, but then returned in to the six-yard box by Alexander Tettey to an offside Grabban. The sight of a grounded Christophe Berra after a tussle with Michael Turner had misled the assistant referee who kept his flag down and Grabban headed over Dean Gerken into the net.

Once more, the majority of the 25,000-plus crowd left the ground wondering when we would beat our rivals again.

Just a month later, we had our third live game of the season with a Monday night fixture at Wigan Athletic.

Town were looking for their first away win of the season after one defeat and two draws in the three away games played to date. Wigan had won just two of their first seven but were unbeaten at the DW Stadium after an opening-day draw against Reading and wins over Blackpool and Birmingham City.

Town took the lead with a cool finish from Luke Hyam midway through the first half and then doubled their advantage through former Wigan player Conor Sammon midway through the second.

A future Ipswich player in the making came off the bench for Wigan in the shape of Martyn Waghorn and he scored from close-range in the 81st minute to set up a tense finish. Fellow Wigan substitute Oriol Riera hit the inside of a post in injury time to have our hearts in our mouths.

The final whistle sounded to immense relief, and we gained a win that in all honesty we thoroughly deserved. After the game, Mick McCarthy hailed the performance as the best he had seen away from home in his two years in charge at that point.

There has not been much to shout about in recent years as an Ipswich fan, and not too many memories to last in the mind either.

But there are a couple of goals I never tire of watching. Both secured Ipswich 1-0 away wins. One would be later in this season at Watford when Richard Chaplow scored in injury time, but that game was not live on TV.

The other was screened, however. The last Saturday of November saw Ipswich away at Charlton Athletic for a lunchtime date on Sky.

Noel Hunt had only joined Ipswich 48 hours before the game, on loan from Leeds United. He would only make the bench for this game and did not come on for Paul Anderson until the 82nd minute.

As the game entered its 95th and final minute, it was Hunt who scored the winner to seal a memorable debut. David McGoldrick's cross after some neat trickery in the area was cleared only as far as Hunt who lashed the ball through a crowded area and into the corner.

It was the last kick of the match and condemned Charlton to their first home defeat of the season, sending Ipswich into second place ahead of the afternoon games.

Hunt raced to the touchline to celebrate and ended up ensconced underneath a body of celebrating Town players. It was a memorable goal indeed.

That win at Charlton would be Mick McCarthy's last on TV for exactly a year as we were then to witness a run that stretched for 11 games and included seven defeats. It would end with a win against Charlton in the 2015/16 season.

But back to 2014/15 and our first live game in the new year would be yet another Saturday lunchtime kick-off at home to Derby County and a clash between two of the top teams in the Championship.

Just one goal would be enough to settle this game, but it was of Chris Martin's 18th of the season that would see the Rams edge to a 1-0 victory. As a result, Derby leapfrogged us into second place and in the process inflicted upon us our first home defeat in almost five months. This would also ignite a sequence of seven games between the two where Derby would win four in succession at Portman Road games, while we would win three in a row at Pride Park Stadium.

Four days later, we would be back for a rare appearance on BBC One as we took on Premier League Southampton in an FA Cup third round replay after the two sides had fought out a 1-1 draw at St Mary's.

A game with little entertainment would see Town once again lose by a single goal as Shane Long's individual moment of magic in the 19th minute was about the only highlight of the game and ensured that it was Southampton who would progress to the fourth round.

Bálint Bajner and Cameron Stewart would both come off the bench in the second half for what in the end would be their final appearances for Ipswich.

The first day of March 2015 saw our 17th live TV encounter with Norwich City – the tenth at Carrow Road.

Once again, Norwich would be too strong for Ipswich and a goal in each half from Bradley Johnson and Lewis Grabban would hand them a 2-0 win and a sixth straight victory.

Johnson's goal came from an effort from the edge of the area, while Grabban's effort had a touch of fortune about it. Substitute Cameron Jerome hit a speculative effort which caught the heel of Grabban and deceived Bartosz Białkowski.

Chris Wood came off the bench for his Town debut and it was the second match of the season between the two where Norwich would have a good stroke of fortune for a goal.

Town were now entering the stage of the season where at one point, they looked a good bet for an automatic promotion place, but certainly looked good for a spot in the play-offs.

By virtue of their good performances, they were once again deemed a viable outfit for live TV and would be in front of the Sky cameras for a visit to Middlesbrough, two weeks after that game at Norwich.

This was initially a game that I was going to attend with my good friends Kevin and Chris. But the lunchtime kick-off made it impossible for us to get there in time on a train from Clacton. We would change our train tickets for another game a few weeks down the line at Wolves.

In the end, I was glad to have missed this game as Middlesbrough ran out 4-1 winners. When Daniel Ayala gave the hosts a third-minute lead, and then when Town were forced into a ninth minute substitution when goalkeeper Dean Gerken had to be replaced by Białkowski, we already had plenty of reason to be worried. But a Daryl Murphy equaliser just a minute later brought us level and we felt that if we could settle ourselves down, we might have been able to make inroads into the game.

It was Middlesbrough though who would make all the running and they scored a second on the half-hour mark through Albert Adomah.

Then two second-half goals from Patrick Bamford sealed a 4-1 scoreline and Town's winless run now stood at four games, while Middlesbrough would go on to make the play-offs.

A 1-0 victory followed three days later at home to Bolton Wanderers and then came that Richard Chaplow goal at Watford and our push for the play-offs was back on track by the time we reached our next live game – a Good Friday fixture at home to Bournemouth.

Like Middlesbrough, this was another clash between two of the division's heavyweights as Bournemouth were battling it out with Watford and Norwich for automatic promotion. That ship had sailed for Town by now which given that we went into the new year at the summit of the league table, it had been a disappointing second half of the season. Even the play-offs were not guaranteed at this stage.

Town included defender Zeki Fryers in their starting line-up for his debut having joined on loan from Crystal Palace.

We got off to the perfect start when Freddie Sears scored after just six minutes. Daryl Murphy was afforded space on the right-hand side of the box and brought a cross under control before playing in Sears to score his 19th goal of the season.

We had Białkowski to thank for keeping our lead intact as the game progressed when he twice denied future Town loanee Ryan Fraser. But Bournemouth would not be denied as they equalised in the 82nd minute through a debutant of their own.

Kenwyne Jones had only been on the field of play for five minutes when he met a Matt Ritchie corner from the left to finally see Białkowski beaten. Matt Clarke came off the bench in the final minute to replace Luke Varney for his last action in an Ipswich shirt and then Białkowski pulled off the save of the match in injury time to deny Yann Kermorgant.

The draw extended Bournemouth's unbeaten run to seven matches and they would go on and win the league. Town meanwhile had now stretched their unbeaten run to three and were once more looking good for a place in the play-offs.

That position had strengthened by the time our next live match came around. Despite losing 2-1 at Huddersfield on Easter Monday, wins over Blackpool (3-2) and Cardiff (3-1), both at Portman Road, meant that we were now going into the last three games of the season in pole position for that top-six finish.

Through my *East Anglian Daily Times* and *Ipswich Star* column, I had at that point interviewed several ex-Ipswich players and other high-profile people connected to Town.

One such person is Ipswich fan and Darts player Kevin Painter. I had interviewed 'The Artist' at the start of 2013, and we met for the first time when Ipswich lost at home to Watford in February 2013.

We have since become particularly good friends and have attended many games together. Kevin lives in Rugby and our live Sky date for our penultimate away game of the season at Wolves was a nice, local affair for him. Not the case for myself, Kevin and Chris travelling from Clacton.

Remember, this was our change of game after our trip to Middlesbrough was messed up by the switch to a Saturday lunchtime kick-off. Having purchased advanced train tickets to Wolverhampton, the following day saw Sky announce this as their live TV game, once again, for the Saturday lunchtime. A slight inconvenience for us, but at least this one was doable.

We caught a train to Rugby where we met Kevin Painter and then another train to Coventry to change for Wolverhampton. By the time we found a Premier Inn bar to drink in near the station, it was a drink that was much needed after the rigmarole of four trains.

If the Middlesbrough and Bournemouth fixtures were of high interest given our positions in the league table at the times that they were played, then the game against Wolves was of equal high relevance. Bournemouth, Watford Middlesbrough, and Norwich were now fighting it out for the two automatic places, while Town, Brentford, Wolves and Derby were all left to scrap for the other two play-off places.

Former Town loanee Richard Stearman had given us a first-half lead with an unfortunate own goal and we were fair value for it. The Wolves fans had been silenced and the game was there for the taking.

After the break though, it was a different story. Within five minutes Wolves levelled through Benik Afobe and as the game wore on, we held on for the draw.

We left the ground the happier of the two sets of fans; Wolves really needed the win.

We went back to Rugby where we met Kevin's mate, and they took us to a sports bar that was only ever five minutes away. It was the longest five-minute walk by the time we finally arrived at the venue.

It had been another one of those excellent away days and with the regular season just having two games remaining we were building up to what would hopefully be an exciting end.

After a 2-1 win at home to Nottingham Forest in our final home game, it all came down to the last day and for Town fans, familiar territory once more.

Sky had our game live as well as Derby v Reading at Pride Park, and Wolves v Millwall at Molineux.

At the start of play, Ipswich sat in fifth place with 78 points, and Derby were a place and a point behind but with a +13-goal difference advantage over us. Wolves and Brentford were both three points behind us but with inferior goal differences. Derby only needed a point to guarantee at least sixth, while for Brentford or Wolves to overtake us we would need to lose and they would have to win, with a big goal difference swing.

With just two minutes on the clock, everything suddenly seemed all good as two goals put us in the driving seat.

Daryl Murphy had given us the lead at Ewood Park when volleying home Jay Tabb's corner for his 26th goal of the season. News then filtered through that Reading had also scored at Derby through Kwesi Appiah.

When we found out that Wolves had gone 1-0 ahead in the 20th minute of their game, there was little for us to worry about. Even when former Town player Jordan Rhodes levelled matters for Blackburn in our game on 36 minutes, there was still not too much concern. But that all started to change five minutes later.

Craig Conway put Blackburn ahead and with Ipswich now losing, it was eyes and ears on what was happening at Derby, while Brentford were 2-0 up at home to Wigan early in their second half, Ipswich were struggling to stay in the game at Blackburn and Mick McCarthy introduced Stephen Hunt and Paul Anderson in place of Tabb and Jonathan Parr to get us going in attack to try and get back level.

And then we had two minutes of torture to endure. Rudy Gestede scored to put Blackburn 3-1 up in the 57th minute, while Wolves scored in the 56th minute of their game to go 2-0 up. Suddenly our goal difference over Wolves was now only three better, with over an hour still to play.

A momentary relief came just a minute later as Millwall pulled one back at Wolves to stretch that goal difference back to four in our favour. This was tension of the highest order and not since those play-off defeats to West Ham in the mid-2000s had things gotten so nervous.

News came through in the 70th minute that Wolves had gone 3-1 up and they were posing a bigger threat to us than Derby who still trailed Reading 1-0. That news got better two minutes later when Reading went 2-0 ahead and Derby's hopes were fading by the minute.

Town pulled a goal back in the 82nd minute when Murphy scored his second of the game, from the penalty spot after Teddy Bishop had been fouled by Tommy Spurr, and at the same time, Millwall had reduced the arrears to 3-2 at Molineux. The nerves were just starting to calm a little.

Reading scored a third at Derby with five minutes remaining and although Wolves scored a fourth in the 91st minute to win their game 4-2, the final whistle at all three significant games sounded to confirm our place in the play-offs for the first time in ten years. We finished level on points with Wolves and Brentford, who won 3-0 to beat us to fifth by one on goal difference, but we were four better off than Wolves who finished in seventh, with Derby dropping to eighth. The excitement of reaching the play-offs was heightened further by the fact that our opponents would be Norwich City.

In my mind, only the 1981 UEFA Cup Final first leg against AZ Alkmaar was a bigger game at Portman Road than the 2014/15 play-off semi-final first leg against Norwich. This game ranked more importantly than the League Cup semi-final, also against Norwich, in 1985.

A glorious, sunny Saturday lunchtime at Portman Road welcomed both the Sky cameras and over 29,000 spectators, while thousands of others watched on eagerly in front of screens and devices in pubs, clubs, and homes across different countries around the world. OK, I am making it sound like the World Cup Final. For Ipswich and Norwich fans, it may as well have been.

Considering that this book includes many of my memories of live TV games stretching back to 1978, I remember nothing about the build-up to this meeting. I dare say that I was completely shot to bits with worry and really did not enjoy the days before kick-off. That is how I normally feel when we play Norwich.

I do recall wondering how our squad, assembled for a total cost of around £110,000, would perform against a Norwich side put together with the help of parachute payments and costing as much as ten times more.

But the performance we put in on that day was magnificent and I could not have been prouder of the team. I thought that we had marginally been the better side when Norwich opened the scoring in the 40th minute through Jonny Howson.

One could have been forgiven for thinking here we go again. We had not beaten Norwich in so long and it was difficult at this point to see where we could overturn going a goal behind to go on and take a lead to Norfolk for the second leg. We did not have to wait long for an answer as to how we could respond.

Freddie Sears made himself room to send a low shot on target that John Ruddy could not hold and as Daryl Murphy and Ruddy both went for the loose ball, it broke to Paul Anderson to slot home.

I have already mentioned the feeling of celebrating this goal, but the noise that then followed was one of the most deafening celebrations I have ever been part of at Portman Road. At times like this, I wondered how football fans do not sustain more severe injuries. I was being pulled by those on my left, right, in front and behind me. It was utter chaos but spine-tingling at the same time.

Before we could even comprehend what had happened, the half-time whistle blew and the teams left the pitch to raucous applause.

Anderson had only been on the pitch for 15 minutes when he scored. He had to come off the bench to replace the unfortunate Luke Varney who had been stretchered off after rupturing his Achilles tendon. Yet Anderson will always be held in the highest regard by most Ipswich fans just for that goal.

The second half was just as tight but with even less goalmouth action, both sides no doubt content to save something in reserve for the second leg. We had not won the match, but the effort was there for all to see. Town players had left nothing behind that day.

That evening, my mate the Artist had a darts exhibition at the United Services club in Harwich. I went along for the craic and the place was full of Ipswich fans who were singing their drunken hearts out all in good nature. I reckoned that they had been at it all day on the drinks. When they saw Kevin, he was treated like a hero, and they were shaking his hand and grabbing selfies.

Kevin told them who I was, and they came over and shook my hand stating they knew me from my column. They were too drunk to think otherwise but it was flattering that my welcoming was as warm as Kevin's.

The week heading to the following Saturday saw the biggest build-up to an Ipswich game since the 2000 play-off final against Barnsley. It was eagerly awaited and at the final whistle, one of us would be off to Wembley again.

It was also our third live TV game to end the season with and our fourth in our final five fixtures.

The first half continued where the first leg had left off. A tight affair with no quarter given and most pleasing for Ipswich fans was that we were giving as good as we were getting and it had remained an absorbing contest up to the interval, despite there being no goals.

As soon as play resumed though, Norwich found an extra gear. Both Jonny Howson and Cameron Jerome came close to scoring in the first minute of the second half and then came the pivotal moment of the whole tie.

Nathan Redmond cut inside Luke Chambers and shot past Bartosz Białkowski before Christophe Berra blocked on the line using his arm and referee Roger East awarded Norwich a penalty before showing Berra an inevitable red card.

Wes Hoolahan sent Białkowski the wrong way to put Norwich ahead and now we were down to ten men.

Rather than collapsing, however, we levelled just ten minutes later. Teddy Bishop sent a long free kick into the area, Daryl Murphy flicked the ball on and there was Tommy Smith to firstly take the ball away from Ruddy, before turning it into the net from close range. Smith ran the length of the field to celebrate in front of the Town fans and once again, it was chaotic emotions spilling out from every Town fan amassed in front of the New Zealander.

It took just four minutes for Norwich to retake the lead and from this moment, it was game over for a gallant Town side. Białkowski saved from Martin Olsson, but the ball found its way to Howson who clipped it out for Nathan Redmond to score from 15 yards. Twelve minutes from time, Jerome scored to seal a 3-1 win on the day. There is no doubt that the dismissal of Berra turned the tie and we were left wondering what could have been if we had kept 11 men on the pitch.

Yet again, I had seen Ipswich fail to win a semi-final. You would think that given this was now the 14th such loss I would be used to it. But in truth, this one hurt more than any other.

This game was the last that we would see of Tyrone Mings, Paul Anderson, Noel Hunt, and Stephen Hunt in an Ipswich shirt. The season had seen us feature 13 times live on TV, but only three of those games saw a win against our name.

Previous semi-final defeats usually meant that we were a good bet the following season to reach the play-offs again. Only in 1987 when we had lost to Charlton Athletic and then in 2005 after defeat to West Ham had we not reached the play-offs again the next season.

Expectations going into 2015/16 were that we would be a good bet to challenge for a place in them once again.

But we were now a much-changed team and unlike the end of the 1990s for example, we were not adding in a gradual manner to quality already in the building.

On the opening day of the new season at Brentford, we had no fewer than six players making their Ipswich debuts. We led 2-0 going into stoppage time only to draw 2-2. Had we won that game, we would have certainly been encouraged by a decent start.

As it was, we were to win our next five league and cup matches and found ourselves at the top of the Championship with a League Cup third round tie to look forward to away at Manchester United.

Our unbeaten run ended with a 3-2 defeat at home to Brighton and Hove Albion before our first live TV game of the season would see a Friday night trip to Reading on Sky.

At this point, Reading had not won at the Madjeski Stadium in seven league matches, a run that stretched back to March in the previous season, and they had not scored in the past six of those games. The omens looked good for a Town win given the impressive start to the season that we had made.

Reading took the lead in the seventh minute through their new £1m summer signing from Legia Warsaw, Orlando Sá, when he glanced home a header from a Nick Blackman cross.

But Town were to find themselves level just three minutes later. Ryan Fraser forced a save from Jonathan Bond, and Freddie Sears was well-placed to tuck home the rebound for his fourth goal of the season.

It was a frenetic start to the game, and just three minutes later, Reading regained the lead. Matěj Vydra, making his Reading debut after joining on-loan from Watford, released Sá who found space for himself before unleashing a drive from 20 yards past Dean Gerken and in off the far post for his second goal.

The game then settled into a pattern where both sides were evenly matched, but Ipswich were just shading the attacking statistics. There was certainly not too much to be worried about at the half-time break.

That all changed though in the second half. Three minutes after the interval, Reading scored a third. Sá miskicked with the goal at his mercy but Town failed to clear the loose ball and Blackman lashed in his fifth goal of the season.

From here, there was no way back for Ipswich despite Brett Pitman heading against the crossbar and Reading took full advantage. On 62 minutes, Sá completed his hat-trick and four minutes from time, Oliver Norwood sent a 30-yard screamer past Gerken to seal a 5-1 win.

This result was a real shock to the system and after the excellent run we had been on nobody could fathom where it had come from.

One week later, we were live again on a Friday night when we hosted Birmingham City. Sandwiched in the middle of these two we had at least atoned the heavy defeat at Reading with a Tuesday night victory away at Leeds United thanks to a Tommy Smith goal.

Birmingham would be the first live TV game that my daughter Angel attended. That meant that I could not be in my usual lower North Stand seat and had to retreat to the upper tier.

I love taking Angel to games, I always have done. But while she was too young to sit in the lower North Stand, it meant relocating either to the middle tier of the Pioneer Stand or the upper tier of the Cobbold Stand. Without a doubt, I get a much better view of games in these loftier positions, but it is always strange to watch on from a different position elsewhere in the ground.

Birmingham took the lead through David Cotterill midway through the first half after he had capitalised on a slip by Christophe Berra.

Town were soon level though, and it was a goal that was a major talking point. Ainsley Maitland-Niles, on loan from Arsenal, used great pace to reach the byline but saw his cross take a deflection into the arms of Birmingham's goalkeeper Tomasz Kuszczak. At the same time, defender Jonathan Spector had slid in to block Maitland-Niles's cross and caught the youngster in his follow through.

Referee Keith Stroud had felt that Spector fouled Maitland-Niles and pointed to the penalty spot.

Brett Pitman stepped up and made no mistake and that was to be the end of the scoring as both sides shared the spoils.

It was the end of November before we would appear live again, and this was for a Saturday lunchtime game at Charlton Athletic.

We had won just twice in the league since the draw with Birmingham and after such a fine start, Town fans were now getting agitated with how the season was progressing, although we were on a rich vein of scoring form with nine goals in three games.

The Charlton match was the first of three successive matches that we would be shown live in the space of 15 days. The hosts were looking for a third win in a row after going 12 without a victory.

Ipswich had made the brighter start, and our efforts were rewarded when we took the lead in the 28th minute as Daryl Murphy headed home to punish some poor Charlton defending.

It got better for Town on the stroke of half-time when Freddie Sears added a second. A low through ball from Luke Chambers found Sears and he beat former Ipswich loanee Stephen Henderson to score his fifth goal of the season.

To cap an excellent performance, victory was sealed in the 68th minute with a third. Sears showed tenacity to win the ball off two defenders and played it inside for Jonathan Douglas to run on to. He played a neat pass across the area, Pitman dummied, and Murphy finished for his second of the game and his sixth goal in three as Town comfortably saw the game out for a 3-0 win.

The following Friday, it was back to Portman Road as we took on Middlesbrough in front of the Sky cameras again.

The moment that we saw striker David Nugent in the opposition line-up, we just knew that Town might be in trouble. And this was another game in which those fears would prove to be right.

Town had the best chances of a quiet first half. Brett Pitman saw an effort from 20 yards beaten away by Dimi Konstantopoulos and then Luke Chambers went even closer but was foiled by the Greek goalkeeper.

After the break, Middlesbrough took control and on 53 minutes they broke the deadlock. Albert Adomah found space on the left-hand side and sent a dangerous cross into the area that was headed in by Cristhian Stuani at the back post.

With 20 minutes remaining Middlesbrough scored a second, and of course it was that man Nugent. Stewart Downing's incisive pass found Nugent, who still had work to do, before his low shot took a slight deflection off Tommy Smith and went into the back of the net via the inside of the post. It was incredibly Nugent's 15th goal in 14 games against Ipswich.

The final whistle brought a few boos from the crowd as Middlesbrough won at Portman Road for the first time since 1993. It was a result that would also see them go to the top of the table ahead of the Saturday afternoon games.

The third successive live match, the following Saturday at MK Dons, would be Town's 150th TV fixture. It also proved to be our last live game of the season even though we were not halfway through December.

I have to say that Stadium MK is one of the nicest grounds that I have been to. Usually, I do not like the new type of grounds, that are typically bowls. But for a bowl this is one of the better grounds.

This game was then of course a Championship fixture. At the time of writing it is nowadays a League One clash.

Another Saturday lunchtime game meant that yet again, we had to catch an early train out of Clacton. My travelling companions on this occasion were Don, Chris, Kevin, and Lewis Snow.

We made sure that we left in suitable time to meet Kevin Painter at Milton Keynes station before we headed to a working men's club for a few cheap drinks. This has been a common find over the years at several away games. I recall when Kevin Mitchell and I had once been to Blackpool when Town won 3-2 thanks to a last–minute goal from Daryl Murphy, prior to that game, we found a local club where we could get a pint of cider and a double vodka and coke for £3.50. Well, football is an expensive hobby, so you must keep the costs down when you can, right?

The club we ended up in I believe was in Bletchley, but quite a walk to the ground. So, we took a taxi to the game and saw Town celebrate that 150 milestone with a 1-0 win.

The goal came as early as the tenth minute through Brett Pitman. Luke Chambers did well to create the space to enable him to send a deep cross into the area where Pitman was on hand to score his sixth goal of the season.

Twice in the first 30 minutes, Daryl Murphy found himself one on one with MK's goalkeeper David Martin, but on both occasions he saw his delicate chips bounce wide.

With 18 minutes remaining, Murphy was once again through and had the chance to wrap up the game but rushed his effort at a half volley and saw his effort go well over the bar.

We were almost paying for that miss as the hosts threw everything at us in the last ten minutes in search of an equaliser. But any attempt that they made on goal was repelled by Dean Gerken. His best three saves came right at the death. Firstly, he denied Ben Reeves, pushing his shot away for a corner, and then he tipped over Samir Carruthers' effort from 30 yards.

And in the dying moments, Rob Hall saw his thunderous effort towards the top corner superbly saved too.

Coming out of the stadium felt like we were the home team. Over 4,000 Ipswich fans were present and there was not an MK Dons supporter to be seen.

The win saw the start of a nine-game run where we lost just once – inevitably at home to Derby.

We then held on to the coat tails of sixth spot for the remainder of the season, yet unlike in previous years, we were not considered serious play-off hopefuls at all by Sky who were not to show us live any more that season.

We finished the season in seventh place, five points behind Sheffield Wednesday.

Despite Mick McCarthy overseeing a further nine live games to come, that 1-0 win at MK Dons would be the last time he would manage a victorious Ipswich side in on TV.

The fourth league game of 2016/17 would be Town's first TV fixture of the new campaign and it would be the 20th live game between Ipswich and Norwich. It was also our first meeting since that epic play-off battle at the end of the 2014/15 season, with Norwich back in the Championship after just one season in the Premier League.

Town had beaten Barnsley 4-2 at Portman Road on the opening day of the season and followed this up with a 2-0 defeat at Brentford, a 0-0 draw at home to Wolves and in the meantime, had been dumped out of the League Cup by Stevenage who had won 1-0 at Portman Road. It is therefore fair to say that we were not in the greatest shape heading into the Norwich game. We had also failed to beat the Canaries in six attempts.

Pre-game saw us as ever in excited mood as I was joined by my friends Kevin, Chris, and Kevin Painter in the fanzone. My mid-morning cider was going down a treat as we were asking one another if this would be the day that we finally beat that lot up the road.

I have tried to hold back in some of my comments in the more recent live fixtures between the two sides that I have written about, when it comes to Norwich having their fair share of luck. After all, you make your own luck and they had benefitted more than what we had.

On this occasion, they were once again enjoying the rub of the green. Within two minutes Jonathan Douglas had the ball in the back of the Norwich net, only for the goal to be ruled out wrongly by the assistant referee. Television replays clearly showed Douglas in an onside position and in today's top-flight game, VAR would have come to our rescue.

Ipswich had not kept a clean sheet in any of the last 16 East Anglian derbies and that became 17 when Cameron Jerome opened the scoring in the 26th minute after his effort from 18 yards went in off the post.

Although this had taken the sting out of our tails to a degree, we were still able to celebrate getting an equaliser that we had thoroughly deserved on the stroke of half-time. And it came from a rare source.

Freddie Sears fed Jonas Knudsen who cut back on to his weaker right foot, aimed for the corner and found it. Once again, we were all over each other in the North Stand, wildly celebrating the goal that we had craved and deserved.

Town had Adam Webster to thank in the 53rd minute when clearing a Steven Whittaker effort off the line and Whittaker came close again in the 75th minute but hit a post after an error by Christophe Berra had gifted him an opportunity.

A draw was about the right result, and we left the ground frustrated that yet again we had failed to beat our enemy.

That game would be the last that we would see of Daryl Murphy in an Ipswich shirt before his £3m move to Newcastle United.

A little under three weeks later, we participated in a Friday night Sky fixture at Reading. After Norwich, we had gotten our season back on track with a 1-0 win at home to Preston North End.

The Reading game was an extraordinary affair with three contentious penalties, all scored, being the main feature.

Referee Jeremy Simpson was at the centre of three major talking points, the first of which came in first-half stoppage time when Grant Ward was penalised for a harsh handball from a Tyler Blackett cross and Garath McCleary scored from the spot.

Five minutes into the second period, Town were awarded a penalty when Blackett and Brett Pitman tussled at the back post and Simpson felt that the Town striker had been impeded. Pitman took the kick himself to level matters and it would be Town who looked the side most likely from there to go on and win the game.

Then in the 90th minute, an incident occurred in the Town penalty area as the players awaited a Reading corner.

Simpson had halted play to have a word with Joey van den Berg and Christophe Berra for grappling with one another as the corner was about to be taken. On resumption of play, Simpson blew for a penalty as van den Berg was once more involved, this time with Knudsen.

On one hand, it was refreshing to see an official clamp down on such behaviour as repeatedly, these incidents occur. But I do not believe I have ever seen another penalty given in these moments.

I have a row b season ticket seat in the North Stand, and I am therefore well-placed to see these incidents when waiting for corners to be sent over. All us fans want is consistency.

Danny Williams stepped up to score the penalty to give Reading a 2-1 win. The whole charade of those decisions certainly left most of us watching totally confused after the game. Mick McCarthy felt aggrieved at all three penalties but unsurprisingly, Reading manager Jaap Stam felt both penalties for his team were fair yet was adamant that Town's should not have been awarded.

Two months went by before we appeared live again, and Nottingham Forest were the visitors to Portman Road for a Saturday evening game just after mid-November.

In the days prior to COVID, Kevin Painter and I would struggle to make kick-offs for most games because if there were 20 minutes still to go, that would usually signal that there was still time for another pint.

Fine if you are at the ground, but not so good if you are inside a hostelry somewhere in the town centre. That game was yet another where kick-off was missed but that proved not to be a terrible thing on this occasion.

It took just 17 seconds for Britt Assombalonga to open the scoring for Forest. It was the fastest goal of the 2016/17 season in the Championship.

When I walked up the steps into the North Stand and looked on to the pitch, I saw Town kicking off and assumed that was to start the game. I then spotted the scoreboard down the far end showing Forest were leading 1-0. For a nanosecond, I was not sure as to exactly what was going on.

On the stroke of half-time, Assombalonga nodded home his second and left a mountain for us to climb after the break.

Despite constant pressure from Town, the Forest back line stood firm to typically achieve their first clean sheet of the season.

As we moved into January 2017, a defeat away at Queens Park Rangers was followed up with a 2-2 home FA Cup draw against Lincoln City, who at the time were still plying their trade in the National League.

Our FA Cup record over the recent years has not been the best and that result was considered a new low. We had been behind in the game twice, and only scraped a replay thanks to an 86th-minute equaliser by Tom Lawrence – his second of the game.

As a result, BBC One chose to screen the replay live on Tuesday, 17 January.

If I had to choose the three most embarrassing results in live TV games, this one would be included and quite possibly sit in pole position ahead of the game that I have already covered when we lost 7-1 at Peterborough United.

Fifty-nine places separated us from Lincoln, but if you knew nothing about football, and happened to watch this game, you could easily be forgiven if those places had been reversed.

Lincoln won in the 90th minute. Ipswich were pressing for a goal at 0-0 and looking to avoid extra time. Then Lincoln substitute Adam Marriott launched a break that suddenly put Nathan Arnold clear.

From the moment he made his first stride, it was easy to fear the worst. Here would come the moment that would embarrass us in front of a watching nation.

The former Grimsby Town winger took the ball calmly around Dean Gerken and rolled in into the net. The final whistle sounded soon after and we lost 1-0. It would also be the last time that we would see Leon Best play for the club.

I want to say that I could not believe what I had seen. Yet I was not remotely surprised. This was the Ipswich we had become accustomed to in cup football.

Town legend Terry Butcher ripped into the performance in the post-match analysis, and who could blame him? Terry spoke for every one of us that night. It was also the last time that we were live on any BBC channel at the time of writing.

The next morning, I took Lola and Angel to school and as we were in the middle of winter, they would be wearing their hats, scarves, and gloves – nothing unusual in that for a pair of nine-year-old girls. But in the case of Angel, I did not know whether to feel sorry for her or admire her.

She was still wearing her Ipswich Town bobble hat. She had watched the game with me the night before. I asked her if she was embarrassed to be wearing that hat and she shrugged her shoulders and just said, 'No, it's what I am used to.' The innocence of youth, hey.

A further seven league matches followed before we were next back on Sky. During this run, we mustered just one victory – a surprising 1-0 win at Aston Villa thanks to an Emyr Huws goal. We only lost twice but the season continued to be hampered by more draws – four of them in fact.

This next live game was at Norwich and much-remembered for the applause from the home fans in the 15th minute as a mark of celebrating our 15 continuous years in the Championship – the longest run of any club in any of the three Football League divisions at that time.

But that was OK, as Town fans responded with a chant of our own referencing that despite these 15 years in the Championship, we were still famous, and they were not.

A stoic first half saw no goals scored and it would be Town who would take the lead in the 63rd minute. Just like the reverse fixture earlier in the season, it was Jonas Knudsen who would once more score our goal – the 200th live TV goal that Ipswich had scored.

Norwich had failed to both cut out a cross and track Knudsen's run as he timed his run to perfection to head home at the far post. Would this be the day that we would finally go on to beat Norwich?

Unfortunately, not, as it took only six minutes for them to reply with a goal from Jacob Murphy.

Another game without a victory but the smallest crumb of comfort came in the fact that at least we were unbeaten in the season against them.

The season petered out for Town as the next 11 games would see only three more wins. That draw at Norwich came in a run of six successive stalemates and we would end the season with a total of 16 – more than any other team in the Championship.

There was still time for one more live game in the season, on the final day away at Nottingham Forest. The Tricky Trees needed to win to avoid relegation to League One.

With Town rooted in 16th place with nothing to play for, all the expectations were on a Forest win. They were in direct competition with Blackburn Rovers as to who would be relegated, the Lancashire club away at Brentford.

As fans, we had been involved in these last-day shenanigans on so many occasions. So, for a while it was enjoyable watching Forest fans suffer as Blackburn had gone 2-0 up inside the first 16 minutes.

But goals either side of half-time from Britt Assombalonga and Chris Cohen brought some relief to Forest fans, and when Assombalonga scored his second on 69 minutes they had wrapped the game up 3-0. It would be the last time that we would see both Christophe Berra and Kieffer Moore play for Ipswich and, this was the final game in a loan spell for striker Dominic Samuel.

Blackburn went on to win 3-1 at Brentford and Forest stayed up on goal difference – just two goals better off than Rovers.

As for Town, it had been an extremely disappointing season and time was running out for Mick McCarthy in the eyes of a growing number of fans.

The 2017/18 season got off to an amazing start when we won our first five games – four in the Championship, which included an exciting 4-3 scoreline, at Millwall, and a win at Luton Town in the League Cup.

We were sitting at the top of the table and worries built up in the previous season had now evaporated. But any thoughts of this season looking like it would be so much better were to take a turn when we then lost three successive games and although we stopped the rot with a 2-0 win at home to Bolton, we lost three of the next four by the time Norwich rolled up in town once more for our first live TV date of the season.

As was becoming the norm for the group that I had pre-match drinks with, Ipswich's waterfront would be our place for a get-together. On this occasion, I was with Jason and Kevin Painter, and we met up with Matt Deller, son of former world darts champion Keith. Normally, I could not stomach cider at 9.30am. But this is always doable when in such company for such an occasion.

Usual chat was around whether this would finally be the day and before any alcohol had been consumed, I would be in the 'probably not' group. A couple of ciders later, I would be 'why not?' I mean, you must at least go to the game with some hope after all.

Ipswich had wasted plenty of early opportunities and the closest we came to scoring was when Jonas Knudsen hit a post to prevent him from netting in three consecutive East Anglian derbies. He was trying his best to become the new Danny Haynes in these games.

The only goal came on the hour mark through James Maddison to seal a fourth successive away win in the Championship for Norwich.

Our fourth defeat in five games saw us slip to 11th and yet again, we left the ground with the same old question of simply: when?

Tom Adeyemi picked up an injury in this game and was not to be seen again in an Ipswich shirt.

Exactly a month later, we were again screened live by Sky as Sheffield Wednesday came to Portman Road. Two wins and a draw in the four matches since Norwich had provided some relief and we went into the Wednesday meeting hoping to build on that run.

It was as early as the third minute when a major talking point arose. Wednesday defender Glenn Loovens caught David McGoldrick in the thigh with a high, studs-up challenge, resulting in a four-inch gash in McGoldrick's groin which subsequently required surgery.

We were anticipating a red card but to the astonishment of many of us watching on, Loovens received no more than a verbal warning – he had even escaped a yellow card.

After a low-key first half, Town took the lead in the 48th minute through Joe Garner before Gary Hooper levelled for Wednesday from the penalty spot on 64 minutes after Jordan Spence had handled.

Six minutes later, Martyn Waghorn scored with a header to put Town back in front. Freddie Sears missed in a one-on-one situation with Keiren Westwood and how Town were made to pay for that miss.

Wednesday threw on their big target man Atdhe Nuhiu in the 87th minute to replace former Ipswich striker Jordan Rhodes. And in the 95th minute, the Kosovan headed home to earn his side a point from a 2-2 draw that they barely deserved.

It would be another three months before we would be seen live on TV again and once more it would be at Norwich. Football can be a cruel game sometimes and as time goes on and the more matches you see, then the list of cruel moments grow. This was one of the cruellest moments in recent years as a Town fan.

Remember, we had not beaten Norwich by this point in almost nine years. Nine games had seen us lose six times and drawn three. It had been 12 years since our last win at Carrow Road.

In any game, there is nothing better than a last-minute winner. It sends you into a frenzied state no matter who the opposition is. But when you believe that is going to be the case away at your close rivals, then the state of frenzy multiplies. Imagine going through those emotions only to have them quashed by an equaliser even later in the game.

I have refused to go to games at Carrow Road for many years now for a multitude of reasons which I will refrain from writing about here.

I have already mentioned that I am a nervous listener and watcher of Ipswich games and on this day, once Luke Chambers had scored in the 89th minute to put us 1-0 ahead, there was no way I could stomach injury time. I simply turned the television off, got in the car and left it ten minutes before I dared to put the radio on to hear about us beating them at last.

When I switched on, I heard Radio Suffolk playing the highlights of the game. It was with great satisfaction to hear Brenner Woolley commentating on that Chambers goal. The next phase of commentary I fully expected to be the moment that referee David Coote blowing the final whistle and Brenner would delightfully describe how Ipswich had finally beaten Norwich.

But that would not be the case. There was more match commentary to come and then Brenner described the moment that Grant Hanley chased a lost cause to keep the ball in play, Bartosz Białkowski was out of his goal and Hanley crossed for Timm Klose to score and the game finished 1-1.

That was real gut-wrenching moment in my life as a Town fan. Forget those 14 semi-final defeats. The urge to see/hear us beat Norwich just once has grown more as each time we play them passes. How can it now be so long since it last happened? Why could we just not keep the ball out of our net for another minute?

As a side note, David McGoldrick came off the bench in the 62nd minute to replace Joe Garner for what would be his final appearance in an Ipswich shirt.

When Town scored, that was the moment that Mick McCarthy screamed obscenities towards the stand housing Ipswich fans. Whether that was just a moment of pure passion or not, it did not go down well with many supporters.

For the next couple of months, relations were strained between McCarthy and the fans, and he left his position after a 1-0 Tuesday night victory at home to Barnsley. That draw at Norwich was the last of his live games.

In 29 TV fixtures, across five seasons, McCarthy only managed to steer us to five wins and they will not be remembered too famously, while that FA Cup defeat at Lincoln will live long in the memory.

Town finished the season in 12th place, two places above Norwich on goal difference.

CHAPTER 7: DOWN AND OUT

Paul Hurst, Paul Lambert and John McGreal (11 games)

Town announced Paul Hurst as their new manager at the end of May 2018 after the Yorkshireman had led Shrewsbury Town to the League One play-off final, where they had lost 2-1 to Rotherham United after extra time.

It was seen at the time as a refreshing appointment by many Ipswich fans who were keen to see a young and upcoming English manager and what he could bring to the club.

Hurst would bring Toto Nsiala and Jon Nolan to Suffolk with him as he started a rebuild in readiness for 2018/19.

By the time we reached the first day of the new season, there were already a few concerns that some of our better players had been released and were replaced with those from divisions below the Championship. The first game of the season at home to Blackburn Rovers saw no fewer than five debutants for Town.

By the time we got to our first live TV game of the season, on 2 October at home to Middlesbrough, the signs were ominous for Hurst, who had failed to win one of his first ten league matches in charge and saw an early exit in the League Cup at the hands of Exeter City.

The atmosphere at Portman Road for this TV fixture was at an all-time low, even more so when Middlesbrough scored twice inside the first 16 minutes. It is hard to believe that there were as many as the official 13,612 stated attendance in the ground. And once those two goals went in, you could hear a pin drop.

Mo Bešić put Boro ahead when he was given too much time and space to run from the halfway line and into the Ipswich area before coolly finishing after his initial effort had been blocked.

And four minutes later, Stuart Downing doubled the lead after a poor pass by Luke Chambers had given him the opportunity to score.

Only some smart goalkeeping by Dean Gerken prevented the visitors from scoring any further goals and the only save that Darren Randolph had to make at the other end was from a low effort by Trevoh Chalobah.

Our winless start was a record matched only once before when we had failed to win any of our opening 14 matches in 2009/10 under Roy Keane.

Winger Jordan Graham played his last game for Ipswich against Middlesbrough, and despite a first win of the season coming in the very next game away at Swansea City – a 3-2 scoreline – Hurst was also on his way out just two further matches down the line and before we had even reached the end of October. He was in charge for just that one live date.

Two days after Hurst's sacking, Town announced Paul Lambert as the new manager. He sat in the stands at Millwall and witnessed a 3-0 defeat and no doubt realised the task in hand to keep Ipswich in the Championship was going to require all his experience.

Lambert's first two games in charge saw two draws – 1-1 at home to Preston North End and 2-2 at Reading – before our next game, and Lambert's first TV match, came on 'Black Friday' at home to West Bromwich Albion.

This was a game that will forever live in my memory. Some of you may remember the ticket story that came off the back of a simple gesture that I had made. It was a story that grew from two tickets to almost 1,000 and was a truly humbling moment in my life.

My daughters Lola and Angel had taken part in a Christmas shoe box appeal that a work colleague of mine at the time had organised. The girls bought some gifts out of their own money for under-privileged children in Romania, an action that had me full of admiration for them both and made me want to do just a little something to help someone myself.

I had no idea what to do really, but once Town announced cheap tickets for the West Brom game, I knew exactly what I wanted to do.

I put a message out on Twitter that I wanted to give a pair of tickets to someone who could not ordinarily afford to go to football. Somebody saw the tweet and offered to do the same if they could send me the tickets. So, between us, we could help a family of four.

Within a week, I had received £2,500 from a total of 108 donors. The story of my simple gesture caught on and suddenly, lots of fellow supporters and businesses wanted to get involved. I even had donations from ex-Ipswich players as well as a generous donation from a current Town player at that time.

Then to top it all, the club agreed to match the donations I had received, and more players donated tickets too. The story had reached everywhere, and I was interviewed on local television on both the BBC and ITV. The story also appeared on the front page of the BBC Sport website.

That was my 15 minutes of fame that we are all meant to have. I had not courted the attention and I was totally overwhelmed by it all to be honest. I will grow old remembering that moment and will never be able to thank all those involved enough.

The scariest part was to come as when I picked up around 1,000 tickets to be distributed to schools and local charities, I really did not know what to do.

But in stepped some real heroes who ensured they were given to exactly the right people. The help afforded to me by Stephen Skeet, Graham Blackburn and Helen Royce was immeasurable. They certainly took a huge weight off my shoulders.

The attendance that night was 22,995, which at the time was the second biggest of the season and only bettered as you would expect by our home game against Norwich. The sight that will stay with me forever was seeing the whole of the bottom tier of the Cobbold Stand full knowing the tickets that were bought through all the donations received had made up much of that support. It certainly had the effect on the Sky cameras to see those seats filled.

West Brom won 2-1 – the days of beating them 3-1 at Portman Road were now long gone – and it was no surprise really. The result moved the Baggies up to second place. Meanwhile, we were still looking for our first home win of the season and were five points adrift at the foot of the Championship.

Jay Rodriguez scored his ninth goal of the season from six yards in the first half, and then Harvey Barnes doubled Albion's lead on 77 minutes.

To their credit, Ipswich kept going and pulled a goal back five minutes from time through Kayden Jackson, and Jack Lankester almost scored an equaliser in injury time but saw his free kick clip a post.

Of course, the result mattered in the great scheme of things, but it was an occasion that was so special for so many people and I felt proud to have played a part in the night that was for them.

A further 13 games were to pass before we would find ourselves live on TV again, for the 24th – and at the time of publication the most recent – live game with Norwich. It would also be the first time that Paul Lambert would come up against his former club, who he had served so well.

Only two wins would come in those 13 games and by then, we were in real trouble. We were nine points away from clawing ourselves out of the relegation zone, the equivalent of three wins. We had only obtained three wins all season and we were now in the second week of February.

The situation was dire, and most Town fans were resigned to our lengthy stay in the Championship ending. But never had we thought it would do so by going into League One.

It took just two minutes for Norwich to score through Onel Hernández. It was Norwich's fastest league goal for eight years.

Teemu Pukki then scored twice in the second half to cap a 3-0 win and our wait for a victory at Norwich had now stretched to ten years.

What the game will be most remembered for was seeing a fired-up Lambert receive a red card after a clash on the touchline with Norwich manager Daniel Farke and one of their coaches, Chris Domogalla.

Our next five games saw us again fail to win but an upturn in performances saw only one defeat. Our consistency was in drawing games which was at that stage of the season not good enough.

Mid-March saw us visit Bristol City for a Tuesday night match live on Sky where I felt that we had put in a decent performance, but again, we could only find our way to yet another draw.

On another night, and with Bristol City one place outside the play-off places, this would have been considered a decent result. But we were 12 points adrift of safety and needed wins.

Town had the better of the opening 20 minutes but fell behind when former Tractor Boy Adam Webster headed in after 32 minutes.

We then deservedly levelled after the break thanks to an own goal by Lloyd Kelly on 68 minutes who diverted Andre Dozzell's cross into his own net. Idris El Mizouni came off the bench in the 75th minute for his Ipswich debut.

There were just nine games remaining after this game and by the time we were live on Sky again, it would be for the final time in the Championship season.

Those nine matches saw just the one win – 2-1 away at Bolton Wanderers – and the fifth in that run would be the day that our relegation to League One was confirmed.

A 1-1 draw at home to Birmingham City sealed our fate despite there still being four games left of the season. Although relegation had been on the cards for so long, it was sad to see us drop to the third tier of English football for the first time since 1957. Despite having so many weeks leading up to this point to prepare for the inevitable, I could not comprehend how we had fallen so far from being that team that was always sniffing around the play-offs to this. Town were down and out.

I shared that damning moment with my daughter Angel, sat up in the top tier of the Cobbold Stand, down the North Stand end.

I stood there after the final whistle watching those in the lower tier of the North Stand, who ordinarily I would have been stood with, give Paul Lambert and his players a reception that ordinarily would be reserved for a team who had achieved something such as winning a cup or promotion. They cheered, clapped, and sung their hearts out and that was on the back of relegation being confirmed.

That just showed how good our support is and if one day we ever return to the big time in my life, I will remember that moment and how the fans stayed behind the team.

That last live game of the season would be our penultimate match, and final away day at Sheffield United, for a Saturday teatime kick-off.

The contrasting fortunes of the two clubs could not have been any different. Town were guaranteed to finish bottom of the league, while the Blades were battling it out with Leeds United to join Norwich in the automatic promotion places and a win for the hosts would also still leave them with a chance of pipping our rivals to the Championship title.

The sight of David McGoldrick starting for United was to rub salt in our wounds too. That was the calibre of player that we had on our books just the year before, and a stark reminder back to the demolition job Paul Hurst had made on our squad that would suffer dire consequences.

Scott Hogan put United in front midway through the first half and Jack O'Connell sealed the win with a second on 71 minutes. It was a farewell game for Dean Gerken who would go on to re-join Colchester United.

We just had one final game left of that traumatic season and the following weekend saw us beat Leeds United 3-2 at Portman Road, which caused a wry smile in that we could win again and not only that, but to a team that would finish their own campaign in third place.

We were all glad to see the back of that season and wondered what a League One tour would hold in store for us.

By the time that we would reach our first live game of the 2019/20 season, away at Accrington Stanley, we were flying high at the top of the table. Our first 11 matches had yielded 27 points from a possible 33 after eight wins and three draws.

Our last league outing before the date on TV with Accrington had seen us win 1-0 away at third-placed Fleetwood Town and, in the process, open a seven-point lead on them. It may have only been early October, but with a near-perfect start, we were already thinking of an instant return to the Championship. The 'HMS Walk the League' supporters, with their 100 points and 100 goals beliefs were already thinking that those targets were well on track.

Until January 2019, we had never played Accrington Stanley. But a third-round tie in the FA Cup at the WHAM Stadium changed that and Accrington won 1-0 to cause an upset for anyone who was not an Ipswich fan.

So, with that meeting still fresh in our minds, a second trip to Stanley mixed with the fact that the game was being screened live by Sky Sports meant that we were treating the prospects of yet another win lightly, no matter how good our start to the season had been.

We were right to be a tad cautious as two Colby Bishop goals in the first half saw us fall to our first defeat of the season.

His first came in the 17th minute when he headed Sam Finley's high, looping cross past Tomáš Holý, and then his second came four minutes before the break from the penalty spot. It was Bishop who himself had been fouled inside the area by Toto Nsiala.

Both sides finished with ten men as Accrington's Ross Sykes clashed with Armando Dobra in an off-the-ball incident.

We did have our moments in front of goal with two efforts being cleared off the line. The first was to prevent an own goal and the second was to thwart Luke Woolfenden.

Town's five-game winning run, where four clean sheets had been kept and only one goal conceded, had ended abruptly.

Despite the defeat, we remained top, a point ahead of Wycombe Wanderers who would incidentally be our next live TV opponents on New Year's Day 2020.

That defeat at Accrington was followed up with a home loss against Rotherham United. Our next seven games saw two wins, three draws and two defeats and the superb start that we had to the campaign was now slipping away.

When we drew 0-0 with Gillingham at Portman Road on Boxing Day, we were still in second place but now six points behind leaders Wycombe.

In the car driving home, we listened intently to Paul Lambert's post-match press conference, and he sounded a broken man. He was very reserved with his answers to

Brenner Woolley's questions and following that, the topic of conversation with my travelling companions was about Lambert's future. Was he going to be sacked? Was he going to walk? Either way, it sounded like his time was ending.

We lost our next game 5-3 at Lincoln City and had now dropped to fourth but still the six points behind Wycombe. It was certainly all set for an interesting clash between two of the division's top teams at Adams Park to start the year.

The big shock for many if you like, was the breaking news that Lambert had signed a new contract which would last until the summer of 2025. Wow. Nobody had seen that coming, especially after how he had sounded on Boxing Day.

A subdued first half saw Wycombe miss a glorious chance to take the lead when Paul Smyth inexplicably put the ball wide of an open goal. That was a massive let-off for Town.

Nine minutes into the second half, Town took the lead. Luke Garbutt took a quick free kick on the left and James Norwood headed home his ninth of the season right in front of us celebrating Ipswich fans.

The lead, however, was to last for only 12 minutes as David Wheeler lobbed a stranded Will Norris after a touch from Adebayo Akinfenwa had played him in. Akinfenwa made a nuisance of himself from the moment he came off the bench just a minute before the goal. The game ended 1-1 and we had now dropped down to fifth.

The matches at Accrington and Wycombe were the only two live TV dates in 2019/20. That was perhaps partly because of the remaining 20 fixtures scheduled after Wycombe, just 13 were played. And with just three wins alongside seven defeats, including a run of four defeats at the cut-off point of the season, Town finished in a disappointing 11th place.

The COVID-19 pandemic had forced the season to end prematurely, and clubs were ranked according to a points-per-game ratio system at the time of the abandonment to determine the final placings. It seemed harsh on Ipswich who had some winnable fixtures remaining, but in hindsight, the early curtailment may have just saved Lambert's job in many people's eyes.

Football resumed a little late at the start of the 2020/21 season, and behind closed doors with no fans allowed to attend due to the ongoing pandemic, with a League Cup tie at home to Bristol Rovers kicking-off Town's season on 5 September.

The following weekend, our first league game of the season, at home to Wigan Athletic, was pushed back to the Sunday afternoon for live coverage on Sky.

Wigan were struggling after financial problems had hit the club in 2019/20 and with a 12-point deduction, they had been relegated to League One. Manager Paul Cook had also resigned, and little did we know then that less than six months on from this game, Cook would become the new Ipswich manager. A couple of weeks before this new season, there were concerns as to whether Wigan would even be able to raise a side after as many as 14 players had departed.

Of those who played that afternoon, Lee Evans, who would join Ipswich the following close season, started, as did former Town player Gary Roberts who would later in the season become a member of Cook's coaching staff at at Portman Road.

It was the visitors who made the brighter start and should have been ahead before Town scored their first league goal of the season. Emeka Obi missed the target from six yards and former Ipswich player Joe Garner saw an overhead kick come back off the crossbar.

That first goal came on 11 minutes when Freddie Sears broke down the left and his bouncing cross was headed home by Teddy Bishop for only his second goal for the club.

Bishop almost scored a second when his effort from outside the area hit a post.

Obi had gone close again for Wigan with another header, but it would be Town who would score the second goal of the game to clinch all three points.

Gwion Edwards replaced Sears in the 73rd minute and seven minutes later, the man who would join Wigan less than a year later executed a smart turn before firing into the net.

Town made an identical start to the season as the one that they had made in 2019/20. They followed up that victory over Wigan with four wins and a draw to top the league once again midway through October before suffering their first defeat of the season away at Doncaster Rovers.

By the time we were live on Sky again for the visit of Swindon Town on 9 January, the similar and familiar traits of the previous season continued.

It had been over three weeks since our last game – a 2-1 win at home to Burton Albion – and the whole festive programme of games was wiped out due to ongoing COVID related problems.

We found ourselves sitting in fifth place after failing to build on another excellent start, but were one of four teams on 32 points, just two points off leaders Hull City.

Swindon were just one place off the foot of the table and presented an ideal opportunity to claim all three points as football resumed. Fans were still not able to attend games, other than three matches in December where a maximum of 2,000 were present at Plymouth and at home to Portsmouth and Burton, it would be the case for the whole season that football would be played behind closed doors.

The Swindon line-up had a couple of familiar faces as former Ipswich players Zeki Fryers and Brett Pitman featured. In their ranks was Dominic Thompson, who would join Town on loan from Brentford during the 2021/22 season.

It was Thompson who would be the main threat to Town with his marauding runs down the left causing all kind of problems.

From one such foray into the Town half in the 16th minute, the Robins took the lead when Thompson's cross was headed home by former Norwich winger Diallang Jaiyesimi.

The closest that Town came to levelling in the first half was through a couple of Alan Judge efforts. The first saw Swindon goalkeeper Mark Travers come off his line to deny Judge and then the diminutive midfielder struck a post with a decent effort from 25 yards.

Half-time came and once again, we were cursing our luck in a live TV game for being behind to one of the division's strugglers.

But we were level on 62 minutes when James Norwood got lucky as the ball struck him and went into the net after coming off Swindon defender Paul Caddis.

Just when we thought that we were able to go on and win, Swindon went back in front five minutes later. In fact, they scored twice in a seven-minute spell to put the game out of our reach.

Thompson was again involved in the build-up to the second goal, which resulted in Scott Twine scoring spectacularly from all of 30 yards, and then another assist from Thompson saw Jaiyesimi score his second of the game when his cross looped into the back of the net.

We were stunned at being 3-1 down and in truth we had put in another performance that was simply not good enough.

We did manage to pull a goal back with three minutes remaining when Norwood found Judge, who tucked the ball past Travers from inside the six-yard box. At the time of writing Judge remains the last player to score for Ipswich in a live TV game.

That unexpected 3-2 defeat saw us drop to eighth and we were now ten points off the top of the table.

Just over two weeks later, Sunderland were the visitors to Portman Road for what turned out to be our last live game of the season and again, at the time of writing, the last live Portman Road fixture.

After that defeat at home to Swindon, we had won away at Burton Albion but lost at home to Peterborough United.

We went into the Sunderland game in ninth place but only two points off the top six. Sunderland were a point ahead of us in seventh.

In what felt like a must-win encounter, our hopes of achieving victory took a huge dent as early as the tenth minute when Kayden Jackson was sent off for serious foul play after a poor challenge on Bailey Wright. Jackson became the tenth Ipswich player to be sent off live on TV, and the last to date.

On the stroke of half-time, Sunderland scored the only goal for a 1-0 win. Charlie Wyke scored his 12th league goal of the season when he connected with a cross from Max Power to glide the ball past Tomáš Holý. Town's best chance saw Sunderland goalkeeper Lee Burge save well from loanee Luke Thomas.

As the game wore on, Town's defence came under constant pressure with Lynden Gooch, Grant Leadbitter and Power all going close to adding a second. It would also be the last time that we would see midfielder Jon Nolan in an Ipswich shirt.

Town dropped another place and were now five points adrift of Charlton Athletic in sixth. Paul Lambert was now under further pressure with calls from many quarters for the Scotsman to be sacked.

One win in his next five games did little to preserve Lambert's chances of remaining in the hotseat and the clamour for him to be relieved of his position grew stronger.

We then pulled off an excellent result with a 1-0 win at promotion-chasing Hull City and followed that up with a 2-1 home win over sixth-placed Doncaster Rovers.

The next evening and on the last day of February 2021, I had sat down and written my latest *East Anglian Daily Times* column and e-mailed that off like I would normally do on a Sunday night.

Around 10pm, I received an e-mail asking for me to write another as news came through that Lambert had left the club with the departure being confirmed as 'by mutual consent'.

Two days later Paul Cook was announced as Ipswich's new manager. He sat in the stands at Accrington's WHAM Stadium where we finally won, 2-1, for the first time under the stewardship of Bryan Klug and Matt Gill.

Cook took charge of the last 16 games of the 2020/21 season and only four would result in an Ipswich win.

Our second season in League One had all the ingredients of the first. A good start followed by an inconsistent season. We had improved our final position however, with ninth place being achieved.

At the beginning of April, Cook dropped his first hints that he would be planning a major squad overhaul in the summer.

Then on 7 April, news came through that Marcus Evans had sold the club after 13 years of ownership, with a group of US investors taking control.

The 'Three Lions' known as Brett Johnson, Berke Bakay and Mark Detmer were at the forefront of the takeover by Gamechanger 20 Ltd, funded by the Arizona state pension fund, with Mike O'Leary named as the new club chairman.

A week later, new CEO Mark Ashton arrived and by the time the transfer window had closed in August at the start of the 2021/22 season, Paul Cook had firmly delivered on his promises of being a demolition man. No fewer than 23 squad players departed while others left on loan. A total of 19 new players were brought in, including former Town favourite Bersant Celina on loan from French club Dijon.

Once more the hopes of Town fans were renewed and were underpinned by new owners and a manager in place with a decent record of getting teams promoted.

Almost 13,000 season tickets were purchased, and an opening-day draw at home to Morecambe attracted a crowd of over 21,000 as fans were allowed to return to games. Nine of Ipswich's new players debuted.

Unlike the two previous seasons in League One, Town were not to get off to a flying start. We failed to win any of our first eight games in three different competitions. We were asked for patience as our new-look squad was taking time to gel.

Nine wins followed in the next 20 games, but we found ourselves sitting in a disappointing 11th place after beating Crewe Alexandra at Portman Road at the end of November.

Concerns were now being raised over Cook's position and when his next two games saw us bow out of the Papa John's Trophy after a penalty shoot-out defeat at the hands of Arsenal's under-21s, followed by a 0-0 draw at home to lowly League Two outfit Barrow in the FA Cup second round, Cook was sacked.

He had been in charge for just nine months and did not manage in a single live TV game for the club. It was disappointing that Cook had not lived up to the standards of his pre-Ipswich managerial career and once again, we were on the hunt for a new boss.

Former Town player John McGreal had recently been brought back to the club to assist Kieron Dyer in managing our under-23s. McGreal was then elevated to the position of caretaker manager of the first team while a replacement for Cook was being sought.

After a defeat at Charlton followed by a creditable draw at Wigan, McGreal took charge in our first live game of the season. ITV 4 was the channel to host our FA Cup replay at Barrow. It was the only replay of the round.

It had been 15 years since Town had progressed through two rounds of the FA Cup in the same season. After beating Oldham Athletic in the first round following a replay in 2021/22, the prospect of reaching the third round looked good when we were drawn to play Barrow at home. But once that game had ended 0-0, it was only a matter of time before the mechanisms inside our heads that were trained to expect the worst started to fire up once more.

And within 35 minutes, we were 2-0 down. Jordan Stevens fired a cleverly worked corner in from the edge of the box on 26 minutes and then Robbie Gotts smashed home from close range.

Town had made nine changes from the side that had drawn at Wigan and yet on paper, we looked strong enough to beat a team struggling in the bottom tier. In the second period we were able to call on Sam Morsy, Luke Woolfenden, Joe Pigott, Conor Chaplin and Janoi Donacien to enhance our chances of getting back into the game. Yet Barrow stood firm and progressed to the next round to face Barnsley.

It would be the last time that we would see Toto Nsiala and Scott Fraser appear for Ipswich and once again, we had the discomfiture of losing on national TV. Not in the same league as those horrible losses to Lincoln City and Peterborough United, but another moment to forget for sure.

McGreal had one more game in charge with a spirited 1-1 draw at home to Sunderland in front of a crowd of over 29,000 as the first of three 'pack out Portman Road' matches for the festive period arrived.

Two days before this game, on 16 December, there had been the announcement of our new manager, who watched the Sunderland match from in the directors' box.

CHAPTER 8: A NEW HOPE

Kieran McKenna (1 game)

The new man entrusted with taking the team forward was 35-year-old Northern Irishman Kieran McKenna. This appointment came as a surprise as not many people could confess to having heard of him.

He joined on a three-and-a-half-year deal to become the 19th overall, and the second youngest manager at the time of appointment in the club's history.

McKenna had been forced to retire from playing due to injury aged just 22 and then set about a coaching career where he gained experience firstly at Tottenham where he was their under-18s manager. He then left Tottenham for Manchester United, again to take charge of their under-18s. He then progressed to the first team setup, serving under José Mourinho, Ole Gunnar Solskjær, and for a short period of time, under Ralf Rangnick.

At the time of his appointment, McKenna had the challenging task of getting Town into a play-off position. The draw with Sunderland had left us ten points adrift.

Just two defeats in his first 14 matches had maintained our hope that we could still yet gate-crash the top six. We had also kept ten clean sheets in that time and had become extremely difficult to beat.

But a run of one win and three draws in a five-match spell between mid-March to mid-April left Town eight points behind sixth-place Sunderland with the Wearsiders having a game in hand. We were ninth, a position that we had held for what seemed like an eternity.

The Easter weekend saw our first league game live on TV of the season when on the Saturday lunchtime we visited Rotherham United, who were still going for automatic promotion.

No fewer than five players were to make their television debuts for Ipswich. Nineteen-year-old centre-back Elkan Baggott started, and he was also making his league debut to become the first Indonesian to play in English league football.

Also starting on TV for the first time were Wes Burns, Tyreeq Bakinson and Dominic Thompson. Macauley Bonne came off the bench for his first live Town game too.

Rotherham had beaten Ipswich at Portman Road 2-0 earlier in the season on a night when their physical presence stood out. But they were on a run of poor form going into this game and it was hoped that Ipswich could capitalise.

James Norwood missed a glorious chance in the ninth minute after Burns had found him with a perfect cross, but he somehow diverted the ball wide from six yards.

It was a miss that would prove costly as an under-par second-half performance saw Rotherham dominate using their physical presence again to eventually carve out a winner in the 78th minute through Michael Smith.

It was a fourth successive 1-0 defeat that Rotherham had inflicted upon us on home soil.

The result meant that it was mathematically impossible for Town to reach the play-offs. Many of us had resigned ourselves to that fact a few weeks beforehand and 2022/23 would see us playing in the third tier for a fourth successive year.

Looking back to the start of the season, the opening six-match spell which saw us take just three points out of a possible 18 from what looked on paper at least, some favourable fixtures, meant that we were always playing catch-up and we could never put a run together to compensate for that poor start.

McKenna made light of the previous inconsistency when he first joined with seven wins in his first ten games. There were also 12 clean sheets kept in his first 17 and all the signs were there that his Ipswich side were a much-improved outfit to the one that he inherited.

Yet the defeats to Cambridge and Rotherham highlighted the need for some strong improvements after finishing the season in a disappointing 11th place.

Town fans would be praying that McKenna's first transfer window and pre-season, coupled with the ongoing investments from Gamechanger 20, would lead to a new hope for a return to the Championship come the end of the 2022/23 season.

THE GAMES

A comprehensive list of Town's live TV matches

Ipswich Town 1 (Osborne 77)
Arsenal 0

Saturday, 6 May 1978, 3pm – FA Cup Final
Wembley Stadium – Attendance: 100,000
Channels: BBC One and ITV
Town manager: Sir Bobby Robson – **Referee:** Derek Nippard

Ipswich: Paul Cooper, George Burley, Mick Mills, Brian Talbot, Allan Hunter, Kevin Beattie, Roger Osborne (Mick Lambert 78), John Wark, Paul Mariner, David Geddis, Clive Woods

Arsenal: Pat Jennings, Pat Rice, Sammy Nelson, David Price, David O'Leary, Willie Young, Liam Brady (Graham Rix 65), Alan Sunderland, Malcolm Macdonald, Frank Stapleton, Alan Hudson

Ipswich Town 1 (Humes 44)
Manchester United 2 (d'Avray 29 og; Anderson 66)

Sunday, 10 January 1988, 3.05pm – FA Cup third round
Portman Road – Attendance: 23,012
Channel: BBC One
Town manager: John Duncan – **Referee:** Brian Stevens

Ipswich: Jon Hallworth, Frank Yallop, Graham Harbey, Ian Atkins, Ian Cranson, Tony Humes, David Lowe, Mark Brennan, Mich d'Avray, Romeo Zondervan (Nigel Gleghorn 86), Jason Dozzell (Mick Stockwell 69)

Manchester United: Chris Turner, Viv Anderson, Mike Duxbury, Steve Bruce, Kevin Moran, Remi Moses (Jesper Olsen 65), Bryan Robson, Gordon Strachan, Brian McClair, Norman Whiteside, Colin Gibson (Peter Davenport 69)

Ipswich Town 0
Liverpool 0

Sunday, 16 February 1992, 1pm – FA Cup fifth round
Portman Road – Attendance: 26,140
Channel: Sky Sports
Town manager: John Lyall – **Referee:** Alf Buksh

Ipswich: Craig Forrest, Gavin Johnson, Neil Thompson, Mick Stockwell, John Wark, David Linighan, Simon Milton, Steve Palmer, Steve Whitton, Jason Dozzell, Chris Kiwomya

Liverpool: Bruce Grobbelaar, Rob Jones, David Burrows, Steve Nicol, Mark Wright, Mike Marsh, Dean Saunders, Ray Houghton, Ian Rush, Jamie Redknapp (István Kozma 55), Steve McManaman

Liverpool 3 (Houghton 45; Mølby 98; McManaman 100)
Ipswich Town 2 (Johnson 82; Dozzell 95), after extra time

Wednesday, 26 February 1992, 7.30pm – FA Cup fifth round replay
Anfield – Attendance: 27,355
Channel: Sky Sports
Town manager: John Lyall – **Referee:** Ken Leach

Liverpool: Bruce Grobbelaar, Rob Jones, Steve Harkness (István Kozma 95), Steve Nicol, Mark Wright, Mike Marsh, Dean Saunders, Ray Houghton, Mark Walters (Ronnie Rosenthal 83), Jan Mølby, Steve McManaman

Ipswich: Craig Forrest, Gavin Johnson, Neil Thompson, Mick Stockwell, John Wark (Romeo Zondervan 117), David Linighan, Simon Milton, Steve Palmer (Paul Goddard 65), Steve Whitton, Jason Dozzell, Chris Kiwomya

Ipswich Town 1 (Wark 45)
Tottenham Hotspur 1 (Cundy 29)

Sunday, 30 August 1992, 4pm – FA Premier League
Portman Road – Attendance: 20,100
Channel: Sky Sports
Town manager: John Lyall – **Referee:** Keith Hackett

Ipswich: Craig Forrest, Phil Whelan, Neil Thompson, Mick Stockwell, John Wark, David Linighan, Geraint Williams, Paul Goddard (Simon Milton 82), Gavin Johnson, Jason Dozzell, Chris Kiwomya

Spurs: Ian Walker, Dean Austin, Justin Edinburgh, Steve Sedgley, Jason Cundy, Neil Ruddock, Darren Anderton, Gordon Durie, Vinny Samways, Teddy Sheringham, Paul Allen (Andy Gray 79)

Norwich City 0
Ipswich Town 2 (Kiwomya 52; Thompson 88)

Monday, 21 December 1992, 7.45pm – FA Premier League
Carrow Road – Attendance: 20,032
Channel: Sky Sports
Town manager: John Lyall – **Referee:** David Elleray

Norwich: Bryan Gunn, Ian Culverhouse, Mark Bowen, Ian Butterworth (Rob Newman 45), John Polston, Daryl Sutch, Gary Megson, Darren Beckford (Chris Sutton 57), Mark Robins, Ruel Fox, Dave Phillips

Ipswich: Clive Baker, Gavin Johnson, Neil Thompson, Mick Stockwell, John Wark, David Linighan, Geraint Williams, Paul Goddard (Phil Whelan 81), Steve Whitton, Jason Dozzell, Chris Kiwomya

Blackburn Rovers 2 (Ripley 6; Whelan 43 og)
Ipswich Town 1 (Milton 68)

Monday, 12 April 1993, 7.45pm – FA Premier League
Ewood Park – Attendance: 14,071
Channel: Sky Sports
Town manager: John Lyall – **Referee:** Keith Hackett

Blackburn: Bobby Mimms, David May, Graeme Le Saux, Tim Sherwood, Colin Hendry, Kevin Moran, Stuart Ripley, Gordon Cowans, Kevin Gallacher, Mike Newell, Jason Wilcox

Ipswich: Clive Baker, Eddie Youds, Gavin Johnson, Geraint Williams, Phil Whelan, David Linighan (Vlado Bozinovski 61), Steve Whitton, Bontcho Guentchev, Simon Milton, Jason Dozzell, Chris Kiwomya

Ipswich Town 3 (Dozzell 21, 57; Stockwell 54)
Norwich City 1 (Sutton 41)

Monday, 19 April 1993, 7.45pm – FA Premier League
Portman Road – Attendance: 21,087
Channel: Sky Sports
Town manager: John Lyall – **Referee:** Vic Callow

Ipswich: Clive Baker, Eddie Youds, Gavin Johnson, Geraint Williams, John Wark, David Linighan, Steve Whitton, Mick Stockwell, Simon Milton, Jason Dozzell, Chris Kiwomya

Norwich: Bryan Gunn, Ian Culverhouse, Ian Crook, Ian Butterworth, John Polston, Mark Bowen, Jeremy Goss, Mark Robins, Chris Sutton, Ruel Fox, Dave Phillips

Ipswich Town 2 (Milton 59; Kiwomya 69)
Tottenham Hotspur 2 (Sheringham 28; Dozzell 85)

Sunday, 26 September 1993, 4pm – FA Premier League
Portman Road – Attendance: 19,437
Channel: Sky Sports
Town manager: John Lyall – **Referee:** Gerald Ashby

Ipswich: Craig Forrest, Mick Stockwell, Neil Thompson, Paul Mason, John Wark, David Linighan, Geraint Williams, Simon Milton, Steve Whitton, Ian Marshall, Chris Kiwomya
Spurs: Erik Thorstvedt, Stephen Carr (Darren Caskey 45), Sol Campbell, Vinny Samways, Colin Calderwood, Gary Mabbutt, Steve Sedgley, Gordon Durie, Jason Dozzell, Teddy Sheringham, Darren Anderton

Ipswich Town 0
Leeds United 0

Sunday, 17 October 1993, 4pm – FA Premier League
Portman Road – Attendance: 17,532
Channel: Sky Sports
Town manager: John Lyall – **Referee:** Martin Bodenham

Ipswich: Craig Forrest, Mick Stockwell, Neil Thompson, Paul Mason, John Wark (Steve Whitton 80), David Linighan, Phil Whelan, Stuart Slater, Steve Palmer, Simon Milton, Chris Kiwomya
Leeds: Mark Beeney, Gary Kelly, Tony Dorigo, David Wetherall, Chris Fairclough, Jon Newsome, David Rocastle (Frank Strandli 82), Rod Wallace, Brian Deane, Gary McAllister, Gary Speed

Wimbledon 0
Ipswich Town 2 (Mason 72; Stockwell 81)

Monday, 25 October 1993, 8pm – FA Premier League
Selhurst Park – Attendance: 7,756
Channel: Sky Sports
Town manager: John Lyall – **Referee:** Alan Gunn

Wimbledon: Hans Segers, Peter Fear, Scott Fitzgerald, Brian McAllister, Alan Kimble, Neal Ardley (Warren Barton 76), Robbie Earle, Lawrie Sanchez, Vinnie Jones, Gary Blissett (John Fashanu 64), Dean Holdsworth
Ipswich: Craig Forrest, Mick Stockwell, Neil Thompson, Paul Mason, John Wark, David Linighan, Geraint Williams (Steve Palmer 78), Stuart Slater, Ian Marshall, Phil Whelan, Chris Kiwomya (Simon Milton 45)

Ipswich Town 1 (Palmer 46)
Wolverhampton Wanderers 2 (Mills 8; Thompson 38)

Wednesday, 2 March 1994, 7.45pm – FA Cup fifth round replay
Portman Road – **Attendance:** 19,385
Channel: Sky Sports
Town manager: John Lyall – **Referee:** Stephen Lodge

Ipswich: Craig Forrest, Mick Stockwell, Neil Thompson, Eddie Youds (Paul Mason 74), John Wark, David Linighan, Geraint Williams (Bontcho Guentchev 80), Stuart Slater, Chris Kiwomya, Ian Marshall, Steve Palmer

Wolves: Mike Stowell, Mark Rankine, Andy Thompson, Mark Venus, Paul Blades, Peter Shirtliff, Robbie Dennison, Darren Ferguson (Paul Cook 80), Lee Mills, David Kelly, Kevin Keen

Ipswich Town 1 (Kiwomya 19) Manchester United 2 (Cantona 36; Giggs 47)

Sunday, 1 May 1994, 4pm – FA Premier League
Portman Road – **Attendance:** 22,478
Channel: Sky Sports
Town manager: John Lyall – **Referee:** Alan Gunn

Ipswich: Craig Forrest, Mick Stockwell, Phil Whelan (Bontcho Guentchev 64), Geraint Williams, John Wark, David Linighan, Simon Milton, Gavin Johnson (Eddie Youds 45), Steve Palmer, Ian Marshall, Chris Kiwomya

Manchester United: Peter Schmeichel (Gary Walsh 30), Denis Irwin, Paul Parker, Steve Bruce, Andrei Kanchelskis, Gary Pallister, Eric Cantona, Paul Ince, Roy Keane, Mark Hughes, Ryan Giggs (Lee Sharpe 83)

Ipswich Town 1 (Wark 45) Norwich City 2 (Newman 12; Bradshaw 53)

Monday, 19 September 1994, 8pm – FA Premier League
Portman Road – **Attendance:** 17,406
Channel: Sky Sports
Town manager: John Lyall – **Referee:** Roger Dilkes

Ipswich: Craig Forrest, Gavin Johnson, Frank Yallop, Steve Sedgley, John Wark, David Linighan, Geraint Williams, Stuart Slater, Simon Milton, Ian Marshall, Chris Kiwomya (Bontcho Guentchev 78)

Norwich: Bryan Gunn, Carl Bradshaw, Mark Bowen, Jon Newsome, John Polston, Rob Newman, Ian Crook (Darren Eadie 70), Jeremy Goss, Neil Adams, Mike Sheron (Efan Ekoku 79), Mike Milligan

Coventry City 2 (Wark 45 og; Cook 76)
Ipswich Town 0

Monday, 10 October 1994, 8pm – FA Premier League
Highfield Road – Attendance: 9,509
Channel: Sky Sports
Town manager: John Lyall – **Referee:** Robert Hart

Coventry: Steve Ogrizovic, Ally Pickering, Steve Morgan, Julian Darby, David Busst, David Rennie, Sean Flynn, Paul Cook, Dion Dublin, Roy Wegerle, Cobi Jones (Peter Ndlovu 83)

Ipswich: Craig Forrest, Frank Yallop, Gavin Johnson, Steve Sedgley, John Wark, David Linighan, Geraint Williams, Stuart Slater (Leo Cotterell 71), Steve Palmer, Chris Kiwomya, Claus Thomsen

Ipswich Town 1 (Wark 52)
Sheffield Wednesday 2 (Bright 9; Hirst 90)

Sunday, 16 October 1994, 4pm – FA Premier League
Portman Road – Attendance: 12,825
Channel: Sky Sports
Town manager: John Lyall – **Referee:** Mike Reed

Ipswich: Craig Forrest, Gavin Johnson, Frank Yallop, Steve Sedgley, John Wark (Eddie Youds 55), Simon Milton, Geraint Williams, Steve Palmer, Bontcho Guentchev, Adrián Paz, Claus Thomsen

Sheffield Wednesday: Kevin Pressman, Ian Nolan, Peter Atherton, Des Walker, Andy Pearce, Chris Bart-Williams (Ian Taylor 73), John Sheridan, Graham Hyde, David Hirst, Mark Bright, Lee Briscoe (Andy Sinton 55)

Norwich City 3 (Cureton 53; Ward 58; Eadie 78)
Ipswich Town 0

Monday, 20 March 1995, 8pm – FA Premier League
Carrow Road – Attendance: 17,510
Channel: Sky Sports
Town manager: George Burley – **Referee:** Paul Durkin

Norwich: Andy Marshall, Robert Ullathorne, Mark Bowen, Jon Newsome, John Polston, Neil Adams (Daryl Sutch 75), Ian Crook, Mike Milligan, Darren Eadie, Ashley Ward, Jamie Cureton (Rob Newman 88)

Ipswich: Craig Forrest, Frank Yallop, Neil Thompson, Phil Whelan, Claus Thomsen, John Wark, Geraint Williams, Alex Mathie, Ian Marshall, Stuart Slater (Lee Chapman 76), Simon Milton

Ipswich Town 0
Luton Town 1 (Oldfield 24)

Sunday, 22 October 1995, 3pm – Division One
Portman Road – Attendance: 9,123
Channel: ITV Anglia
Town manager: George Burley – **Referee:** Trevor West

Ipswich: Craig Forrest, Mick Stockwell, Mauricio Taricco, David Linighan, Tony Mowbray, Geraint Williams, Gus Uhlenbeek, Steve Sedgley (Adam Tanner 27), Alex Mathie (Neil Gregory 81), Ian Marshall, Stuart Slater
Luton: Ian Feuer, Trevor Peake, Marvin Johnson, Steve Davis, Ceri Hughes, Johnny Vilstrup (Gary Waddock 51), Graham Alexander, Scott Oakes, David Oldfield, Dwight Marshall (Bontcho Guentchev 87), Richard Harvey (Gavin Johnson 77)

Norwich City 2 (Newsome 9; Fleck 71)
Ipswich Town 1 (Wark 82)

Sunday, 19 November 1995, 3pm – Division One
Carrow Road – Attendance: 17,862
Channel: ITV Anglia
Town manager: George Burley – **Referee:** Kevin Lynch

Norwich: Bryan Gunn, Carl Bradshaw (Daryl Sutch 13), Robert Ullathorne, Neil Adams, Jon Newsome, Spencer Prior, Mark Bowen, Robert Fleck, Ashley Ward, Mike Milligan (Ade Akinbiyi 53), Keith O'Neill
Ipswich: Craig Forrest, Mick Stockwell, Tony Vaughan, Tony Mowbray, John Wark, Geraint Williams, Claus Thomsen, Simon Milton (Neil Gregory 55), Gus Uhlenbeek (Adam Tanner 79), Alex Mathie, Paul Mason

Wolverhampton Wanderers 2 (Goodman 60, 70) Ipswich Town 2 (Marshall 30; Mowbray 90)

Sunday, 3 December 1995, 2.55pm – Division One
Molineux – Attendance: 20,867
Channels: ITV Anglia, ITV Central
Town manager: George Burley – **Referee:** George Cain

Wolves: Mike Stowell, Mark Rankine, Andy Thompson, Darren Ferguson, Brian Law, Dean Richards, Mark Venus, Don Goodman, Steve Bull, Mark Atkins, Neil Emblen (Paul Birch 82)
Ipswich: Fred Barber, Mauricio Taricco (Paul Mason 74), Neil Thompson, Steve Sedgley, Tony Mowbray, Claus Thomsen (Gus Uhlenbeek 74), Mick Stockwell, Simon Milton, Geraint Williams, Alex Mathie, Ian Marshall

Ipswich Town 4 (Wark 6; Milton 11; Marshall 13, 85)
Leicester City 2 (Roberts 55, 75)

Sunday, 3 March 1996, 3pm – Division One
Portman Road – Attendance: 9,817
Channels: ITV Anglia, ITV Central
Town manager: George Burley – Referee: Ken Leach

Ipswich: Richard Wright, Gus Uhlenbeek, Mauricio Taricco, Claus Thomsen, John Wark, Geraint Williams, Paul Mason (James Scowcroft 73), Steve Sedgley, Alex Mathie, Ian Marshall, Simon Milton
Leicester: Kevin Poole, Simon Grayson, Mike Whitlow, Brian Carey, Steve Walsh, Garry Parker, Neil Lennon, Scott Taylor (Jamie Lawrence 69), Steve Claridge, Iwan Roberts, Neil Lewis (Emile Heskey 82)

Ipswich Town 2 (Marshall 23; Ullathorne 86 og)
Norwich City 1 (Cureton 62)

Sunday, 14 April 1996, 3pm – Division One
Portman Road – Attendance: 20,355
Channel: ITV Anglia
Town manager: George Burley – Referee: Jim Rushton

Ipswich: Richard Wright, Gus Uhlenbeek, Mauricio Taricco, Mick Stockwell (Richard Appleby 73), John Wark (Tony Vaughan 85), Geraint Williams, Paul Mason, Steve Sedgley, James Scowcroft, Ian Marshall, Simon Milton
Norwich: Bryan Gunn, Carl Bradshaw, Robert Ullathorne, Ian Crook, John Polston, Rob Newman, Neil Adams, Robert Fleck, Ade Akinbiyi (Spencer Prior 19), Mike Milligan (Andrew Johnson 86), Darren Eadie (Jamie Cureton 61)

Ipswich Town 0
Millwall 0

Sunday, 5 May 1996, 3pm – Division One
Portman Road – Attendance: 17,290
Channels: ITV Anglia, ITV Meridian
Town manager: George Burley – Referee: Kevin Lynch

Ipswich: Richard Wright, Mick Stockwell, Mauricio Taricco, Claus Thomsen, John Wark (Tony Vaughan 67), Geraint Williams, Paul Mason (James Scowcroft 29), Steve Sedgley, Alex Mathie, Ian Marshall, Simon Milton
Millwall: Kasey Keller, Ricky Newman, Ben Thatcher, Bobby Bowry, Jason van Blerk, Keith Stevens, Jim Connor, Dave Savage (Lucas Neill 71), Maurice Doyle, Chris Malkin, Mickey Weir (Tony Witter 84)

Manchester City 1 (Lomas 25)
Ipswich Town 0

Friday, 16 August 1996, 7.45pm – Division One
Maine Road – Attendance: 29,126
Channel: Sky Sports 3
Town manager: George Burley – **Referee:** Terry Heilbron

Manchester City: Eike Immel, Ian Brightwell, Michael Frontzeck, Steve Lomas, Kit Symons, Michael Brown, Nicky Summerbee, Martin Phillips (Gerry Creaney 67), Mikheil Kavelashvili (Scott Hiley 83), Georgi Kinkladze, Uwe Rösler

Ipswich: Richard Wright, Mick Stockwell (Adam Tanner 84), Mauricio Taricco, Claus Thomsen, Tony Vaughan (Alex Mathie 67), Steve Sedgley, Gus Uhlenbeek, Geraint Williams, Paul Mason, Ian Marshall, Bobby Petta

Ipswich Town 2 (Sedgley 56; Mathie 72)
Charlton Athletic 1 (Allen 34)

Friday, 20 September 1996, 7.45pm – Division One
Portman Road – Attendance: 10,558
Channel: Sky Sports 3
Town manager: George Burley – **Referee:** Gurnam Singh

Ipswich: Craig Forrest, Mick Stockwell, Tony Vaughan, Claus Thomsen, Steve Sedgley, Stuart Niven (Danny Sonner 87), Gus Uhlenbeek, Chris Swailes, Alex Mathie (Richard Naylor 79), James Scowcroft, Simon Milton

Charlton: Mike Sammon, Anthony Barness, Jamie Stuart, Steve Brown (Kevin Nicholls 67), Phil Chapple, Stuart Balmer, Shaun Newton (David Whyte 83), Carl Leaburn, Bradley Allen, Paul Mortimer, Ricky Otto (Paul Sturgess 81)

Norwich City 3 (Johnson 19, 34; Polston 67)
Ipswich Town 1 (Sonner 46)

Friday, 11 October 1996, 7.45pm – Division One
Carrow Road – Attendance: 20,256
Channel: Sky Sports 3
Town manager: George Burley – **Referee:** Clive Wilkes

Norwich: Bryan Gunn, Danny Mills, Rob Newman, Darren Eadie, John Polston, Daryl Sutch, Neil Adams, Robert Fleck (Ade Akinbiyi 72), Mike Milligan, Andrew Johnson (Ian Crook 80), Keith O'Neill

Ipswich: Richard Wright, Mauricio Taricco, Tony Vaughan, Tony Mowbray, Steve Sedgley, Geraint Williams, Mick Stockwell, Danny Sonner, Alex Mathie, James Scowcroft, Simon Milton (Richard Naylor 68)

Ipswich Town 2 (Taricco 32; Mason 42)
Norwich City 0

Friday, 18 April 1997, 7.45pm – Division One
Portman Road – Attendance: 22,397
Channel: Sky Sports 3
Town manager: George Burley – **Referee:** Uriah Rennie

Ipswich: Richard Wright, Mick Stockwell, Mauricio Taricco, Steve Sedgley, Chris Swailes, Geraint Williams, Gus Uhlenbeek, Tony Vaughan, Neil Gregory, Niklas Gudmundsson, Paul Mason (Kieron Dyer 88)

Norwich: Andy Marshall, Matt Jackson, Rob Newman, Ian Crook, Carl Bradshaw (John Polston 32), Daryl Sutch, Neil Adams, Robert Fleck, Darren Eadie, Danny Mills, Keith O'Neil (Karl Simpson 84)

Ipswich Town 2 (Scowcroft 32; Gudmundsson 73)
Sheffield United 2 (Kachuro 9; Walker 77)
after extra time; 3-3 on aggregate – Sheffield United won on away goals

Wednesday, 14 May 1997, 7.45pm – Division One play-off semi-final second leg
Portman Road – Attendance: 21,467
Channel: Sky Sports 3
Town manager: George Burley – **Referee:** Terry Heilbron

Ipswich: Richard Wright, Mick Stockwell, Mauricio Taricco, Steve Sedgley, Chris Swailes (Kieron Dyer 91), Geraint Williams, Gus Uhlenbeek, Tony Vaughan, Niklas Gudmundsson (Neil Gregory 85), James Scowcroft, Paul Mason

Sheffield United: Alan Kelly, Chris Short, Lee Sandford, Mitch Ward, Carl Tiler, David Holdsworth, David White (Don Hutchison 53), Nicky Henry, Jan Åge Fjørtoft, Petr Kachuro (Andy Walker 68; Roger Nilsen 110), Dane Whitehouse

Norwich City 2 (Eadie 8; Cundy 59 og)
Ipswich Town 1 (Stein 73)

Friday, 26 September 1997, 7.45pm – Division One
Carrow Road – Attendance: 18,911
Channel: Sky Sports 2
Town manager: George Burley – **Referee:** John Brandwood

Norwich: Andy Marshall, Craig Fleming, Daryl Sutch, Peter Grant, Keith Scott, Neil Adams, Matt Jackson, Robert Fleck, Darren Eadie, Mike Milligan (Craig Bellamy 66), Adrian Forbes (Adrian Coote 82)

Ipswich: Richard Wright, Mick Stockwell, Mark Venus (David Kerslake 51), Geraint Williams, Tony Mowbray, Jason Cundy, Kieron Dyer, Matt Holland, Mark Stein, James Scowcroft (Alex Mathie 21), Bobby Petta

Ipswich Town 2 (Legg 50; Gregory 87)
Sheffield United 2 (Taylor 9; Ward 79)

Sunday, 9 November 1997, 1pm – Division One
Portman Road – Attendance: 9,695
Channel: Sky Sports 2
Town manager: George Burley – **Referee:** Mick Pierce

Ipswich: Richard Wright, Mick Stockwell, Adam Tanner (Danny Sonner 68), Geraint Williams, Tony Mowbray, Jason Cundy, Kieron Dyer, Matt Holland, Alex Mathie (Neil Gregory 79), Jason Dozzell, Andrew Legg
Sheffield United: Simon Tracey (Mitch Ward 60), Vassilis Borbokis, Don Hutchinson, Paul McGrath, Carl Tiler, David Holdsworth, Mark Patterson, Nicky Marker, Gareth Taylor, Brian Deane, Dane Whitehouse

Nottingham Forest 2 (Cooper 53; van Hooijdonk 58)
Ipswich Town 1 (Scowcroft 46)

Sunday, 5 April 1998, 12.05pm – Division One
City Ground – Attendance: 22,292
Channel: Sky Sports 2
Town manager: George Burley – **Referee:** William Burns

Forest: Dave Beasant, Thierry Bonalair, Alan Rogers, Colin Cooper, Steve Chettle, Andy Johnson (Jon Olav Hjelde 86), Steve Stone, Scot Gemmill, Pierre van Hooijdonk, Kevin Campbell, Chris Bart-Williams
Ipswich: Richard Wright, Mick Stockwell, Mauricio Taricco, Kieron Dyer, Tony Mowbray (Alex Mathie 78), Jason Cundy, Jamie Clapham, Matt Holland, David Johnson, James Scowcroft, Bobby Petta (Gus Uhlenbeek 61)

Ipswich Town 2 (Holland 48; Mathie 61)
Sunderland 0

Tuesday, 28 April 1998, 7.45pm – Division One
Portman Road – Attendance: 20,902
Channel: Sky Sports 2
Town manager: George Burley – **Referee:** Ken Leach

Ipswich: Richard Wright, Mick Stockwell, Mauricio Taricco, Kieron Dyer (Danny Sonner 80), Mark Venus, Jason Cundy, Jamie Clapham, Matt Holland, David Johnson (James Scowcroft 71), Alex Mathie, Bobby Petta (Gus Uhlenbeek 84)
Sunderland: Lionel Pérez, Darren Holloway (Danny Dichio 75), Chris Makin, Lee Clark (Alex Rae 63), Jody Craddock, Darren Williams, Nicky Summerbee, Kevin Ball, Niall Quinn, Kevin Phillips, Allan Johnston

Ipswich Town 0
Charlton Athletic 1 (Clapham 12 og)

Sunday, 10 May 1998, 1pm – Division One play-off semi-final first leg
Portman Road – Attendance: 21,681
Channel: Sky Sports 2
Town manager: George Burley – **Referee:** Mick Fletcher

Ipswich: Richard Wright, Mick Stockwell, Mauricio Taricco, Kieron Dyer, Mark Venus, Jason Cundy, Jamie Clapham (Gus Uhlenbeek 67), Matt Holland, David Johnson, Alex Mathie, Bobby Petta (James Scowcroft 67)
Charlton: Saša Ilić, Danny Mills, Mark Bowen, Keith Jones (Steve Brown 85), Richard Rufus, Eddie Youds, Shaun Newton, Mark Kinsella, Mark Bright (Steve Jones 65), Clive Mendonca, Neil Heaney (Anthony Barness 75)

Grimsby Town 0
Ipswich Town 0

Sunday, 9 August 1998, 4pm – Division One
Blundell Park – Attendance: 7,211
Channel: Sky Sports 2
Town manager: George Burley – **Referee:** Alan Wiley

Grimsby: Aidan Davison, John McDermott, Tony Gallimore, Peter Handyside, Richard Smith, Tommy Widdrington, Stacy Coldicott, Kingsley Black (David Smith 74), Lee Nogan, Jack Lester, Paul Groves
Ipswich: Richard Wright, Mick Stockwell, Mauricio Taricco, Jamie Clapham, Tony Mowbray, Mark Venus, Kieron Dyer, Matt Holland, David Johnson, Marco Holster (Alex Mathie 56), Bobby Petta (Danny Sonner 87)

Ipswich Town 0
Sunderland 2 (Mullin 12; Phillips 36)

Saturday, 29 August 1998, 6pm – Division One
Portman Road – Attendance: 15,813
Channel: Sky Sports 2
Town manager: George Burley – **Referee:** Mark Halsey

Ipswich: Richard Wright, Mick Stockwell (Marco Holster 14), Mauricio Taricco, Jamie Clapham, Tony Mowbray, Mark Venus, Kieron Dyer, Matt Holland, David Johnson, Alex Mathie (James Scowcroft 64), Bobby Petta
Sunderland: Thomas Sørensen, Darren Williams, Michael Gray, Kevin Ball, Andy Melville, Paul Butler, Nicky Summerbee, John Mullin, Danny Dichio, Kevin Phillips Allan Johnston (Jody Craddock 90)

Sheffield United 1 (Devlin 78)
Ipswich Town 2 (Abou 49; Naylor 89)

Sunday, 20 December 1998, 1pm – Division One
Bramall Lane – Attendance: 12,944
Channel: Sky Sports 2
Town manager: George Burley – **Referee:** Rob Styles

Sheffield United: Alan Kelly, Vassilis Borbokis, Wayne Quinn, Robert Ford (Pail Devlin 74), Shaun Derry, Jonathan O'Connor, Curtis Woodhouse, Marcelo, Nicky Marker, Ian Hamilton (Lee Morris 59), Andy Campbell

Ipswich: Richard Wright, John Kennedy, Titus Bramble, Jamie Clapham (Lee Hodges 90), Tony Mowbray, Adam Tanner (Wayne Brown 85), Kieron Dyer, Matt Holland, Samassi Abou, Richard Naylor, Bobby Petta

Sunderland 2 (Quinn 27, 33)
Ipswich Town 1 (Holland 36)

Sunday, 17 January 1999, 1pm – Division One
Stadium of Light – Attendance: 39,835
Channel: Sky Sports 2
Town manager: George Burley – **Referee:** Eddie Wolstenholme

Sunderland: Thomas Sørensen, Chris Makin, Michael Gray, Kevin Ball, Andy Melville, Paul Butler, Alex Rae (Michael Bridges 62), Lee Clark, Niall Quinn, Kevin Phillips (Danny Dichio 74), Allan Johnston

Ipswich: Richard Wright, Fabian Wilnis, Manuel Thétis, Jamie Clapham, Titus Bramble, Mark Venus, Kieron Dyer, Matt Holland, David Johnson, Richard Naylor, Jim Magilton

Ipswich Town 1 (Magilton 39)
Stockport County 0

Tuesday, 20 April 1999, 7.45pm – Division One
Portman Road – Attendance: 17,056
Channel: Sky Sports 2
Town manager: George Burley – **Referee:** Rob Styles

Ipswich: Richard Wright, Mick Stockwell (Bobby Petta 85), Manuel Thétis, Jamie Clapham, Tony Mowbray, Mark Venus, Kieron Dyer (Jason Cundy 89), Matt Holland, David Johnson (Richard Naylor 73), James Scowcroft, Jim Magilton

Stockport: Carlo Nash, Tony Dinning, Jim Gannon, Dave Smith, Michael Flynn, Martin McIntosh, Thomas Bennett (Rob Matthews 85), Colin Woodthorpe, Brett Angell, Kevin Cooper (Ian Thomas-Moore 46), Anthony Ellis

Birmingham City 1 (Furlong 60)
Ipswich Town 0

Sunday, 2 May 1999, 1pm – Division One
St Andrew's – Attendance: 27,685
Channel: Sky Sports 2
Town manager: George Burley – **Referee:** Roy Pearson

Birmingham: Kevin Poole, Gary Rowett, Martin Grainger, Graham Hyde (Darren Purse 89), David Holdsworth, Michael Johnson, Jonathan McCarthy, Steve Robinson, Paul Furlong (Dele Adebola 62), Bryan Hughes, Lee Bradbury (Peter Ndlovu 79)

Ipswich: Richard Wright, Fabian Wilnis, Manuel Thétis (Mick Stockwell 61), Jamie Clapham, Tony Mowbray, Mark Venus, Kieron Dyer, Matt Holland, David Johnson, James Scowcroft, Jim Magilton

Ipswich Town 4 (Magilton 18; Scowcroft 32; Dyer 45; Naylor 79)
Sheffield United 1 (Donis 63)

Sunday, 9 May 1999, 1.30pm – Division One
Portman Road – Attendance: 21,689
Channel: Sky Sports 3
Town manager: George Burley – **Referee:** Paul Taylor

Ipswich: Richard Wright, Fabian Wilnis, Jamie Clapham, Jim Magilton (Mick Stockwell 80), Tony Mowbray, Mark Venus, Kieron Dyer, Matt Holland, David Johnson (Richard Naylor 67), James Scowcroft, Bobby Petta (Manuel Thétis 70)

Sheffield United: Alan Kelly, Shaun Derry (Ian Hamilton 73), Robert Kozluk, Traianos Dellas, Anders Jacobsen (Wayne Quinn 46), Olivier Tébily, Giorgios Donis, Jonathan Hunt, Marcelo, Paul Devlin (Petr Kachuro 62), Lee Morris

Bolton Wanderers 1 (Johansen 84)
Ipswich Town 0

Sunday, 16 May 1999, 1pm – Division One play-off semi-final first leg
Reebok Stadium – Attendance: 18,295
Channel: Sky Sports 2
Town manager: George Burley – **Referee:** Mark Halsey

Bolton: Steve Banks, Neil Cox, Robbie Elliott, Per Frandsen, Andy Todd, Mark Fish (Gudni Bergsson 65), Michael Johansen, Claus Jensen, Eidur Gudjohnsen (Bo Hansen 73), Bob Taylor, Ricardo Gardner (Paul Warhurst 73)

Ipswich: Richard Wright, Fabian Wilnis, Manuel Thétis, Jamie Clapham, Tony Mowbray, Mark Venus, Kieron Dyer, Matt Holland, David Johnson (Richard Naylor 77), James Scowcroft, Jim Magilton

Brentford 0
Ipswich Town 2 (Johnson 64; Clapham 70)

Wednesday, 11 August 1999, 8pm – League Cup first round first leg
Griffin Park – Attendance: 4,825
Channel: Sky Sports 2
Town manager: George Burley – **Referee:** Paul Rejer

Brentford: Andy Woodman, Danny Boxall, Ijah Anderson, Rob Quinn (Martin Rowlands 73), Darren Powell, Hermann Hreidarsson, Paul Evans, Gavin Mahon, Lloyd Owusu (Tony Folan 82), Andy Scott (Derek Bryan 71), Scott Partridge
Ipswich: Richard Wright, Mick Stockwell, Jamie Clapham, Manuel Thétis, Mark Venus, John McGreal, Matt Holland, Jermaine Wright, James Scowcroft, David Johnson (Jonas Axeldal 89), Richard Naylor (Fabian Wilnis 69)

Swindon Town 1 (Grazioli 16)
Ipswich Town 4 (Johnson 44, 74; Naylor 55, 68)

Sunday, 15 August 1999, 1pm – Division One
County Ground – Attendance: 6,195
Channel: Sky Sports 2
Town manager: George Burley – **Referee:** Gary Willard

Swindon: Frank Talia, Mark Robinson (Adam Willis 80), Gareth Hall, Craig Taylor, Robin Hulbert (Mark Walters 59), James Williams, Bobby Howe, George Ndah, Iffy Onuora (Chris Hay 82), Giuliano Grazioli, Frazer McHugh
Ipswich: Richard Wright, Fabian Wilnis, Jamie Clapham, Manuel Thétis, Mark Venus (Wayne Brown 88), John McGreal, Matt Holland, Jermaine Wright, Mick Stockwell, David Johnson (Jonas Axeldal 84), Richard Naylor

Ipswich Town 2 (Johnson 43; Croft 67)
Manchester City 1 (Goater 50)

Sunday, 26 September 1999, 1pm – Division One
Portman Road – Attendance: 19,406
Channels: Sky Sports 2, Sky Sports Xtra
Town manager: George Burley – **Referee:** Andy D'Urso

Ipswich: Richard Wright, Fabian Wilnis (Wayne Brown 77), Gary Croft, Manuel Thétis, Mark Venus, Mick Stockwell (Richard Naylor 83), Matt Holland, Jermaine Wright (Jamie Clapham 46), James Scowcroft, David Johnson, Jim Magilton
Manchester City: Nicky Weaver, Lee Crooks, Danny Tiatto (Danny Granville 78), Gerard Wiekens, Richard Jobson, Kevin Horlock, Mark Kennedy, Jeff Whitley, Paul Dickov, Shaun Goater, Ian Bishop (Terry Cooke 73)

Nottingham Forest 0
Ipswich Town 1 (Holland 79)

Sunday, 5 December 1999, 1pm – Division One
City Ground – Attendance: 15,724
Channel: Sky Sports 2
Town manager: George Burley – **Referee:** Rob Styles

Forest: Dave Beasant, Chris Doig, Jim Brennan, Jon Olav Hjelde, Carlos Merino (Andrew Gray 46), Riccardo Scimeca, David Prutton, Nigel Quashie, Mikkel Beck (Dougie Freedman 76), Stern John, Chris Bart-Williams
Ipswich: Richard Wright, Gary Croft, Jamie Clapham, Tony Mowbray, Wayne Brown, John McGreal, Matt Holland, Jim Magilton, James Scowcroft, David Johnson, Mick Stockwell (Jermaine Wright 66)

Ipswich Town 0
Southampton 1 (Richards 40)

Monday, 13 December 1999, 8pm – FA Cup third round
Portman Road – Attendance: 14,383
Channel: Sky Sports 2
Town manager: George Burley – **Referee:** Graham Barber

Ipswich: Richard Wright, Fabian Wilnis (Jermaine Wright 46), Jamie Clapham, Tony Mowbray, Wayne Brown, John McGreal, Matt Holland, Jim Magilton, James Scowcroft, David Johnson (Jonas Axeldal 65), Mick Stockwell (Richard Naylor 72)
Southampton: Paul Jones, Jo Tessem, Wayne Bridge, Jason Dodd, Claus Lundekvam, Dean Richards, Stuart Ripley, Trond Egil Soltvedt, Marians Pahars, Mark Hughes (James Beattie 77), Matt Oakley

Birmingham City 1 (Mowbray 17 og)
Ipswich Town 1 (Johnson 45)

Sunday, 27 February 2000, 1pm – Division One
St Andrew's – Attendance: 20,493
Channel: Sky Sports 2
Town manager: George Burley – **Referee:** Anthony Leake

Birmingham: Ian Bennett, Gary Rowett, Simon Charlton (Peter Ndlovu 46), Bryan Hughes, Darren Purse, Michael Johnson, David Holdsworth, Michael Carrick (Jeremy Gill 77), Dele Adebola, Isaiah Rankin (Stan Lazaridis 68), Martin Grainger
Ipswich: Richard Wright, Michael Clegg, Jamie Clapham, Tony Mowbray, Wayne Brown, John McGreal, Matt Holland, Jim Magilton, James Scowcroft, David Johnson, Marcus Stewart

West Bromwich Albion 1 (Hughes 43)
Ipswich Town 1 (Holland 68)

Tuesday, 4 April 2000, 7.45pm – Division One
The Hawthorns – Attendance: 12,536
Channels: Sky Sports 3, Sky Sports Xtra
Town manager: George Burley – **Referee:** Clive Wilkes

West Brom: Brian Jensen, Des Lyttle, Jason van Blerk, Sean Flynn, Neil Clement, Tony Butler, James Quinn, Richard Sneekes, Bob Taylor, Lee Hughes (Fabian de Freitas 46), Georges Santos

Ipswich: Richard Wright, Gary Croft, Jamie Clapham, Tony Mowbray, Mark Venus, Mick Stockwell (Martijn Reuser 51), Matt Holland, Jim Magilton, James Scowcroft, David Johnson (Marcus Stewart 60), Jermaine Wright

Ipswich Town 1 (Johnson 26)
Crystal Palace 0

Tuesday, 25 April 2000, 7.45pm – Division One
Portman Road – Attendance: 18,798
Channel: Sky Sports 2
Town manager: George Burley – **Referee:** Paul Robinson

Ipswich: Richard Wright, Fabian Wilnis, Jamie Clapham, Tony Mowbray, Manuel Thétis (Jermaine Wright 75), Wayne Brown, Matt Holland, Jim Magilton, James Scowcroft (Richard Naylor 88), David Johnson, Martijn Reuser

Crystal Palace: Matt Gregg, Jamie Smith, Ashley Cole, Dean Austin, Wayne Carlisle, Andy Linighan, Hayden Mullins, Craig Foster, Clinton Morrison, Stephen Thomson, Leon McKenzie

Bolton Wanderers 2 (Holdsworth 5; Gudjohnsen 26)
Ipswich Town 2 (Stewart 36, 65)

Sunday, 14 May 2000, 1pm – Division One play-off semi-final first leg
Reebok Stadium – Attendance: 18,814
Channels: Sky Sports 3, Sky Sports Xtra
Town manager: George Burley – **Referee:** Rob Styles

Bolton: Jussi Jääskeläinen, Gudni Bergsson, Mike Whitlow, Paul Warhurst, Mark Fish, Paul Ritchie (Jimmy Phillips 61), Michael Johansen (Robbie Elliott 75), Claus Jensen, Eidur Gudjohnsen (Bo Hansen 61), Dean Holdsworth, Allan Johnston

Ipswich: Richard Wright, Fabian Wilnis (Gary Croft 85), Jamie Clapham, Tony Mowbray (Wayne Brown 29), Manuel Thétis, Mark Venus, Matt Holland, Jim Magilton, James Scowcroft, David Johnson (Martijn Reuser 33), Marcus Stewart

Barnsley 2 (R. Wright 6 og; Hignett 78)
Ipswich Town 4 (Mowbray 28; Naylor 52; Stewart 58; Reuser 90)

Monday, 29 May 2000, 1pm – Division One play-off final
Wembley Stadium – Attendance: 73,427
Channel: Sky Sports 2
Town manager: George Burley – **Referee:** Terry Heilbron

Barnsley: Kevin Miller, John Curtis (Nicky Eaden 71), Darren Barnard, Chris Morgan, Steve Chettle, Keith Brown, Matty Appleby, Craig Hignett, Neil Shipperley, Bruce Dyer (Gjorgji Hristov 64), Eric Tinkler (Geoff Thomas 60)
Ipswich: Richard Wright, Gary Croft, Jamie Clapham, Mark Venus, Tony Mowbray, John McGreal, Matt Holland, Jermaine Wright (Fabian Wilnis 89), David Johnson (Richard Naylor 22), Jim Magilton, Marcus Stewart (Martijn Reuser 83)

Coventry City 0
Ipswich Town 1 (Wilnis 90)

Monday, 20 November 2000, 8pm – FA Premier League
Highfield Road – Attendance: 19,322
Channel: Sky Sports 1
Town manager: George Burley – **Referee:** David Elleray

Coventry: Chris Kirkland, Paul Telfer, Paul Williams, Gary Breen, Mohammed Konjić, Marc Edworthy, David Thompson, Youssef Chippo, Mustapha Hadji, Craig Bellamy, Cédric Roussel (John Aloisi 68)
Ipswich: Richard Wright, Fabian Wilnis, Jamie Clapham, John McGreal (Titus Bramble 70), Hermann Hreidarsson, Mark Venus, Matt Holland, Jim Magilton, James Scowcroft, Jermaine Wright (Martijn Reuser 68), Marcus Stewart

Ipswich Town 3 (Stewart 9; Armstrong 62; Clapham 88)
Tottenham Hotspur 0

Saturday, 30 December 2000, midday – FA Premier League
Portman Road – Attendance: 22,234
Channel: Sky Sports 1
Town manager: George Burley – **Referee:** Matt Messias

Ipswich: Richard Wright, Fabian Wilnis (John McGreal 82), Mark Venus, Hermann Hreidarsson, Titus Bramble, Matt Holland, Jermaine Wright, James Scowcroft, Alun Armstrong (David Johnson 80), Marcus Stewart (Jamie Clapham 85), Martijn Reuser
Spurs: Neil Sullivan, Sol Campbell, Chris Perry, Alton Thelwell, Tim Sherwood (Simon Davies 80), Darren Anderton, Willem Korsten (Serhiy Rebrov 80), Øyvind Leonhardsen, Stephen Clemence, Ledley King, Gary Doherty

Ipswich Town 2 (Stewart 80; Scowcroft 90)
Leicester City 0

Sunday, 14 January 2001, 4pm – FA Premier League
Portman Road – Attendance: 22,002
Channel: Sky Sports 1
Town manager: George Burley – **Referee:** Mike Riley

Ipswich: Richard Wright, Fabian Wilnis, John McGreal, Hermann Hreidarsson, Titus Bramble, Jamie Clapham (Martijn Reuser 89), Jim Magilton, Matt Holland, Alun Armstrong (Jermaine Wright 82), Marcus Stewart, James Scowcroft
Leicester: Simon Royce, Gary Rowett, Callum Davidson, Andy Impey, Matt Elliott, Matt Jones (Arnar Gunnlaugsson 85), Robbie Savage, Ade Akinbiyi (Richard Cresswell 62), Trevor Benjamin (Phil Gilchrist 75), Muzzy Izzet, Steve Guppy

Ipswich Town 3 (Reuser 59, 72; Burchill 75)
Bradford City 1 (Carbone 27)

Sunday, 4 March 2001, 4pm – FA Premier League
Portman Road – Attendance: 21,820
Channels: Sky Sports 1, Sky Sports Xtra
Town manager: George Burley – **Referee:** Andy D'Urso

Ipswich: Richard Wright, Fabian Wilnis, Titus Bramble, Hermann Hreidarsson (Jamie Clapham 77), John McGreal, Jermaine Wright (Nabil Abidallah 85), Martijn Reuser, Jim Magilton (Alun Armstrong 46), Matt Holland, Mark Burchill, James Scowcroft
Bradford: Gary Walsh, Andy O'Brien, David Wetherall, Robert Molenaar, Andy Myers, Gary Locke (Gunnar Halle 29), Stuart McCall, David Hopkin, Eoin Jess, Ashley Ward, Benito Carbone

Southampton 0
Ipswich Town 3 (Stewart 33, 68, 71)

Monday, 2 April 2001, 8pm – FA Premier League
The Dell – Attendance: 15,244
Channel: Sky Sports 1
Town manager: George Burley – **Referee:** Alan Wiley

Southampton: Paul Jones, Tahar El Khalej, Claus Lundekvam, Dean Richards, Wayne Bridge, Jo Tessem, Matt Oakley, Chris Marsden (Matt Le Tissier 75), Dan Petrescu (Jason Dodd 59), James Beattie, Marians Pahars (Uwe Rösler 75)
Ipswich: Richard Wright, Titus Bramble, Chris Makin, Hermann Hreidarsson, John McGreal, Jermaine Wright, Jamie Clapham, Matt Holland, Martijn Reuser (Mark Venus 76), James Scowcroft (Alun Armstrong 68), Marcus Stewart (Mark Burchill 86)

Charlton Athletic 2 (Svensson 12; Rufus 57)
Ipswich Town 1 (Reuser 20)

Monday, 30 April 2001, 8pm – FA Premier League
The Valley – **Attendance:** 20,043
Channel: Sky Sports 1
Town manager: George Burley – **Referee:** Rob Styles

Charlton: Saša Ilić, Mark Fish, Chris Powell, Andrew Todd, Richard Rufus, Claus Jensen (Paul Konchesky 87), Scott Parker (Graham Stuart 38), John Robinson, Mark Kinsella, Shaun Bartlett, Mathias Svensson (Kevin Lisbie 77)
Ipswich: Richard Wright, Titus Bramble, Chris Makin, Hermann Hreidarsson, John McGreal, Jermaine Wright, Jim Magilton, Matt Holland, Martijn Reuser, Alun Armstrong, Marcus Stewart (Mark Burchill 66)

Ipswich Town 2 (Holland 78; Reuser 85)
Manchester City 1 (Goater 74)

Monday, 7 May 2001, 8pm – FA Premier League
Portman Road – **Attendance:** 25,004
Channel: Sky Sports 1
Town manager: George Burley – **Referee:** Stephen Lodge

Ipswich: Richard Wright, Titus Bramble, Chris Makin, Hermann Hreidarsson (Jamie Clapham 63), John McGreal, Jermaine Wright (Richard Naylor 71), Jim Magilton, Matt Holland, Martijn Reuser, Alun Armstrong, James Scowcroft
Manchester City: Carlo Nash, Laurent Charvet, Richard Dunne, Steve Howey, Danny Granville, Jeff Whitley, Gerard Wiekens, Tony Grant (Shaun Goater 46; Spencer Prior 76), Danny Tiatto, Paulo Wanchope, Paul Dickov (Mark Kennedy 57)

Ipswich Town 1 (Armstrong 15)
Blackburn Rovers 1 (Jansen 54)

Sunday, 16 September 2001, 4pm – FA Premier League
Portman Road – **Attendance:** 22,126
Channels: Sky Sports 1, Sky Sports Xtra
Town manager: George Burley – **Referee:** Graham Poll

Ipswich: Matteo Sereni, Chris Makin, John McGreal, Hermann Hreidarsson, Titus Bramble, Matt Holland, Jim Magilton, Marcus Stewart, Alun Armstrong (Richard Naylor 64), Martijn Reuser (Pablo Couñago 89), Finidi George (Fabian Wilnis 79)
Blackburn: Brad Friedel, Lucas Neill, Henning Berg, Martin Taylor, Alan Mahon, Keith Gillespie, Garry Flitcroft, Tugay Kerimoğlu, Damien Duff, Matt Jansen, Corrado Grabbi (Marcus Bent 84)

Ipswich Town 1 (Bramble 85)
Torpedo Moscow 1 (Vyazmikin 14)

Thursday, 20 September 2001, 8pm – UEFA Cup first round first leg
Portman Road – **Attendance:** 21,201
Channel: BBC One
Town manager: George Burley – **Referee:** Orhan Erdemir

Ipswich: Matteo Sereni, Chris Makin (Martijn Reuser 67), John McGreal (Jamie Clapham 46), Hermann Hreidarsson, Titus Bramble, Matt Holland, Jim Magilton, Jermaine Wright, Marcus Stewart, Pablo Couñago (Richard Naylor 56), Finidi George

Torpedo: Roman Berezovsky, Vyacheslav Dayev, Andrei Malay, Nikola Jolović, Alyaksandar Lukhvich, Edik Sajaia, Vladimir Leonchenko, Sergei Kormiltsev, Konstantin Zyryanov, Dmitri Vyazmikin (Vyacheslav Kamoltsev 89), Aleksandr Shirko (Igor Semshov 82)

Torpedo Moscow 1 (Vyazmikin 65)
Ipswich Town 2 (George 47, Stewart 54);
Ipswich won 3-2 on aggregate

Thursday, 27 September 2001, 6pm – UEFA Cup first round second leg
BSA Luzhniki – **Attendance:** 10,000
Channel: Channel 5
Town manager: George Burley – **Referee:** Pascal Garibian

Torpedo: Roman Berezovsky, Vyacheslav Dayev, Andrei Malay, Nikola Jolović (Jovica Lakić 81), Alyaksandar Lukhvich, Edik Sajaia (Andrei Gashkin 56), Vladimir Leonchenko, Sergei Kormiltsev (Igor Semshov 40), Konstantin Zyryanov, Dmitri Vyazmikin, Aleksandr Shirko

Ipswich: Matteo Sereni, Chris Makin, John McGreal, Hermann Hreidarsson, Mark Venus, Jamie Clapham (Tommy Miller 86), Finidi George (Jermaine Wright 70), Matt Holland, Jim Magilton, Alun Armstrong (Richard Naylor 83), Marcus Stewart

Ipswich Town 1 (Stewart 22)
Leeds United 2 (Keane 70; Venus 86 og)

Sunday, 30 September 2001, 4pm – FA Premier League
Portman Road – **Attendance:** 22,643
Channel: Sky Sports 1
Town manager: George Burley – **Referee:** Andy D'Urso

Ipswich: Matteo Sereni, Chris Makin (Fabian Wilnis 88), John McGreal, Mark Venus, Hermann Hreidarsson, Jermaine Wright (Pablo Couñago 87), Matt Holland, Jim Magilton, Finidi George (Jamie Clapham 72), Alun Armstrong, Marcus Stewart

Leeds: Nigel Martyn, Danny Mills, Rio Ferdinand, Dominic Matteo, Ian Harte, Lee Bowyer, David Batty, Eirik Bakke, Harry Kewell, Robbie Keane, Mark Viduka

Ipswich Town 0
Helsingborgs IF 0

Thursday, 18 October 2001, 8.05pm – UEFA Cup second round second leg
Portman Road – Attendance: 22,254
Channel: BBC One
Town manager: George Burley – **Referee:** Wolfgang Sowa

Ipswich: Matteo Sereni, Fabian Wilnis (Jamie Clapham 87), John McGreal, Mark Venus, Hermann Hreidarsson, Jermaine Wright, Matt Holland, Jim Magilton (Sixto Peralta 58), Finidi George, Martijn Reuser (Pablo Couñago 57), Marcus Stewart

Helsingborgs: Sven Andersson, Mikael Gustavsson, Jozo Matovac, Ola Nilsson, Jesper Jansson, Christoffer Andersson (Mattias Lindström 58), Hans Eklund, Lars Bakkerud, Michael Hansson, Rade Prica (Ulrik Jansson 85), Alvaro Santos

Ipswich Town 2 (Hreidarsson 63; Holland 90)
West Ham United 3 (Di Canio 22; Kanouté 72; Defoe 90)

Sunday, 28 October 2001, 2pm – FA Premier League
Portman Road – Attendance: 22,834
Channel: ITV Sport Select
Town manager: George Burley – **Referee:** Steve Dunn

Ipswich: Matteo Sereni, Chris Makin, Thomas Gaardsøe, Mark Venus, Hermann Hreidarsson, Jamie Clapham (Sixto Peralta 46), Matt Holland, Jermaine Wright (Jim Magilton 87), Alun Armstrong (Pablo Couñago 55), Martijn Reuser, Marcus Stewart

West Ham: Shaka Hislop, Hayden Foxe, Christian Dailly, Scott Minto, Sébastien Schemmel, Trevor Sinclair, Don Hutchison, Michael Carrick, Nigel Winterburn, Frédéric Kanouté, Paolo Di Canio (Jermain Defoe 88)

Helsingborgs IF 1 (Eklund 7)
Ipswich Town 3 (Hreidarsson 69; Stewart 81, 88);
Ipswich won 3-1 on aggregate

Thursday, 1 November 2001, 7.45pm – UEFA Cup second round second leg
Olympia de Helsingborg – Attendance: 9,484
Channel: BBC Two
Town manager: George Burley – **Referee:** Eduardo Iturralde González

Helsingborgs: Sven Andersson, Ola Nilsson, Mikael Gustavsson, Jozo Matovac, Lars Bakkerud, Michael Hansson, Rade Prica, Christoffer Andersson, Jesper Jansson, Hans Eklund (Bjørn Johansen 31), Alvaro Santos

Ipswich: Matteo Sereni, Fabian Wilnis (Chris Makin 38), Jamie Clapham, Hermann Hreidarsson, Mark Venus, Titus Bramble, Jim Magilton, Matt Holland, Sixto Peralta (Tommy Miller 88), Richard Naylor (Darren Bent 73), Marcus Stewart

Ipswich Town 1 (Holland 45)
Bolton Wanderers 2 (Bergsson 6; Ricketts 25)

Sunday, 18 November 2001, 4pm – FA Premier League
Portman Road – **Attendance:** 22,335
Channels: Sky Sports 1, Sky Sports Xtra
Town manager: George Burley – **Referee:** Steve Bennett

Ipswich: Matteo Sereni, Chris Makin (Ulrich Le Pen 79), Titus Bramble, Hermann Hreidarsson, Mark Venus, Sixto Peralta, Matt Holland, Jim Magilton (Jermaine Wright 45), Martijn Reuser, Darren Bent (Richard Naylor 87), Pablo Couñago

Bolton: Jussi Jääskeläinen, Bruno N'Gotty, Mike Whitlow, Gudni Bergsson, Paul Warhurst (Gareth Farrelly 66), Per Frandsen, Ricardo Gardner, Kevin Nolan, Michael Ricketts, Rodney Wallace (Dean Holdsworth 69), Simon Charlton

Ipswich Town 1 (Armstrong 81)
Inter Milan 0

Thursday, 22 November 2001, 7.45pm – UEFA Cup third round first leg
Portman Road – **Attendance:** 24,569
Channel: BBC Two
Town manager: George Burley – **Referee:** Kim Milton Nielsen

Ipswich: Matteo Sereni, Chris Makin, Titus Bramble, Hermann Hreidarsson, Mark Venus, Jermaine Wright, Matt Holland, Sixto Peralta (Martijn Reuser 88), Jamie Clapham (Thomas Gaardsøe 89), Pablo Couñago, Richard Naylor (Alun Armstrong 77)

Inter Milan: Francesco Toldo, Javier Zanetti, Ivan Córdoba, Luigi Di Biagio (Georgatos 76), Vratislav Greško, Clarence Seedorf, Cristiano Zanetti, Emre Belözoğlu (Sérgio Conceição 67), Javier Farinós, Mohamed Kallon, Nicola Ventola (Adriano 56)

Newcastle United 4 (Robert 18; Ameobi 26; Shearer 37, 40)
Ipswich Town 1 (Bent 77)

Tuesday, 27 November 2001, 7.45pm – League Cup fourth round
St James' Park – **Attendance:** 32,576
Channel: ITV Sport Channel
Town manager: George Burley – **Referee:** Alan Wiley

Newcastle: Stephen Harper, Aaron Hughes (Andy O'Brien 45), Sylvain Distin, Nikos Dabizas, Robbie Elliott, Nolberto Solano, Robert Lee (Clarence Acuña 71), Gary Speed, Laurent Robert (Lomana Lualua 79), Shola Ameobi, Alan Shearer

Ipswich: Matteo Sereni, Fabian Wilnis, Chris Makin, John McGreal, Hermann Hreidarsson, Jamie Clapham, Matt Holland, Tommy Miller (Thomas Gaardsøe 45), Jermaine Wright, Pablo Couñago (Richard Naylor 45), Alun Armstrong (Darren Bent 71)

Inter Milan 4 (Vieri 19, 34, 71; Kallon 46)
Ipswich Town 1 (Armstrong 79);
Inter Milan won 4-2 on aggregate

Thursday, 6 December 2001, 8pm – UEFA Cup third round second leg
San Siro – Attendance: 25,358
Channel: Channel 5
Town manager: George Burley – **Referee:** Alain Sars

Inter Milan: Francesco Toldo, Javier Zanetti, Ivan Córdoba, Luigi Di Biagio, Vratislav Greško, Okan Buruk, Emre Belözoğlu (Sérgio Conceição 90), Javier Farinós, Andrés Guglielminpietro, Christian Vieri (Ronaldo 79), Mohamed Kallon
Ipswich: Matteo Sereni, Chris Makin, Titus Bramble, Hermann Hreidarsson, Mark Venus, Finidi George (Pablo Couñago 61), Matt Holland, Jim Magilton (Sixto Peralta 71), Jamie Clapham, Richard Naylor (Alun Armstrong 46), Jermaine Wright

Aston Villa 2 (Ángel 44, 70) Ipswich Town 1 (George 18)

Monday, 17 December 2001, 8pm – FA Premier League
Villa Park – Attendance: 29,320
Channel: Sky Sports 1
Town manager: George Burley – **Referee:** Mike Dean

Aston Villa: Peter Schmeichel, Gareth Barry, Olof Mellberg, Alan Wright, Steve Staunton, George Boateng, Steve Stone, Lee Hendrie (Dion Dublin 67), Jlloyd Samuel, Juan Pablo Ángel (Darius Vassal 84), Paul Merson
Ipswich: Matteo Sereni, Chris Makin, John McGreal, Mark Venus, Hermann Hreidarsson, Jermaine Wright, Matt Holland, Jim Magilton, Finidi George (Jamie Clapham 65), Alun Armstrong (Marcus Bent 80), Richard Naylor

Ipswich Town 1 (Bent 83)
Manchester City 4 (Berkovic 43; Goater 65, 86; Huckerby 90)

Sunday, 27 January 2002, kick-off: 7.00pm – FA Cup fourth round
Portman Road – Attendance: 21,199
Chanel: BBC One
Town manager: George Burley – **Referee:** Graham Poll

Ipswich: Andy Marshall, Fabian Wilnis (Alun Armstrong 65), Hermann Hreidarsson (Ulrich Le Pen 80), John McGreal, Titus Bramble, Matt Holland, Jermaine Wright, Martijn Reuser (Jamie Clapham 53), Sixto Peralta, Marcus Stewart, Marcus Bent
Manchester City: Nicky Weaver, Shaun Wright-Phillips, Niclas Jensen, Gerard Wiekens, Richard Dunne, Stuart Pearce, Ali Benarbia, Eyal Berkovic, Darren Huckerby, Shaun Goater, Kevin Horlock

Arsenal 2 (Ljunbgerg 68, 78)
Ipswich Town 0

Sunday, 21 April 2002, 4pm – FA Premier League
Highbury – Attendance: 38,058
Channel: Sky Sports 1
Town manager: George Burley – **Referee:** Alan Wiley

Arsenal: David Seaman, Lauren, Martin Keown, Tony Adams, Ashley Cole, Ray Parlour, Patrick Vieira, Edu (Nwankwo Kanu 56), Fredrik Ljungberg, Dennis Bergkamp (Gilles Grimaldi 76), Thierry Henry
Ipswich: Andy Marshall, Titus Bramble, John McGreal, Hermann Hreidarsson, Jamie Clapham, Finidi George (Sixto Peralta 50), Matt Holland, Tommy Miller, Martijn Reuser (Darren Ambrose 85), Marcus Stewart, Marcus Bent (Alun Armstrong 85)

Ipswich Town 0
Manchester United 1 (van Nistelrooy 45)

Saturday, 27 April 2002, 5.35pm – FA Premier League
Portman Road – Attendance: 28,433
Channels: Sky Sports 1, Sky Sports Xtra
Town manager: George Burley – **Referee:** Rob Styles

Ipswich: Andy Marshall, Titus Bramble, John McGreal, Hermann Hreidarsson, Jamie Clapham, Finidi George (Fabian Willis 53), Tommy Miller, Matt Holland, Sixto Peralta, Martijn Reuser (Darren Bent 70), Marcus Bent (Alun Armstrong 85)
Manchester United: Roy Carroll, Phil Neville, Wes Brown, John O'Shea, Denis Irwin, Michael Stewart (Paul Scholes 46), Roy Keane, Nicky Butt, Luke Chadwick (Mikaél Silvestre 79), Ruud van Nistelrooy (Ole Gunnar Solskjær 60), Diego Forlán

Liverpool 5 (Riise 13, 35; Owen 46; Šmicer 57; Anelka 88)
Ipswich Town 0

Saturday, 11 May 2002, 3pm – FA Premier League
Anfield – Attendance: 44,088
Channel: Sky Sports 2
Town manager: George Burley – **Referee:** Steve Dunn

Liverpool: Jerzy Dudek, Abel Xavier (Nicolas Anelka 84), Jamie Carragher, Dietmar Hamann, Stéphane Henchoz, Sami Hyypiä, Steven Gerrard (Vladimir Šmicer 33), Danny Murphy (Gary McAllister 82), Emile Heskey, Michael Owen, John Arne Riise
Ipswich: Andy Marshall, Titus Bramble, John McGreal (Fabian Willis 39), Hermann Hreidarsson, Mark Venus, Martijn Reuser, Matt Holland, Tommy Miller, Jamie Clapham, Darren Bent (Marcus Stewart 69), Marcus Bent (Alun Armstrong 82)

Walsall 0
Ipswich Town 2 (Ambrose 37; M. Bent 62)

Saturday, 10 August 2002, 5.35pm – Division One
Bescot Stadium – Attendance: 5,253
Channel: Sky Sports 2
Town manager: George Burley – **Referee:** Howard Webb

Walsall: Jimmy Walker, Darren Bazeley, Ian Roper, Matt Carbon, Zigor Aranalde, Darren Wrack, Steve Corica, Danny Sonner, Pedro Matías (Herivelto 63), Jorge Leitão (Dani Rodrigues 77), Gary Birch
Ipswich: Andy Marshall, Fabian Wilnis (Jermaine Wright 45), Thomas Gaardsøe, Hermann Hreidarsson, Jamie Clapham, Darren Bent, Jim Magilton, Matt Holland, Darren Ambrose, Marcus Bent (Alun Armstrong 62), Pablo Couñago (Tommy Miller 45)

Ipswich Town 1 (Couñago 90)
Norwich City 1 (Mackay 79)

Sunday, 15 September 2002, midday – Division One
Portman Road – Attendance: 29,112
Channel: Sky Sports 1
Town manager: George Burley – **Referee:** Paul Durkin

Ipswich: Andy Marshall, John McGreal, Hermann Hreidarsson, Mark Venus, Jermaine Wright, Darren Ambrose, Matt Holland, Jim Magilton (Pablo Couñago 82), Jamie Clapham, Marcus Bent (Alun Armstrong 66), Darren Bent
Norwich: Robert Green, Steen Nedergaard (Neil Emblen 76), Malky Mackay, Darren Kenton, Adam Drury, Phil Mulryne, Alex Notman (Darel Russell 20), Gary Holt, Paul Heckingbottom, Iwan Roberts, Paul McVeigh (David Nielsen 89)

Leicester City 1 (Dickov 55)
Ipswich Town 2 (Gaardsøe 84; Ambrose 88)

Thursday, 26 December 2002, kick-off: 6.05pm – Division One
Walkers Stadium – Attendance: 31,426
Channel: Sky Sports 2
Town manager: Joe Royle – **Referee:** Scott Mathieson

Leicester: Ian Walker, Andy Impey, Matt Heath, Matt Elliott, Alan Rogers, James Scowcroft, Muzzy Izzet, Billy McKinlay (Trevor Benjamin 89), Jordan Stewart, Brian Deane (Nicky Summerbee 82), Paul Dickov
Ipswich: Andy Marshall, Hermann Hreidarsson, Thomas Gaardsøe, Chris Makin, Fabian Wilnis (Darren Ambrose 58), Jamie Clapham, Matt Holland, Tommy Miller, Jim Magilton (Jermaine Wright 72), Pablo Couñago, Marcus Bent (Richard Naylor 70)

Ipswich Town 3 (Reuser 11; Miller 27; Couñago 30)
Portsmouth 0

Friday, 18 April 2003, 5.15pm – Division One
Portman Road – Attendance: 29,396
Channel: Sky Sports 1
Town manager: Joe Royle – Referee: Eddie Wolstenholme

Ipswich: Andy Marshall, Chris Makin, Fabian Wilnis, Matt Richards, Thomas Gaardsøe, Jim Magilton (Jermaine Wright 69), Martijn Reuser (Ian Westlake 82), Matt Holland, Tommy Miller, Pablo Couñago, Marcus Bent (Alun Armstrong 82)

Portsmouth: Shaka Hislop, Hayden Foxe, Linvoy Primus, Arjan de Zeeuw (Gary O'Neil 68), Gianluca Festa, Nigel Quashie, Steve Stone, Tim Sherwood, Svetoslav Todorov, Lee Bradbury (Vincent Péricard 60), Paul Merson (Kevin Harper 68)

Ipswich Town 1 (Richards 43)
Stoke City 0

Saturday, 18 October 2003, 5.35pm – Division One
Portman Road – Attendance: 22,122
Channel: Sky Sports Xtra
Town manager: Joe Royle – Referee: Paul Armstrong

Ipswich: Kelvin Davis, Fabian Wilnis, Matt Richards, Chris Bart-Williams, Alan Mahon (Ian Westlake 12), Jim Magilton (Tommy Miller 46), Georges Santos, Jermaine Wright, Pablo Couñago, Shefki Kuqi, Richard Naylor

Stoke: Neil Cutler, Paul Williams, Clive Clarke (Chris Greenacre 89), Clint Hill (Gareth Owen 77), Darel Russell, Karl Henry, John Halls, Keith Andrews, Ade Akinbiyi (Kris Commons 81), Gifton Noel-Williams, Carl Asaba

Ipswich Town 1 (Kuqi 60)
Wigan Athletic 3 (Roberts 18; Ellington 33; Teale 53)

Saturday, 7 February 2004, 5.35pm – Division One
Portman Road – Attendance: 22,093
Channel: Sky Sports 1
Town manager: Joe Royle – Referee: Paul Taylor

Ipswich: Kelvin Davis, Drissa Diallo, Matt Richards, Jim Magilton, Martijn Reuser (Georges Santos 46), Chris Bart-Williams (Ian Westlake 59), Jermaine Wright, Tommy Miller, Pablo Couñago (Darren Bent 46), Shefki Kuqi, Richard Naylor

Wigan: John Filan, Leighton Baines, Ian Breckin, Jason De Vos, Nicky Eaden, Alan Mahon, Jimmy Bullard, Jason Jarrett (Lee McCulloch 71), Nathan Ellington (Steve McMillan 83), Jason Roberts, Gary Teale

Ipswich Town 4 (Bowditch 5, 24, 61; Wright 90)
Watford 1 (Fitzgerald 45)

Saturday, 20 March 2004, midday – Division One
Portman Road – Attendance: 23,524
Channel: Sky Sports 1
Town manager: Joe Royle – **Referee:** Paul Robinson

Ipswich: Kelvin Davis, Fabian Wilnis, Matt Richards, John McGreal, Matt Elliott, Ian Westlake, Jim Magilton (Scott Mitchell 82), Jermaine Wright, Tommy Miller, Dean Bowditch, Darren Bent (Shefki Kuqi 82)
Watford: Lenny Pidgeley, Sean Dyche, Jerel Ifil, Paul Mayo, Chris Baird, Micah Hyde, Paul Devlin, Gavin Mahon, Neal Ardley (Lee Cook 73), Heidar Helguson, Scott Fitzgerald (Danny Webber 86)

Ipswich Town 2 (Miller 43; Bent 78)
West Bromwich Albion 3 (Koumas 71; Dyer 73; Horsfield 90)

Sunday, 4 April 2004, 4.05pm – Division One
Portman Road – Attendance: 24,608
Channel: Sky Sports 1
Town manager: Joe Royle – **Referee:** Graham Laws

Ipswich: Kelvin Davis, Fabian Wilnis, Matt Richards, Matt Elliott, Georges Santos, Ian Westlake, Jim Magilton, Jermaine Wright, Tommy Miller, Dean Bowditch, Darren Bent
West Brom: Russell Hoult (Joe Murphy 46), Darren Moore, Thomas Gaardsøe, Adam Chambers, Paul Robinson, Mark Kinsella (Lloyd Dyer 67), Andy Johnson, Sean Gregan, Artim Šakiri (Jason Koumas 46), Lee Hughes, Geoff Horsfield

Sheffield United 1 (Gray 64)
Ipswich Town 1 (Westlake 71)

Friday, 30 April 2004, 7.45pm – Division One
Bramall Lane – Attendance: 24,184
Channel: Sky Sports 2
Town manager: Joe Royle – **Referee:** Eddie Ilderton

Sheffield United: Paddy Kenny, Chris Morgan, Robert Kozluk (Simon Francis 90), Robert Page, Alan Wright, Andrew Gray, Phil Jagielka, Michael Tonge, Stuart McCall (Peter Ndlovu 73), Jack Lester (Izale McLeod 46), Wayne Allison
Ipswich: Kelvin Davis, Fabian Wilnis, Matt Richards, John McGreal, Matt Elliott, Ian Westlake, Jim Magilton, Jermaine Wright, Tommy Miller (Martijn Reuser 67), Dean Bowditch (Richard Naylor 46), Darren Bent

Ipswich Town 1 (Kuqi 26)
Cardiff City 1 (Bullock 41)

Sunday, 9 May 2004, 1pm – Division One
Portman Road – Attendance: 28,703
Channel: Sky Sports 1
Town manager: Joe Royle – **Referee:** Richard Beeby

Ipswich: Kelvin Davis, Fabian Wilnis, Matt Richards, John McGreal, Matt Elliott, Ian Westlake, Jim Magilton (Martijn Reuser 57), Jermaine Wright, Tommy Miller, Shefki Kuqi (Richard Naylor 57), Darren Bent

Cardiff: Martyn Margetson, Tony Vidmar, Gary Croft, Danny Gabbidon (Chris Barker 90), Lee Bullock, John Robinson (Paul Parry 74), Richard Langley, Willie Boland, James Collins, Alan Lee, Robert Earnshaw

Ipswich Town 1 (Bent 57)
West Ham United 0

Saturday, 15 May 2004, 12.15pm – Division One play-off semi-final first leg
Portman Road – Attendance: 28,435
Channel: Sky Sports 1
Town manager: Joe Royle – **Referee:** Mark Clattenburg

Ipswich: Kelvin Davis, Fabian Wilnis, Matt Richards, John McGreal (Shefki Kuqi 83), Matt Elliott, Ian Westlake, Jim Magilton (Chris Bart-Williams 76), Jermaine Wright, Tommy Miller, Darren Bent (Dean Bowditch 69), Richard Naylor

West Ham: Stephen Bywater, Andy Melville, Tomáš Řepka, Hayden Mullins, Christian Dailly, Steve Lomas, Michael Carrick, Matthew Etherington (Nigel Reo-Coker 90), David Connolly, Marlon Harewood (Brian Deane 78), Bobby Zamora (Jobi McAnuff 69)

West Ham United 2 (Etherington 50; Dailly 72)
Ipswich Town 0

West Ham won 2-1 on aggregate
Saturday, 15 May 2004, 12.15pm – Division One play-off semi-final second leg
Boleyn Ground, Upton Park – Attendance: 34,002
Channel: Sky Sports 1
Town manager: Joe Royle – **Referee:** Neale Barry

West Ham: Stephen Bywater, Andy Melville, Tomáš Řepka, Hayden Mullins, Christian Dailly, Steve Lomas, Michael Carrick, Matthew Etherington, David Connolly (Nigel Reo-Coker 82), Marlon Harewood, Bobby Zamora (Brian Deane 57)

Ipswich: Kelvin Davis, Fabian Wilnis, Matt Richards, Matt Elliott, Ian Westlake, Jim Magilton (Martijn Reuser 72), Jermaine Wright, Tommy Miller, Darren Bent, Shefki Kuqi (Alun Armstrong 46), Richard Naylor

Ipswich Town 2 (Bent 83; Couñago 90)
Millwall 0

Sunday, 12 September 2004, 1pm – Championship
Portman Road – Attendance: 21,246
Channel: Sky Sports 1
Town manager: Joe Royle – **Referee:** Anthony Bates

Ipswich: Kelvin Davis, Fabian Wilnis, Drissa Diallo, Jason de Vos, Richard Naylor, Ian Westlake, Jim Magilton, Kevin Horlock, Tommy Miller, Darren Bent, Shefki Kuqi (Pablo Couñago 67)
Millwall: Graham Stack, Marvin Elliott, Matt Lawrence, Darren Ward, Josh Simpson, Adrian Serioux, Dennis Wise (Kevin Muscat 72), Jody Morris, David Livermore, Barry Hayles (Stefan Moore 57), Mark McCammon (Neil Harris 62)

Coventry City 1 (Suffo 77)
Ipswich Town 2 (Bowditch 70; Mills 87 og)

Sunday, 3 October 2004, 1pm – Championship
Highfield Road – Attendance: 12,608
Channel: Sky Sports 1
Town manager: Joe Royle – **Referee:** Clive Penton

Coventry: Luke Steele, Andrew Whing, Richard Shaw, Matthew Mills, Steve Staunton, Andy Morrell (Claus Jørgensen 79), Michael Doyle, Tim Sherwood (Patrick Suffo 73), Stephen Hughes, Graham Barrett (Bjarni Gudjonsson 61), Stern John
Ipswich: Lewis Price, Drissa Diallo, Matt Richards, Jason de Vos, Richard Naylor, Tommy Miller, Jim Magilton, Jermaine Wright, Dean Bowditch, Darren Bent, Shefki Kuqi (Ian Westlake 76)

Sunderland 2 (Elliott 60; Brown 75)
Ipswich Town 0

Sunday, 21 November 2004, 1pm – Championship
Stadium of Light – Attendance: 31,723
Channel: Sky Sports 1
Town manager: Joe Royle – **Referee:** Paul Robinson

Sunderland: Thomas Myhre, Stephen Wright, Steven Caldwell, Gary Breen, George McCartney, Jeff Whitley (Liam Lawrence 46), Darren Carter, Julio Arca, Dean Whitehead, Stephen Elliott (Michael Bridges 76), Marcus Stewart (Chris Brown 57)
Ipswich: Kelvin Davis, Drissa Diallo, Fabian Wilnis, Jason de Vos, Richard Naylor, Dean Bowditch (Pablo Couñago 43), Jim Magilton, Kevin Horlock, Ian Westlake, Darren Bent, Shefki Kuqi (Darryl Knights 80)

Ipswich Town 2 (Naylor 66; Bent 89)
Wigan Athletic 1 (Baines 56)

Tuesday, 21 December 2004, 7.45pm – Championship
Portman Road – Attendance: 28,286
Channel: Sky Sports 1
Town manager: Joe Royle – **Referee:** Richard Beeby

Ipswich: Kelvin Davis, Fabian Wilnis, Matt Richards, Jason de Vos, Richard Naylor, Ian Westlake, Jim Magilton, Darren Currie, Tommy Miller, Darren Bent, Shefki Kuqi
Wigan: John Filan, Nicky Eaden, Matt Jackson, Ian Breckin, Leighton Baines, Gary Teale (David Graham 78), Jimmy Bullard, Alan Mahon (David Wright 80), Lee McCulloch, Nathan Ellington, Jason Roberts

Ipswich Town 1 (Kuqi 34)
Stoke City 0

Tuesday, 28 December 2004, 12.15pm – Championship
Portman Road – Attendance: 26,217
Channel: Sky Sports 1
Town manager: Joe Royle – **Referee:** Lee Mason

Ipswich: Kelvin Davis, Fabian Wilnis, Matt Richards, Jason de Vos, Richard Naylor, Ian Westlake, Jim Magilton (Kevin Horlock 76), Darren Currie, Tommy Miller, Darren Bent, Shefki Kuqi
Stoke: Steve Simonsen, Lewis Buxton, Wayne Thomas, Michael Duberry, Clint Hill, Darel Russell (John Eustace 73), David Brammer (Karl Henry 55), Clive Clarke, Carl Asaba, Gifton Noel-Williams (Chris Greenacre 74), Ade Akinbiyi

Preston North End 1 (Nugent 36)
Ipswich Town 1 (Miller 69)

Friday, 18 February 2005, 7.45pm – Championship
Deepdale – Attendance: 14,418
Channel: Sky Sports 3
Town manager: Joe Royle – **Referee:** Matt Messias

Preston: Gavin Ward (Chris Neal 83), Graham Alexander, Chris Lucketti, Youl Mawéné, Callum Davidson (Dickson Etuhu 75), Chris Sedgwick, Brian O'Neil, Paul McKenna, Matt Hill, David Nugent (Patrick Agyemang 75), Richard Cresswell
Ipswich: Kelvin Davis, Fabian Wilnis, David Unsworth, Jason de Vos, Richard Naylor, Darren Currie (Jim Magilton 46), Tommy Miller, Kevin Horlock (Dean Bowditch 46), Ian Westlake, Darren Bent, James Scowcroft

Wolverhampton Wanderers 2 (Cameron 5; Cort 22)
Ipswich Town 0

Monday, 11 April 2005, 7.45pm – Championship
Molineux – Attendance: 25,882
Channel: Sky Sports 1
Town manager: Joe Royle – **Referee:** Steve Dunn

Wolves: Michael Oakes, Rob Edwards, Jody Craddock, Joleon Lescott, Lee Naylor, Seol Ki-hyeon, Paul Ince, Seyi Olofinjana, Colin Cameron, Kenny Miller, Carl Cort (Leon Clarke 46)
Ipswich: Kelvin Davis, Fabian Wilnis, Matt Richards (Darren Currie 46), David Unsworth, Jason de Vos, Richard Naylor, Jim Magilton, Tommy Miller, Ian Westlake (Pablo Couñago 75), Darren Bent, Shefki Kuqi (James Scowcroft 46)

Ipswich Town 2 (Naylor 66; Bent 89)
Sunderland 2 (Elliott 71; Robinson 84)

Sunday, 17 April 2005, midday – Championship
Portman Road – Attendance: 29,230
Channel: Sky Sports 1
Town manager: Joe Royle – **Referee:** Steve Bennett

Ipswich: Kelvin Davis, Fabian Wilnis, David Unsworth, Jason de Vos, Richard Naylor, Ian Westlake, Kevin Horlock (Jim Magilton 76), Darren Currie (Pablo Couñago 82), Tommy Miller, Darren Bent, Shefki Kuqi
Sunderland: Michael Ingham, Stephen Wright, Steven Caldwell, Gary Breen, George McCartney, Liam Lawrence (Sean Thornton 76), Carl Robinson, Julio Arca, Dean Whitehead, Chris Brown (Brian Deane 69), Marcus Stewart (Stephen Elliott 69)

Brighton and Hove Albion 1 (Virgo 10)
Ipswich Town 1 (Kuqi 4)

Sunday, 8 May 2005, 1pm – Championship
Withdean Stadium – Attendance: 6,848
Channel: Sky Sports 2
Town manager: Joe Royle – **Referee:** Bryn Markham-Jones

Brighton: Alan Blayney, Adam El-Abd, Guy Butters, Paul Reid, Dan Harding, Gary Hart (Chris McPhee 82), Charlie Oatway, Richard Carpenter, Leon Knight (Jake Robinson 88), Dean Hammond, Adam Virgo
Ipswich: Kelvin Davis, Fabian Wilnis (Drissa Diallo 40; James Scowcroft 75), David Unsworth, Jason de Vos, Richard Naylor, Jim Magilton, Tommy Miller, Ian Westlake, Darren Currie (Pablo Couñago 64), Darren Bent, Shefki Kuqi

West Ham United 2 (Harewood 7; Zamora 13)
Ipswich Town (Walker 45 og; Kuqi 74)

Saturday, 14 May 2005, 12.15pm – Championship play-off Semi-Final 1ˢᵗ Leg
Boleyn Ground, Upton Park – Attendance: 33,723
Channel: Sky Sports 1
Town manager: Joe Royle – **Referee:** Uriah Rennie

West Ham: Jimmy Walker, Tomáš Řepka, Anton Ferdinand, Elliott Ward, Chris Powell, Nigel Reo-Coker, Shaun Newton (Serhiy Rebrov 86), Hayden Mullins, Matthew Etherington, Bobby Zamora (Mark Noble 76), Marlon Harewood

Ipswich: Kelvin Davis, Fabian Wilnis, Drissa Diallo (Matt Richards 46), Jason de Vos, Richard Naylor, Jim Magilton, Tommy Miller, Ian Westlake, Kevin Horlock (Darren Currie 46), Darren Bent, Shefki Kuqi

Ipswich Town 0 West Ham United 2 (Zamora 61, 72)
West Ham won 4-2 on aggregate

Wednesday, 18 May 2005, 7.45pm – Championship play-off semi-final second leg
Portman Road – Attendance: 30,010
Channel: Sky Sports 1
Town manager: Joe Royle – **Referee:** Steve Dunn

Ipswich: Kelvin Davis, Fabian Wilnis, Matt Richards, Jason de Vos, Richard Naylor, Jim Magilton (Dean Bowditch 75), Tommy Miller, Ian Westlake, Darren Currie, Darren Bent, Shefki Kuqi

West Ham: Jimmy Walker, Tomáš Řepka (Christian Dailly 76), Anton Ferdinand, Elliott Ward, Chris Powell, Nigel Reo-Coker, Carl Fletcher, Hayden Mullins, Matthew Etherington (Mark Noble 89), Bobby Zamora (Shaun Newton 79), Marlon Harewood

Ipswich Town 0
Preston North End 4 (Nugent 31, 34; Jones 45; Agyemang 85)

Monday, 29 August 2005, 12.45pm – Championship
Portman Road – Attendance: 22,551
Channel: Sky Sports 1
Town manager: Joe Royle – **Referee:** Brian Curson

Ipswich: Lewis Price, Sito, Matt Richards, Fabian Wilnis, Aidan Collins, Jim Magilton (Jimmy Juan 52), Darren Currie, Kevin Horlock (Dean McDonald 40), Owen Garvan (Jaime Peters 51), Ian Westlake, Sam Parkin

Preston: Carlo Nash, Graham Alexander, Chris Lucketti, Claude Davis, Matt Hill, Brian O'Neil, David Jones (Dickson Etuhu 56), Paul McKenna, Tyrone Mears, David Nugent (Chris Sedgwick 74), Danny Dichio (Patrick Agyemang 82)

Reading 2 (Naylor 18 og; Doyle 47)
Ipswich Town 0

Sunday, 16 October 2005, 1.30pm – Championship
Madejski Stadium – Attendance: 17,581
Channel: Sky Sports 1
Town manager: Joe Royle **– Referee:** Steve Tanner

Reading: Marcus Hahnemann, Chris Makin, Ibrahima Sonko, Ivar Íngimarsson, Nicky Shorey, Glen Little (John Oster 72), Brynjar Gunnarsson, James Harper, Bobby Convey (Stephen Hunt 81), Leroy Lita, Kevin Doyle (Dave Kitson 64)
Ipswich: Lewis Price, Sito, Fabian Wilnis, Jason de Vos (Adam Proudlock 46), Richard Naylor, Jay McEveley, Jim Magilton, Darren Currie (Dean Bowditch 83), Kevin Horlock, Nicky Forster (Owen Garvan 69), Sam Parkin

Cardiff City 2 (Ricketts 30; Koumas 90)
Ipswich Town 1 (Juan 86)

Monday, 28 November 2005, 7.45pm – Championship
Ninian Park – Attendance: 8,724
Channel: Sky Sports 1
Town manager: Joe Royle **– Referee:** Andre Marriner

Cardiff: Neil Alexander, Rhys Weston, Neil Cox, Glenn Loovens, Chris Barker, Jason Koumas, Jeff Whitley, Joe Ledley, Paul Parry, Cameron Jerome, Michael Ricketts (Alan Lee 88)
Ipswich: Lewis Price, Sito, Fabian Wilnis, Jason de Vos, Jay McEveley (Kevin Horlock 15), Jim Magilton (Billy Clarke 65; Darren Currie 86), Matt Richards, Jimmy Juan, Gavin Williams, Nicky Forster, Richard Naylor

Norwich City 1 (Johansson 33)
Ipswich Town 2 (Juan 38; Haynes 88)

Sunday, 5 February 2006, kick-off: 11.15am – Championship
Carrow Road – Attendance: 25,402
Channel: Sky Sports 1
Town manager: Joe Royle **– Referee:** Keith Stroud

Norwich: Robert Green, Craig Fleming (Jason Shackell 71), Zesh Rehman, Gary Doherty, Adam Drury, Andy Hughes (Darren Huckerby 45), Dickson Etuhu (Carl Robinson 45), Youssef Safri, Paul McVeigh, Robert Earnshaw, Jonatan Johansson
Ipswich: Lewis Price, Fabian Wilnis, Jason de Vos, Richard Naylor, Matt Richards, Gavin Williams (Danny Haynes 25; Sito 89), Jimmy Juan, Owen Garvan, Scott Barron, Darren Currie, Alan Lee

Queens Park Rangers 1 (Gallen 58)
Ipswich Town 3 (Walton 62; de Vos 68; Bowditch 86)

Friday, 25 August 2006, 7.45pm – Championship
Loftus Road – Attendance: 10,918
Channel: Sky Sports 1
Town manager: Jim Magilton – **Referee:** Lee Mason

QPR: Paul Jones, Matthew Rose, Damion Stewart, Zesh Rehman, Mauro Milanese (Shabazz Baidoo 77), Kevin Gallen, Steve Lomas (Marc Bircham 72), Nick Ward, Lee Cook, Ray Jones, Dexter Blackstock
Ipswich: Lewis Price, Fabian Wilnis, Alex Bruce, Jason de Vos, Dan Harding, Gavin Williams (Darren Currie 89), Simon Walton, Mark Noble, Matt Richards, Alan Lee (Danny Haynes 83), Billy Clarke (Dean Bowditch 77)

Colchester United 1 (Duguid 9)
Ipswich Town 0

Friday, 29 September 2006, 7.45pm – Championship
Layer Road – Attendance: 6,065
Channel: Sky Sports 2
Town manager: Jim Magilton – **Referee:** Lee Probert

Colchester: Aidan Davison, Greg Halford, Pat Baldwin, Wayne Brown, Chris Barker, Richard Garcia, Kevin Watson, Kem Izzet, Karl Duguid, Chris Iwelumo, Jamie Cureton
Ipswich: Lewis Price, Sito, Richard Naylor, Jason de Vos, Dan Harding, Mark Noble, Simon Walton (Dean Bowditch 86), Sylvain Legwinski, Darren Currie, Jon Macken (Billy Clarke 63), Alan Lee

Ipswich Town 5 (Legwinski 20; Peters 54; Lee 66, 76, 90)
Luton Town 0

Sunday, 29 October 2006, 1.15pm – Championship
Portman Road – Attendance: 20,975
Channel: Sky Sports 1
Town manager: Jim Magilton – **Referee:** Iain Williamson

Ipswich: Shane Supple, Fabian Wilnis, Dan Harding, Jason de Vos (Richard Naylor 70), Alex Bruce, Jaime Peters (Danny Haynes 88), Simon Walton, Sylvain Legwinski, Matt Richards, Alan Lee, Billy Clarke (Gary Roberts 68)
Luton: Marlon Beresford, Kevin Foley, Keith Keane, Leon Barnett, Lewis Emanuel (Ahmet Brković 60), Carlos Edwards, Steve Robinson, David Bell, Dean Morgan (Russell Perrett 79), Rowan Vine, Warren Feeney (Adam Boyd 69)

Ipswich Town 3 (Legwinski 40; Haynes 77, 90)
Norwich City 1 (Chadwick 26)

Sunday, 19 November 2006, 11.30am – Championship
Portman Road – Attendance: 27,276
Channel: Sky Sports 1
Town manager: Jim Magilton – **Referee:** Trevor Kettle

Ipswich: Mike Pollitt, Matthew Bates, Dan Harding, Jason de Vos, Alex Bruce, Gary Roberts, Simon Walton, Sylvain Legwinski, Matt Richards, Alan Lee, Billy Clarke (Danny Haynes 76)
Norwich: Paul Gallacher, Adam Drury, Jason Shackell, Gary Doherty, Jürgen Colin, Darren Huckerby, Dickson Etuhu, Carl Robinson, Andy Hughes (Dion Dublin 61), Luke Chadwick (Robert Eagle 83), Robert Earnshaw

Ipswich Town 1 (Walters 72)
Crystal Palace 0

Sunday, 26 August 2007, 1.15pm – Championship
Portman Road – Attendance: 19,382
Channel: Sky Sports 1
Town manager: Jim Magilton – **Referee:** Andy D'Urso

Ipswich: Neil Alexander, David Wright, Dan Harding, Jason de Vos, Alex Bruce, Jon Walters, Tommy Miller, Owen Garvan, Gary Roberts (Danny Haynes 73), Alan Lee (Sylvain Legwinski 79), Pablo Couñago (Billy Clarke 87)
Crystal Palace: Julián Speroni, Matt Lawrence, Mark Hudson, Leon Cort, Tony Craig, Tom Soares, Carl Fletcher (Dougie Freedman 73), Stuart Green (Shefki Kuqi 64), Mark Kennedy, Clinton Morrison (Jeff Hughes 73), James Scowcroft

Ipswich Town 4 (de Vos 10; Couñago 24, 57; Walters 40)
Coventry City 1 (Hughes 69)

Saturday, 22 September 2007, 5.20pm – Championship
Portman Road – Attendance: 18,840
Channel: Sky Sports 1
Town manager: Jim Magilton – **Referee:** Trevor Kettle

Ipswich: Neil Alexander, David Wright, Dan Harding, Jason de Vos, Alex Bruce (Chris Casement 78), Jon Walters, Tommy Miller, Owen Garvan, Gary Roberts (Jaime Peters 74), Alan Lee, Pablo Couñago (Billy Clarke 88)
Coventry: Dimi Konstantopoulos, Gary Borrowdale, Arjan de Zeeuw, Marcus Hall, Issac Osbourne, Jay Tabb (Kevin Thornton 78), Stephen Hughes, Michael Doyle, Ellery Cairo (Robbie Simpson 83), Leon Best, Dele Adebola (Michael Mifsud 56)

Norwich City 2 (Garvan 56 og; Cureton 67)
Ipswich Town 2 (Lee 27; Couñago 41)

Sunday, 4 November 2007, 12.45pm – Championship
Carrow Road – Attendance: 25,461
Channel: Sky Sports 1
Town manager: Jim Magilton – **Referee:** Rob Styles

Norwich: David Marshall, Jon Otsemobor, Jason Shackell, Martin Taylor, Simon Lappin, Luke Chadwick (Lee Croft 76), Julien Brellier, Darel Russell, Darren Huckerby, Dion Dublin (John Harrison 46), Jamie Cureton (Jimmy Smith 82)

Ipswich: Neil Alexander, David Wright, Dan Harding, Jason de Vos, Fabian Wilnis, Jon Walters, Sylvain Legwinski (Danny Haynes 75), Owen Garvan, Billy Clarke (Gary Roberts 82), Alan Lee, Pablo Couñago (Liam Trotter 74)

Coventry City 2 (Gray 11; Adebola 64)
Ipswich Town 1 (Haynes 42)

Saturday, 29 December 2007, 5.20pm – Championship
Ricoh Arena – Attendance: 18,346
Channel: Sky Sports 1
Town manager: Jim Magilton – **Referee:** Iain Williamson

Coventry: Andy Marshall, Isaac Osbourne, Arjan de Zeeuw, Ben Turner, Gary Borrowdale, Jay Tabb (Kevin Thornton 51), Stephen Hughes (Elliott Ward 89), Michael Doyle, Julian Gray (Liam Davis 46), Dele Adebola, Michael Misfud

Ipswich: Neil Alexander, Fabian Wilnis, David Wright, Chris Casement (Liam Trotter 89), Jason de Vos, Tommy Miller, Owen Garvan, Danny Haynes, Jon Walters, Alan Lee (Jordan Rhodes 81), Pablo Couñago (Gavin Williams 72)

Ipswich Town 1 (Lee 70)
Hull City 0

Sunday, 4 May 2008, 2pm – Championship
Portman Road – Attendance: 28,233
Channel: Sky Sports 2
Town manager: Jim Magilto – **Referee:** Andre Marriner

Ipswich: Stephen Bywater, Danny Simpson, David Wright, Jason de Vos, Alex Bruce, Jon Walters, Tommy Miller, Owen Garvan, Alan Quinn (Alan Lee 69), Shefki Kuqi (Danny Haynes 52), Pablo Couñago (Veliče Šumulikoski 80)

Hull: Boaz Myhill, Sam Ricketts, Michael Turner, Wayne Brown, Andy Dawson, Caleb Folan (Nick Barmy 64), Ian Ashbee, Dean Marney, Brian Hughes (Craig Fagan 61), Fraizer Campbell, Dean Windass

Watford 2 (Eustace 58; O'Toole 87)
Ipswich Town 1 (Couñago 2)

Saturday, 30 August 2008, 5.20pm – Championship
Vicarage Road – Attendance: 16,345
Channel: Sky Sports 1
Town manager: Jim Magilton – **Referee:** Lee Probert

Watford: Mart Poom, Lloyd Doyley, Leigh Bromby, Jay DeMerit, Jordan Parkes (John-Joe O'Toole 87), Jobi McAnuff, Lee Williamson (Damien Francis 82), John Eustace, Jon Harley, Tommy Smith, Tamás Priskin (Liam Henderson 81)
Ipswich: Richard Wright, Moritz Volz, Ben Thatcher, Gareth McAuley, Richard Naylor, Tommy Miller, Iván Campo, Liam Trotter (Veliče Šumulikoski 82), Jon Walters, Kevin Lisbie (Danny Haynes 66), Pablo Couñago (Jordan Rhodes 74)

Ipswich Town 1 (Stead 23)
Crystal Palace 1 (Moses 25)

Saturday, 27 September 2008, 5.20pm – Championship
Portman Road – Attendance: 19,032
Channel: Sky Sports 1
Town manager: Jim Magilton – **Referee:** Darren Deadman

Ipswich: Richard Wright, Alex Bruce, David Wright, Gareth McAuley, Richard Naylor, Tommy Miller, Veliče Šumulikoski (Iván Campo 71), David Norris (Owen Garvan 57), Jon Walters, Kevin Lisbie, Jon Stead (Pablo Couñago 62)
Crystal Palace: Julián Speroni, Danny Butterfield, Paddy McCarthy, José Fonte, Clint Hill, Nick Carle (Carl Fletcher 81), Ben Watson, Shaun Derry, Paul Ifill (Shefki Kuqi 68), Victor Moses, Craig Beattie (Sean Scannell 74)

Doncaster Rovers 1 (Martin 42)
Ipswich Town 0

Saturday, 15 November 2008, 5.20pm – Championship
Keepmoat Stadium – Attendance: 10,823
Channel: Sky Sports 1
Town manager: Jim Magilton – **Referee:** Kevin Friend

Doncaster: Neil Sullivan, Matt Mills, Shelton Martis, Sam Hird (John Spicer 57), James O'Connor, Richie Wellens, Brian Stock, Martin Woods, James Chambers, Paul Heffernan (Lewis Guy 77), Jason Price (Gareth Taylor 83)
Ipswich: Richard Wright, Moritz Volz, David Wright, Alex Bruce, Richard Naylor, David Norris, Owen Garvan, Veliče Šumulikoski, Alan Quinn (Darren Ambrose 53), Jon Walters (Jon Stead 54), Kevin Lisbie (Pablo Couñago 70)

Norwich City 2 (Croft 61; Pattison 82)
Ipswich Town 0

Sunday, 7 December 2008, 1.15pm – Championship
Carrow Road – Attendance: 25,472
Channel: Sky Sports 1
Town manager: Jim Magilton – **Referee:** Lee Probert

Norwich: David Marshall, Jon Otsemobor, Gary Doherty, Elliot Omozusi, Ryan Bertrand, Lee Croft (Darel Russell 85), Sammy Clingan, Matty Pattison, David Bell (Mark Fotheringham 89), Wes Hoolahan (Arturo Lupoli 90), Leroy Lita
Ipswich: Richard Wright, Moritz Volz, David Wright, Alex Bruce, Gareth McAuley, David Norris, Owen Garvan (Richard Naylor 84), Veliče Šumulikoski, Darren Ambrose (Danny Haynes 62), Jon Walters, Pablo Couñago (Jon Stead 66)

Queens Park Rangers 1 (Di Carmine 3)
Ipswich Town 3 (Stead 14; Couñago 61; Walters 70)

Saturday, 21 February 2009, 5.20pm – Championship
Loftus Road – Attendance: 13,904
Channel: Sky Sports 1
Town manager: Jim Magilton – **Referee:** Stuart Attwell

QPR: Lee Camp, Damien Delaney (Dexter Blackstock 67), Gavin Mahon, Fitz Hall, Mikele Leigertwood, Wayne Routledge, Kaspars Gorkšs, Matt Connolly, Lee Cook, Liam Miller (Ángelo Balanta 73), Samuel Di Carmine (Heidar Helguson 55)
Ipswich: Richard Wright, David Wright, Ben Thatcher, Alex Bruce, Gareth McAuley, David Norris, Tommy Miller, Luciano Civelli (Jon Walters 61), Alan Quinn, Jon Stead (Kevin Lisbie 69), Pablo Couñago (Owen Garvan 82)

Coventry City 2 (Morrison 10, 24)
Ipswich Town 1 (Walters 29)

Sunday, 9 August 2009, 12.45pm – Championship
Ricoh Arena – Attendance: 16,279
Channel: Sky Sports 1
Town manager: Roy Keane – **Referee:** Russell Booth

Coventry: Keiren Westwood, Stephen Wright, Patrick van Aanholt, Ben Turner, Sammy Clingan, David Bell (Jordan Clarke 63), Isaac Osbourne, Aron Gunnarsson, Michael McIndoe (Elliott Ward 82), Leon Best (Freddy Eastwood 61), Clinton Morrison
Ipswich: Richard Wright, Gareth McAuley, Alex Bruce, Pim Balkestein, Damien Delaney, Lee Martin, David Norris (Owen Garvan 56), Jaime Peters (Tamás Priskin 67), Liam Trotter, Jon Stead (Connor Wickham 66), Jon Walters

West Bromwich Albion 2 (Mulumbu 10; Koren 38)
Ipswich Town 0

Saturday, 22 August 2009, 5.20pm – Championship
The Hawthorns – Attendance: 19,390
Channel: Sky Sports 2
Town manager: Roy Keane – **Referee:** Steve Tanner

West Brom: Scott Carson, Joe Mattock (Craig Beattie 75), Jonas Olsson, Marek Čech, Shelton Martis, Shaun Cummings, Robert Koren (Borja Valero 84), Chris Brunt (Jerome Thomas 55), Youssouf Mulumbu, Chris Wood, Luke Moore
Ipswich: Richard Wright, David Wright, Tommy Smith, Alex Bruce, Pim Balkestein, Owen Garvan (Jack Colback 46), Lee Martin, Liam Trotter, Jon Stead (Alan Quinn 46), Jon Walters, Connor Wickham (Tamás Priskin 71)

Ipswich Town 0
Newcastle United 4 (Nolan 30, 32, 51; R. Taylor 34)

Saturday, 26 September 2009, 5.30pm – Championship
Portman Road – Attendance: 27,059
Channel: BBC Two
Town manager: Roy Keane – **Referee:** Mike Jones

Ipswich: Richard Wright, Alex Bruce (Tommy Smith 39), Liam Rosenior, Pim Balkestein, Damien Delaney (Jaime Peters 60), Grant Leadbitter, Jack Colback, Carlos Edwards, Liam Trotter, Tamás Priskin (Pablo Couñago 61), Jon Walters
Newcastle: Steve Harper, Fabricio Coloccini (Peter Løvenkrands 68), José Enrique, Zurab Khizanishvili, Ryan Taylor (Ryan Donaldson 78), Steven Taylor, Kevin Nolan, Nicky Butt, Alan Smith, Andy Carroll, Nile Ranger (Marlon Harewood 65)

Ipswich Town 0
Sheffield Wednesday 0

Saturday, 21 November 2009, 5.20pm – Championship
Portman Road – Attendance: 19,636
Channel: BBC One
Town manager: Roy Keane – **Referee:** Andy D'Urso

Ipswich: Asmir Begović, David Wright, Liam Rosenior, Alex Bruce (Gareth McAuley 57), Damien Delaney, Grant Leadbitter, Owen Garvan, Lee Martin (Alan Quinn 57), Carlos Edwards, Tamás Priskin, Jon Walters (Jon Stead 76)
Sheffield Wednesday: Lee Grant, Tommy Spurr, Lewis Buxton, Richard Hinds, Frankie Simek, Michael Gray, Darren Potter, James O'Connor, Jermaine Johnson (Leon Clarke 61), Marcus Tudgay, Luke Varney

Leicester City 1 (Howard 38)
Ipswich Town 1 (Norris 1)

Sunday, 10 January 2010, 3pm – Championship
Walkers Stadium – Attendance: 20,758
Channel: Sky Sports 1
Town manager: Roy Keane – **Referee:** Mark Haywood

Leicester: Chris Weale, Robbie Neilson, Ryan McGivern, Michael Morrison, Wayne Brown, Matt Oakley, Andy King, Lloyd Dyer (Martyn Waghorn 71), Richie Wellens (Paul Gallagher 70), Steve Howard (Yann Kermorgant 83), Matty Fryatt
Ipswich: Arran Lee-Barrett, Damien Delaney, Gareth McAuley, Alex Bruce (Liam Rosenior 57), Pim Balkestein, Grant Leadbitter, David Norris, Jaime Peters, Jack Colback (Stern John 83), Jon Walters, Connor Wickham (Owen Garvan 73)

Norwich City 4 (Holt 13, 35, 76; Hoolahan 78)
Ipswich Town 1 (Delaney 29)

Sunday, 28 November 2010, 1.15pm – Championship
Carrow Road – Attendance: 26,532
Channel: Sky Sports 1
Town manager: Roy Keane – **Referee:** Keith Hill

Norwich: John Ruddy, Russell Martin, Leon Barnett, Elliott Ward, Andrew Crofts, Andrew Surman (Wes Hoolahan 64), Henri Lansbury (Korey Smith 80), David Fox, Simon Lappin, Grant Holt (Simeon Jackson 85), Chris Martin
Ipswich: Márton Fülöp, Damien Delaney, Darren O'Dea, Tommy Smith, Gianni Zuiverloon (Rory Fallon 69), Grant Leadbitter, Carlos Edwards, David Norris, Jack Colback, Jason Scotland (Colin Healy 42), Tamás Priskin (Troy Brown 81)

Ipswich Town 1 (Townsend 50)
Swansea City 3 (Beattie 64, 86; Allen 70)

Saturday, 4 December 2010, 12.45pm – Championship
Portman Road – Attendance: 16,978
Channel: Sky Sports 2
Town manager: Roy Keane – **Referee:** Andy D'Urso

Ipswich: Brian Murphy, Tommy Smith, Troy Brown, Gianni Zuiverloon, Darren O'Dea (Shane O'Connor 72), Grant Leadbitter, Carlos Edwards, Andros Townsend (Jaime Peters 82), Jack Colback, Jason Scotland, Tamás Priskin (Rory Fallon 66)
Swansea: Dorus De Vries, Ashley Williams, Neil Taylor, Alan Tate, Ángel Rangel, Andrea Orlandi (Darren Pratley 75), Nathan Dyer (Stephen Dobbie 88), Scott Sinclair, Joe Allen, Mark Gower, Craig Beattie

Ipswich Town 3 (Norris 6; Scotland 27, 39)
Leicester City 0

Saturday, 18 December 2010, 5.20pm – Championship
Portman Road – Attendance: 16,728
Channel: Sky Sports 2
Town manager: Roy Keane – Referee: Stuart Attwell

Ipswich: Márton Fülöp, Tommy Smith, Mark Kennedy, Damien Delaney, Gianni Zuiverloon, Shane O'Connor (Carlos Edwards 77), Grant Leadbitter, David Norris, Jack Colback, Jason Scotland (Jake Livermore 69), Rory Fallon (Connor Wickham 62)
Leicester: Chris Kirkland, Miguel Vítor, Kyle Naughton, Curtis Davies (Jack Hobbs 70), Andy King, Lloyd Dyer (Steve Howard 28), Richie Wellens, Yuki Abe, Greg Cunningham, Paul Gallagher (Matty Fryatt 65), Darius Vassell

Ipswich Town 1 (Priskin 78)
Arsenal 0

Wednesday, 12 January 2011, 7.45pm – League Cup semi-final first leg
Portman Road – Attendance: 29,146
Channel: Sky Sports 1
Town manager: Ian McParland – Referee: Martin Atkinson

Ipswich: Márton Fülöp, Darren O'Dea, Mark Kennedy, Gareth McAuley, Damien Delaney, Jaime Peters, Carlos Edwards, David Norris, Colin Healy, Connor Wickham, Tamás Priskin (Ronan Murray 90)
Arsenal: Wojciech Szczęsny, Laurent Koscielny, Johan Djourou, Emmanuel Eboué, Kieran Gibbs, Cesc Fàbregas, Theo Walcott, Denílson, Jack Wilshere (Alex Song 68), Andrey Arshavin (Carlos Vela 80), Nicklas Bendtner (Marouane Chamakh 68)

Arsenal 3 (Bendtner 61; Koscielny 64; Fàbregas 77)
Ipswich Town 0

Arsenal won 3-1 on aggregate

Tuesday, 25 January 2011, 7.45pm – League Cup semi-final second leg
Emirates Stadium – Attendance: 59,387
Channel: BBC Two
Town manager: Paul Jewell – Referee: Mark Halsey

Arsenal: Wojciech Szczęsny, Bacary Sagna (Emmanuel Eboué 18), Laurent Koscielny, Johan Djourou, Gaël Clichy, Cesc Fàbregas, Denílson, Jack Wilshere, Andrey Arshavin (Theo Walcott 84), Robin van Persie (Samir Nasri 84), Nicklas Bendtner
Ipswich: Márton Fülöp, Darren O'Dea, Mark Kennedy, Gareth McAuley, Damien Delaney, Grant Leadbitter, Carlos Edwards, David Norris, Colin Healy (Shane O'Connor 74), Connor Wickham, Tamás Priskin (Jason Scotland 53)

Cardiff City 0
Ipswich Town 2 (Bullard 67, 86)

Saturday, 5 March 2011, 5.20pm – Championship
Cardiff City Stadium – Attendance: 21,347
Channel: Sky Sports 2
Town manager: Paul Jewell – **Referee:** Anthony Bates

Cardiff: Stephen Bywater, Kevin McNaughton, Mark Hudson, Dekel Keinan, Paul Quinn (Darcy Blake 85), Peter Whittingham, Stephen McPhail, Jay Emmanuel-Thomas (Chris Burke 80), Michael Chopra (Jon Parkin 87), Jay Bothroyd, Craig Bellamy
Ipswich: Márton Fülöp, Carlos Edwards, Mark Kennedy (Darren O'Dea 29), Gareth McAuley, Damien Delaney, Grant Leadbitter, David Norris, Lee Martin, Jimmy Bullard, Connor Wickham (Luciano Civelli 89), Jason Scotland (Tamás Priskin 84)

Peterborough United 7 (Taylor 30, 40; Tomlin 38, 42, 90; McCann 48, 56)
Ipswich Town 1 (Andrews 23)

Saturday, 20 August 2011, 5.20pm – Championship
London Road – Attendance: 7,928
Channel: Sky Sports 2
Town manager: Paul Jewell – **Referee:** Graham Scott

Peterborough: Paul Jones, Mark Little (Ben Gordon 57), Ryan Bennett, Scott Wootton, Craig Alcock, Grant McCann, Tommy Rowe, Lee Frecklington (Ryan Tunnicliffe 62), Lee Tomlin, George Boyd, Paul Taylor
Ipswich: David Stockdale, Josh Carson (Tommy Smith 46), Aaron Cresswell, Jack Ainsley, Damien Delaney, Grant Leadbitter, Carlos Edwards, Jay Emmanuel-Thomas (Mark Kennedy 54), Lee Martin, Keith Andrews, Michael Chopra (Nathan Ellington 71)

Ipswich Town 3 (Cranie 6 og; Andrews 15; Scotland 67)
Coventry City 0

Monday, 19 September 2011, 7.45pm – Championship
Portman Road – Attendance: 15,650
Channel: Sky Sports 1
Town manager: Paul Jewell – **Referee:** Craig Pawson

Ipswich: David Stockdale, Carlos Edwards, Aaron Cresswell, Danny Collins, Ibrahima Sonko (Damien Delaney 35), Grant Leadbitter, Lee Bowyer, Keith Andrews, Jimmy Bullard, Michael Chopra (Daryl Murphy 82), Jason Scotland (Jay Emmanuel-Thomas 86)
Coventry: Joe Murphy, Richard Keogh, Chris Hussey, Martin Crainie, Cyrus Christie (Nathan Cameron 76), Sammy Clingan, David Bell, Carl Baker, Gaël Bigirimana (Gary McSheffrey 44), Lukas Jutkiewicz, Cody McDonald (Roy O'Donovan 69)

Barnsley 3 (Davies 14, 89; Vaz Té 39)
Ipswich Town 5 (Andrews 46, 49; Collins 66; Chopra 68; Scotland 83)

Saturday, 10 December 2011, 5.20pm – Championship
Oakwell – Attendance: 9,107
Channel: Sky Sports 2
Town manager: Paul Jewell – **Referee:** Gary Sutton

Barnsley: Luke Steele, Bobby Hassell, Stephen Foster, Scott Wiseman, Jim McNulty, Jim O'Brien (Nile Ranger 71), David Perkins, Jacob Butterfield, Danny Drinkwater (Matt Done 17), Craig Davies, Ricardo Vaz Té (Danny Haynes 66)
Ipswich: David Stockdale, Carlos Edwards, Aaron Cresswell, Danny Collins, Ibrahima Sonko, Lee Bowyer, Lee Martin (Josh Carson 83), Keith Andrews, Michael Chopra (Nathan Ellington 80), Jason Scotland, Daryl Murphy (Reece Wabara 89)

Ipswich Town 1 (Campbell 45)
Cardiff City 2 (Helguson 62, 87)

Saturday, 6 October 2012, 5.20pm – Championship
Portman Road – Attendance: 16,434
Channel: Sky Sports 1
Town manager: Paul Jewell – **Referee:** Eddie Ilderton

Ipswich: Scott Loach, Carlos Edwards, Luke Chambers, Danny Higginbotham, Aaron Cresswell, Jay Emmanuel-Thomas, Lee Martin, Richie Wellens (Massimo Luongo 72), Andy Drury, DJ Campbell (Jason Scotland 58), Daryl Murphy (Bilel Mohsni 89)
Cardiff: David Marshall, Kevin McNaughton (Ben Turner 89), Andrew Taylor, Mark Hudson, Matthew Connolly, Peter Whittingham, Don Cowie, Craig Noone (Craig Conway 54), Aron Gunnarsson, Joe Mason (Rudy Gestede 63), Heidar Helguson

Ipswich Town 1 (Murphy 40) Barnsley 1 (O'Brien 69)

Friday, 1 November 2013, 7.45pm – Championship
Portman Road – Attendance: 18,361
Channel: Sky Sports 1
Town manager: Mick McCarthy – **Referee:** Andy D'Urso

Ipswich: Dean Gerken, Luke Chambers, Aaron Cresswell, Christophe Berra, Tommy Smith, Luke Hyam, Paul Anderson (Jay Tabb 68), Cole Skuse, Daryl Murphy, David McGoldrick (Frank Nouble 81), Ryan Tunnicliffe (Paul Taylor 81)
Barnsley: Jack Butland, Scott Wiseman, Tom Kennedy, David Fox, Jean-Yves Mvoto, Martin Cranie, Paddy McCourt (Kelvin Etuhu 80), David Perkins, Marcus Pedersen (Jason Scotland 73), Chris O'Grady, Jacob Mellis (Jim O'Brien 42)

Burnley 1 (Kightly 53)
Ipswich Town 0

Saturday, 26 April 2014, 12.15pm – Championship
Turf Moor – Attendance: 14,574
Channel: Sky Sports 1
Town manager: Mick McCarthy – **Referee:** James Linington

Burnley: Tom Heaton, Kieran Trippier, Ben Mee, David Jones, Michael Duff, Jason Shackell, Michael Kightly (Junior Stanislas 62), Dean Marney, Danny Ings (Keith Treacy 90), Ashley Barnes, Scott Arfield (Ross Wallace 80)

Ipswich: Dean Gerken, Luke Chambers, Aaron Cresswell, Christophe Berra, Tommy Smith, Frazer Richardson (Paul Taylor 64), Paul Green, Cole Skuse, Daryl Murphy, Jonny Williams, Stephen Hunt (Frank Nouble 65)

Ipswich Town 2 (Murphy 32; McGoldrick 61)
Fulham 1 (Hoogland 86)

Saturday, 9 August 2014, 5.15pm – Championship
Portman Road – Attendance: 17,218
Channel: Sky Sports 1
Town manager: Mick McCarthy – **Referee:** Stephen Martin

Ipswich: Dean Gerken, Luke Chambers, Tyrone Mings, Christophe Berra, Tommy Smith, Luke Hyam (Kevin Bru 81), Jay Tabb, Cole Skuse (Anthony Wordsworth 69), Elliott Hewitt, Bálint Bajner (David McGoldrick 43), Daryl Murphy

Fulham: Jesse Joronen, Kostas Stafylidis, Shaun Hutchinson (Patrick Roberts 73), Nikolay Bodurov, Tim Hoogland, Emerson Hyndman, Cameron Burgess, Chris David (Thomas Eisfield 46), Scott Parker, Ross McCormack (Cauley Woodrow 56), Moussa Dembélé

Ipswich Town 0
Norwich City 1 (Grabban 23)

Saturday, 23 August 2014, 12.15pm – Championship
Portman Road – Attendance: 25,245
Channel: Sky Sports 1
Town manager: Mick McCarthy – **Referee:** Keith Stroud

Ipswich: Dean Gerken, Luke Chambers, Tyrone Mings, Christophe Berra, Tommy Smith, Luke Hyam (Kevin Bru 70), Paul Anderson (Conor Sammon 71), Cole Skuse, Jay Tabb (Alex Henshall 71), David McGoldrick, Daryl Murphy

Norwich: John Ruddy, Russell Martin, Steven Whittaker, Reece Johnson, Ryan Bennett (Javi Garrido 6), Michael Turner, Kyle Lafferty (Elliott Bennett 52), Alexander Tettey, Lewis Grabban, Wes Hoolahan (Gary O'Neil 82), Nathan Redmond

Wigan Athletic 1 (Waghorn 81)
Ipswich Town 2 (Hyam 20; Sammon 63)

Monday, 22 September 2014, 7.45pm – Championship
DW Stadium – Attendance: 12,817
Channel: Sky Sports 1
Town manager: Mick McCarthy – **Referee:** Andy Woolmer

Wigan: Scott Carson, Iván Ramis, James Perch, Rob Kiernan, Emmerson Boyce, Adam Forshaw, Don Cowie, William Kvist, Callum McManaman (James McClean 35), Andy Delort (Martyn Waghorn 71), Shaun Maloney (Oriol Riera 63)
Ipswich: Dean Gerken, Jonathan Parr, Tyrone Mings, Luke Chambers, Christophe Berra, Luke Hyam, Teddy Bishop (Darren Ambrose 80), Cole Skuse (Kevin Bru 59), David McGoldrick (Tommy Smith 89), Daryl Murphy, Conor Sammon

Charlton Athletic 0
Ipswich Town 1 (N. Hunt 90)

Saturday, 29 November 2014, 12.15pm – Championship
The Valley – Attendance: 16,613
Channel: Sky Sports 1
Town manager: Mick McCarthy – **Referee:** Darren Bond

Charlton: Nick Pope, Chris Solly, Tal Ben Haim, André Bikey, Morgan Fox, Johann Gudmundsson (Frédéric Bulot 90), Francis Coquelin, Johnnie Jackson (Lawrie Wilson 75), Jordan Cousins, Callum Harriott (George Țucudean 85), Igor Vetokele
Ipswich: Bartosz Białkowski, Jonathan Parr, Tyrone Mings, Luke Chambers, Tommy Smith, Jay Tabb, Stephen Hunt (Conor Sammon 75), Cole Skuse, David McGoldrick, Daryl Murphy, Paul Anderson (Noel Hunt 82)

Ipswich Town 0
Derby County 1 (Martin 56)

Saturday, 10 January 2015, 12.15pm – Championship
Portman Road – Attendance: 20,861
Channel: Sky Sports 1
Town manager: Mick McCarthy – **Referee:** Kevin Wright

Ipswich: Bartosz Białkowski, Luke Chambers, Tyrone Mings, Christophe Berra, Tommy Smith, Luke Hyam, Paul Anderson (Noel Hunt 67), Teddy Bishop (Kevin Bru 71), Jay Tabb (Stephen Hunt 55), David McGoldrick, Daryl Murphy
Derby: Lee Grant, Cyrus Christie, Richard Keogh, Jake Buxton, Craig Forsyth, Jeff Hendrick (Craig Bryson 79), John Eustace, Will Hughes, Johnny Russell (Ryan Shotton 90), Chris Martin, Jordon Ibe (Simon Dawkins 85)

Ipswich Town 0
Southampton 1 (Long 19)

Wednesday, 14 January 2015, kick-off: 7.55pm – FA Cup third round replay
Portman Road – Attendance: 27,933
Channel: BBC One
Town manager: Mick McCarthy – **Referee:** Graham Scott

Ipswich: Bartosz Białkowski, Luke Chambers, Jonathan Parr, Christophe Berra, Tommy Smith, Luke Hyam, Darren Ambrose (Cameron Stewart 81), Kevin Bru, Stephen Hunt (Tyrone Mings 54), David McGoldrick (Bálint Bajner 62), Daryl Murphy

Southampton: Fraser Forster, Florin Gardoş, José Fonte, Ryan Bertrand, Nathaniel Clyne, James Ward-Prowse, Victor Wanyama (Steven Davis 46), Harrison Reed, Matt Targett, Shane Long, Dusan Tadić (Graziano Pellè 66)

Norwich City 2 (Johnson 23; Grabban 61)
Ipswich Town 0

Sunday, 1 March 2015, 2.05pm – Championship
Carrow Road – Attendance: 27,005
Channel: Sky Sports 3
Town manager: Mick McCarthy – **Referee:** Paul Tierney

Norwich: John Rudd, Steven Whittaker, Russell Martin, Sébastien Bassong, Martin Olsson, Alexander Tettey, Bradley Johnson, Nathan Redmond (Cameron Jerome 60; Gary Hooper 90), Jonathan Howson, Wes Hoolahan (Graham Dorrans 82), Lewis Grabban

Ipswich: Bartosz Białkowski, Luke Chambers, Tyrone Mings, Tommy Smith, Christophe Berra, Richard Chaplow (Luke Varney 46), Kevin Bru (Jonathan Parr 69), Cole Skuse, Jay Tabb, Freddie Sears, Daryl Murphy (Chris Wood 78)

Middlesbrough 4 (Ayala 3; Adomah 29; Bamford 63, 78)
Ipswich Town 1 (Murphy 10)

Saturday, 14 March 2015, 12.15pm – Championship
Riverside Stadium – Attendance: 18,909
Channel: Sky Sports 1
Town manager: Mick McCarthy – **Referee:** Mike Jones

Middlesbrough: Dimi Konstantopoulos, Tomás Kalas, Ben Gibson, Daniel Ayala (Jonathan Woodgate 23), George Friend, Adam Clayton, Grant Leadbitter (Emilio López 87), Albert Adomah, Patrick Bamford, Adam Reach, Jelle Vossen (Adam Forshaw 67)

Ipswich: Dean Gerken (Bartosz Białkowski 9), Luke Chambers, Tyrone Mings, Tommy Smith, Christophe Berra, Jonathan Parr, Cole Skuse, Teddy Bishop (Luke Varney 83), Jay Tabb (Chris Wood 68), Freddie Sears, Daryl Murphy

Ipswich Town 1 (Sears 6)
Bournemouth 1 (Jones 82)

Friday, 3 April 2015, 5.15pm – Championship
Portman Road – Attendance: 22,672
Channel: Sky Sports 1
Town manager: Mick McCarthy – **Referee:** Robert Madley

Ipswich: Bartosz Białkowski, Luke Chambers, Zeki Fryers, Christophe Berra, Tommy Smith, Teddy Bishop (Richard Chaplow 56), Cole Skuse, Jay Tabb, Luke Varney (Matt Clarke 89), Freddie Sears (Chris Wood 78), Daryl Murphy

Bournemouth: Artur Boruc, Simon Francis, Tommy Elphick, Steve Cook (Kenwyne Jones 78), Charlie Daniels, Matt Ritchie, Andrew Surman, Harry Arter, Ryan Fraser (Adam Smith 77), Brett Pitman (Yann Kermorgant 64), Callum Wilson

Wolverhampton Wanderers 1 (Afobe 50)
Ipswich Town 1 (Stearman 21 og)

Saturday, 18 April 2015, 12.15pm – Championship
Molineux – Attendance: 23,409
Channel: Sky Sports 1
Town manager: Mick McCarthy – **Referee:** Stuart Attwell

Wolves: Carl Ikeme, Dominic Iorfa, Danny Batth, Richard Stearman, Scott Golbourne, Rajiv van La Parra (James Henry 63), David Edwards, Kevin McDonald, Bakary Sako, Nouha Dicko, Benik Afobe

Ipswich: Dean Gerken, Luke Chambers, Tyrone Mings, Tommy Smith, Christophe Berra, Jonathan Parr (Paul Anderson 65), Cole Skuse, Teddy Bishop (Stephen Hunt 73), Jay Tabb, Freddie Sears (Chris Wood 82), Daryl Murphy

Blackburn Rovers 3 (Rhodes 36; Conway 41; Gestede 57)
Ipswich Town 2 (Murphy 2, 82)

Saturday, 2 May 2015, 12.15pm – Championship
Ewood Park – Attendance: 16,469
Channel: Sky Sports 2
Town manager: Mick McCarthy – **Referee:** Graham Scott

Blackburn: David Martin, Adam Henley, Darragh Lenihan, Tommy Spurr, Marcus Olsson, Lee Williamson, David Dunn (Ben Marshall 75), Craig Conway, Corry Evans, Jordan Rhodes, Rudy Gestede (Joshua King 71)

Ipswich: Bartosz Białkowski, Luke Chambers, Tyrone Mings, Tommy Smith, Christophe Berra, Jonathan Parr (Paul Anderson 53), Cole Skuse, Teddy Bishop (Kevin Bru 83), Jay Tabb (Stephen Hunt 46), Freddie Sears, Daryl Murphy

Ipswich Town 1 (Anderson 45)
Norwich City 1 (Howson 40)

Saturday, 9 May 2015, 12.15pm – Championship play-off semi-final first leg
Portman Road – Attendance: 29,166
Channel: Sky Sports 1
Town manager: Mick McCarthy – **Referee:** Anthony Taylor

Ipswich: Bartosz Białkowski, Luke Chambers, Tyrone Mings, Christophe Berra, Tommy Smith, Teddy Bishop (Jonathan Parr 76), Cole Skuse, Kevin Bru (Jay Tabb 71), Luke Varney (Paul Anderson 30), Freddie Sears, Daryl Murphy

Norwich: John Ruddy, Steven Whittaker, Russell Martin, Sébastien Bassong, Martin Olsson, Alexander Tettey, Graham Dorrans (Wes Hoolahan 68), Nathan Redmond, Jonny Howson, Bradley Johnson, Cameron Jerome (Gary Hooper 85)

Norwich City 3 (Hoolahan 49; Redmond 63; Jerome 75)
Ipswich Town 1 (Smith 59)

Norwich won 4-2 on aggregate

Saturday, 16 May 2015, 12.15pm – Championship play-off semi-final second leg
Carrow Road – Attendance: 26,994
Channel: Sky Sports 1
Town manager: Mick McCarthy – **Referee:** Roger East

Norwich: John Ruddy, Steven Whittaker, Russell Martin, Sébastien Bassong, Martin Olsson, Nathan Redmond, Alexander Tettey, Jonny Howson, Bradley Johnson (Elliott Bennett 86), Wes Hoolahan (Graham Dorrans 73), Cameron Jerome (Gary Hooper 82)

Ipswich: Bartosz Białkowski, Luke Chambers, Tyrone Mings, Christophe Berra, Tommy Smith, Teddy Bishop (David McGoldrick 70), Cole Skuse, Kevin Bru (Jay Tabb 70), Paul Anderson (Noel Hunt 82), Freddie Sears, Daryl Murphy

Reading 5 (Sá 7, 13, 62; Blackman 48; Norwood 86)
Ipswich Town 1 (Sears 10)

Friday, 11 September 2015, 8pm – Championship
Madejski Stadium – Attendance: 16,809
Channel: Sky Sports 5
Town manager: Mick McCarthy – **Referee:** Roger East

Reading: Jonathan Bond, Chris Gunter, Paul McShane, Anton Ferdinand, Jordan Obita, Aaron Tshibola, Oliver Norwood, Stephen Quinn, Nick Blackman (Ola John 77), Orlando Sá (Hal Robson-Kanu 81), Matěj Vydra (Lucas Piazon 76)

Ipswich: Dean Gerken, Luke Chambers, Jonas Knudsen, Christophe Berra, Tommy Smith, Jonathan Douglas, Cole Skuse, Ryan Fraser (Ainsley Maitland-Niles 65), David McGoldrick, Freddie Sears, Brett Pitman (Daryl Murphy 65)

Ipswich Town 1 (Pitman 32)
Birmingham City 1 (Cotterill 21)
Friday, 18 September 2015, 7.45pm – Championship
Portman Road – Attendance: 18,973
Channel: Sky Sports 5
Town manager: Mick McCarthy – **Referee:** Keith Stroud

Ipswich: Dean Gerken, Luke Chambers, Jonas Knudsen, Christophe Berra, Tommy Smith, Larsen Touré (David McGoldrick 70), Jonathan Douglas, Cole Skuse, Ainsley Maitland-Niles (Ryan Fraser 79), Brett Pitman (Daryl Murphy 65), Freddie Sears
Birmingham: Tomasz Kuszczak, Neal Eardley (Paul Caddis 45), Michael Morrison, Jonathan Spector, Jonathan Grounds, Maikel Kieftenbeld, Stephen Gleeson, David Cotterill, Andrew Shinnie (Jacques Maghoma 72), Demarai Gray (Paul Robinson 84), Clayton Donaldson

Charlton Athletic 0
Ipswich Town 3 (Murphy 28, 68; Sears 45)
Saturday, 28 November 2015, 12.30pm – Championship
The Valley – Attendance: 15,870
Channels: Sky Sports 1 and 5
Town manager: Mick McCarthy – **Referee:** Scott Duncan

Charlton: Stephen Henderson, Tareiq Holmes-Dennis, Patrick Bauer, Naby Sarr, Morgan Fox (Ricardo Vaz Té 46), Jordan Cousins, Alou Diarra, Johnnie Jackson (Chris Solly 12), Johann Gudmundsson, Ademola Lookman, Simon Makienok (Reza Ghoochannejhad 72)
Ipswich: Dean Gerken, Luke Chambers, Jonas Knudsen, Christophe Berra, Tommy Smith, Jonathan Douglas, Cole Skuse, Ainsley Maitland-Niles (Giles Coke 83), Freddie Sears (Tommy Oar 89), Brett Pitman, Daryl Murphy

Ipswich Town 0
Middlesbrough 2 (Stuani 53; Nugent 73)
Friday, 4 December 2015, 7.45pm – Championship
Portman Road – Attendance: 17,662
Channel: Sky Sports 1
Town manager: Mick McCarthy – **Referee:** Tim Robinson

Ipswich: Dean Gerken, Luke Chambers, Jonas Knudsen, Christophe Berra, Tommy Smith, Jonathan Douglas, Cole Skuse, Ainsley Maitland-Niles (Giles Coke 62), Brett Pitman (David McGoldrick 85), Freddie Sears, Daryl Murphy
Middlesbrough: Dimi Konstantopoulos, Emilio Nsue, Daniel Ayala, Ben Gibson, George Friend, Adam Clayton, Grant Leadbitter, Cristhian Stuani (Adam Forshaw 84), Stewart Downing, Albert Adomah, David Nugent

Milton Keynes Dons 0
Ipswich Town 1 (Pitman 10)
Saturday, 12 December 2015, 12.30pm – Championship
Stadium MK
Attendance: 13,520
Channel: Sky Sports 1
Town manager: Mick McCarthy – Referee: Roger East

MK Dons: David Martin, Jordan Spence (Robert Hall 85), Kyle McFadzean, Anthony Kay, Dean Lewington, Darren Potter, Samir Carruthers, Carl Baker (Daniel Powell 61), Dean Bowditch (Ben Reeves 61), Josh Murphy, Nicky Maynard

Ipswich: Dean Gerken, Luke Chambers, Jonas Knudsen, Christophe Berra, Tommy Smith, Jonathan Douglas, Cole Skuse, Ainsley Maitland-Niles (Jonathan Parr 77), Daryl Murphy, Freddie Sears (David McGoldrick 85), Brett Pitman

Ipswich Town 1 (Knudsen 45)
Norwich City 1 (Jerome 26)
Sunday, 21 August 2016, midday – Championship
Portman Road – Attendance: 23,350
Channel: Sky Sports 2
Town manager: Mick McCarthy – Referee: David Coote

Ipswich: Bartosz Białkowski, Luke Chambers, Jonas Knudsen, Christophe Berra, Adam Webster, Jonathan Douglas, Cole Skuse, Kevin Bru (Teddy Bishop 70), Grant Ward, Freddie Sears (Luke Varney 89), Daryl Murphy

Norwich: Michael McGovern, Ivo Pinto (Steven Whittaker 46), Ryan Bennett, Timm Klose, Robbie Brady, Alexander Tettey, Youssouf Mulumbu (Jacob Murphy 61), Steven Naismith (Sergi Canós 80), Jonny Howson, Wes Hoolahan, Cameron Jerome

Reading 2 (McCleary 45; Williams 90)
Ipswich Town 1 (Pitman 50)
Friday, 9 September 2016, 8pm – Championship
Madejski Stadium – Attendance: 15,146
Channel: Sky Sports 1
Town manager: Mick McCarthy – Referee: Jeremy Simpson

Reading: Ali Al-Habsi, Chris Gunter, Paul McShane, Liam Moore, Tyler Blackett (Jordan Obita 82), Danny Williams, Joey van den Berg, George Evans (Stephen Quinn 59), Garath McCleary (John Swift 66), Yann Kermorgant, Roy Beerens

Ipswich: Bartosz Białkowski, Luke Chambers, Jonas Knudsen, Christophe Berra, Tommy Smith, Jonathan Douglas, Cole Skuse, Grant Ward (Luke Varney 86), Kevin Bru (Teddy Bishop 68), Freddie Sears, Brett Pitman

Ipswich Town 0
Nottingham Forest 2 (Assombalonga 1, 45)

Saturday, 19 November 2016, 5.30pm – Championship
Portman Road – **Attendance:** 15,417
Channel: Sky Sports 1
Town manager: Mick McCarthy – **Referee:** Peter Bankes

Ipswich: Bartosz Białkowski, Josh Emmanuel (Luke Varney 70), Jonas Knudsen, Christophe Berra, Luke Chambers, Teddy Bishop (Jonny Williams 46), Cole Skuse, Tom Lawrence, Grant Ward (Kevin Bru 46), Freddie Sears, David McGoldrick
Forest: Vladimir Stojković, Matt Mills, Damien Perquis, Joe Worrall, Eric Lichaj, Pajtim Kasami, Henri Lansbury, Thomas Lam (Jorge Grant 85), Daniel Pinillos (Michael Mancienne 63), Ben Osborn, Britt Assombalonga (Apostolos Vellios 56)

Lincoln City 1 (Arnold 90)
Ipswich Town 0

Tuesday, 17 January 2017, 8.05pm – FA Cup third round replay
Sincil Bank – **Attendance:** 9,054
Channel: BBC One
Town manager: Mick McCarthy – **Referee:** Ben Toner

Lincoln: Paul Farman, Bradley Wood, Luke Waterfall, Sean Raggett, Sam Habergham, Terry Hawkridge (Jamie McCombe 90), Alex Woodyard, Alan Power, Nathan Arnold (Jack Muldoon 90), Theo Robinson (Adam Marriott 80), Matt Rhead
Ipswich: Dean Gerken, Josh Emmanuel, Jonas Knudsen, Christophe Berra, Luke Chambers, Paul Digby, Jonathan Douglas, Cole Skuse, Grant Ward (Andre Dozzell 75), Tom Lawrence, Leon Best (Freddie Sears 75)

Norwich City 1 (Jacob Murphy 69)
Ipswich Town 1 (Knudsen 63)

Sunday, 26 February 2017, midday – Championship
Carrow Road – **Attendance:** 27,107
Channel: Sky Sports 2
Town manager: Mick McCarthy – **Referee:** Oliver Langford

Norwich: John Ruddy, Ivo Pinto, Russell Martin, Timm Klose, Mitchell Dijks, Jonny Howson, Alexander Tettey, Jacob Murphy, Wes Hoolahan (Alex Pritchard 79), Steven Naismith (Josh Murphy 76), Cameron Jerome
Ipswich: Bartosz Białkowski, Jordan Spence, Jonas Knudsen, Luke Chambers, Christophe Berra, Myles Kenlock (Tommy Smith 56), Cole Skuse, Grant Ward, Emyr Huws (Toumani Diagouraga 81), David McGoldrick, Freddie Sears (Kieffer Moore 75)

Nottingham Forest 3 (Assombalonga 43, 69; Cohen 57)
Ipswich Town 0

Sunday, 7 May 2017, midday – Championship
City Ground – Attendance: 28,249
Channel: Sky Sports 3
Town manager: Mick McCarthy – Referee: Andy Davies

Forest: Jordan Smith, Joe Worrall, Matt Mills, Michael Mancienne, Eric Lichaj, Chris Cohen (Matty Cash 85), David Vaughan, Ben Osborn, Jamie Ward (Ben Brereton 79), Mustapha Carayol (Zach Clough 14), Britt Assombalonga
Ipswich: Bartosz Białkowski, Jordan Spence, Myles Kenlock (Josh Emmanuel 46), Luke Chambers, Christophe Berra (Adam Webster 81), Emyr Huws, Cole Skuse, Danny Rowe, Grant Ward, Freddie Sears (Kieffer Moore 68), Dominic Samuel

Ipswich Town 0
Norwich City 1 (Maddison 59)

Sunday, 22 October 2017, midday – Championship
Portman Road – Attendance: 24,928
Channels: Sky Sports Football and Sky Sports Main Event
Town manager: Mick McCarthy – Referee: Tim Robinson

Ipswich: Bartosz Białkowski, Jordan Spence, Jonas Knudsen, Luke Chambers, Adam Webster, Cole Skuse, Tom Adeyemi (Flynn Downes 67), Tristan Nydam (Freddie Sears 77), Martyn Waghorn, David McGoldrick, Joe Garner (Bersant Celina 76)
Norwich: Angus Gunn, Ivo Pinto, Christoph Zimmermann (Grant Hanley 65), Timm Klose, Harrison Reed, Wes Hoolahan (James Husband 78), Marco Stiepermann, Tom Trybull, James Maddison (Mario Vrančić 88), Cameron Jerome, Yanic Wildschut

Ipswich Town 2 (Garner 48; Waghorn 70)
Sheffield Wednesday 2 (Hooper 64; Nuhiu 90)

Wednesday, 22 November 2017, 7.45pm – Championship
Portman Road – Attendance: 15,702
Channels: Sky Sports Football and Sky Sports Main Event
Town manager: Mick McCarthy – Referee: Keith Stroud

Ipswich: Bartosz Białkowski, Jordan Spence, Myles Kenlock, Luke Chambers, Adam Webster, Cole Skuse, Callum Connolly, Bersant Celina (Emyr Huws 67), Martyn Waghorn (Grant Ward 78), David McGoldrick (Freddie Sears 45), Joe Garner
Sheffield Wednesday: Keiren Westwood, Jack Hunt, Morgan Fox (Steven Fletcher 60), Glenn Loovens, Tom Lees, Jacob Butterfield, Barry Bannan, Adam Reach, Ross Wallace (Kieran Lee 62), Jordan Rhodes (Atdhe Nuhiu 87), Gary Hooper

Norwich City 1 (Klose 90)
Ipswich Town 1 (Chambers 89)

Sunday, 18 February 2018, midday – Championship
Carrow Road – Attendance: 27,100
Channels: Sky Sports Football and Sky Sports Main Event
Town manager: Mick McCarthy – **Referee:** David Coote

Norwich: Angus Gunn, Christoph Zimmermann, Timm Klose, Jamal Lewis, Grant Hanley, Harrison Reed (Onel Hernández 89), Moritz Leitner, Josh Murphy (Dennis Srbeny 84), James Maddison, Alexander Tettey (Mario Vrančić 89), Nélson Oliveira
Ipswich: Bartosz Białkowski, Dominic Iorfa (Jordan Spence 79), Jonas Knudsen, Luke Chambers, Adam Webster, Cameron Carter-Vickers, Callum Connolly, Cole Skuse, Stephen Gleeson (Luke Hyam 67), Martyn Waghorn, Joe Garner (David McGoldrick 62)

Ipswich Town 0
Middlesbrough 2 (Bešić 12; Downing 16)

Tuesday, 2 October 2018, 7.45pm – Championship
Portman Road – Attendance: 13,612
Channels: Sky Sports Football and Sky Sports Main Event
Town manager: Paul Hurst – **Referee:** Andy Madley

Ipswich: Dean Gerken, Janoi Donacien, Jonas Knudsen, Luke Chambers, Toto Nsiala, Trevoh Chalobah, Cole Skuse, Jon Nolan, Jordan Graham, Grant Ward, Kayden Jackson
Middlesbrough: Darren Randolph, George Friend, Daniel Ayala, Ryan Shotton, Aden Flint, Jonny Howson, Stewart Downing, George Saville, Mo Bešić (Sam McQueen 82), Martin Braithwaite (Paddy McNair 69), Jordan Hugill (Britt Assombalonga 65)

Ipswich Town 1 (Jackson 85)
West Bromwich Albion 2 (Rodriguez 26; Barnes 77)

Friday, 23 November 2018, 7.45pm – Championship
Portman Road – Attendance: 22,995
Channels: Sky Sports Football and Sky Sports Main Event
Town manager: Paul Lambert – **Referee:** Keith Stroud

Ipswich: Bartosz Białkowski, Jordan Spence, Jonas Knudsen, Luke Chambers, Matthew Pennington, Trevoh Chalobah, Cole Skuse, Gwion Edwards (Jack Lankester 77), Jordan Roberts (Kayden Jackson 85), Flynn Downes (Teddy Bishop 64), Freddie Sears
West Brom: Sam Johnstone, Kieran Gibbs, Tosin Adarabioyo, Craig Dawson, Ahmed Hegazy, James Morrison (Gareth Barry 89), Jake Livermore, Matt Phillips, Harvey Barnes, Hal Robson-Kanu (Dwight Gayle 75), Jay Rodriguez

Norwich City 3 (Hernández 2; Pukki 65, 80)
Ipswich Town 0

Sunday, 10 February 2019, midday – Championship
Carrow Road – Attendance: 27,040
Channels: Sky Sports Football and Sky Sports Main Event
Town manager: Paul Lambert – **Referee:** Peter Bankes

Norwich: Tim Krul, Ben Godfrey, Christoph Zimmermann, Jamal Lewis, Max Aarons, Mario Vrančić (Alexander Tettey 51), Emiliano Buendia, Marco Stiepermann (Todd Cantwell 85), Tom Trybull, Onel Hernández, Teemu Pukki (Jordan Rhodes 88)
Ipswich: Bartosz Białkowski, James Bree, Jonas Knudsen, Luke Chambers, Matthew Pennington, Trevoh Chalobah, Cole Skuse (Teddy Bishop 74), Jon Nolan (Flynn Downes 85), Alan Judge, Will Keane, Freddie Sears (Ellis Harrison 43)

Bristol City 1 (Webster 32)
Ipswich Town 1 (Kelly 68 og)

Tuesday, 12 March 2019, 7.45pm – Championship
Ashton Gate – Attendance: 18,411
Channels: Sky Sports Football and Sky Sports Main Event
Town manager: Paul Lambert – **Referee:** Darren Bond

Bristol City: Stefan Marinović, Adam Webster, Lloyd Kelly, Tomás Kalas, Jack Hunt, Josh Brownhill, Niclas Eliasson (Matty Taylor 83), Marlon Pack, Famara Diedhiou, Andreas Weimann (Kasey Palmer 73), Jamie Paterson (Callum O'Dowda 73)
Ipswich: Bartosz Białkowski, Josh Emmanuel, Myles Kenlock, Luke Chambers, Toto Nsiala, Trevoh Chalobah, Gwion Edwards, Jon Nolan (Cole Skuse 75), Andre Dozzell (Teddy Bishop 86), Alan Judge (Idris El Mizouni 75), Kayden Jackson

Sheffield United 2 (Hogan 24; O'Connell 71)
Ipswich Town 0

Saturday, 27 April 2019, 5.15pm – Championship
Bramall Lane – Attendance: 30,140
Channels: Sky Sports Football and Sky Sports Main Event
Town manager: Paul Lambert – **Referee:** Tim Robinson

Sheffield United: Dean Henderson, George Baldock, Enda Stevens, Jack O'Connell, Chris Basham, John Egan, John Fleck, Oliver Norwood, Mark Duffy (John Lundstram 85), Scott Hogan (Billy Sharp 63), David McGoldrick (Gary Madine 78)
Ipswich: Dean Gerken, James Bree, Myles Kenlock, Luke Chambers, Toto Nsiala, Cole Skuse, Teddy Bishop, Flynn Downes, Alan Judge, Will Keane (Trevoh Chalobah 8), Kayden Jackson (Andre Dozzell 68)

Accrington Stanley 2 (Bishop 17, 41)
Ipswich Town 0

Sunday, 20 October 2019, midday – League One
Wham Stadium – Attendance: 3,567
Channels: Sky Sports Football and Sky Sports Main Event
Town manager: Paul Lambert **– Referee:** Seb Stockbridge

Accrington: Dimitar Evtimov, Callum Johnson, Mark Hughes, Ross Sykes, Séamus Conneely, Jerome Opoku (Aji Alese 67), Jordan Clark, Sam Finley, Sean McConville (Joe Pritchard 77), Offrande Zanzala (Dion Charles 75), Colby Bishop
Ipswich: Tomáš Holý, Luke Chambers, Luke Garbutt, Toto Nsiala (Danny Rowe 46), Luke Woolfenden, Gwion Edwards, Cole Skuse, Jon Nolan, Alan Judge (Anthony Georgiou 66), Andre Dozzell (Armando Dobra 46), Kayden Jackson

Wycombe Wanderers 1 (Wheeler 66)
Ipswich Town 1 (Norwood 54)

Wednesday, 1 January 2020, 3pm – League One
Adams Park – Attendance: 8,523
Channels: Sky Sports Football, Sky Sports Main Event and Sky Sports Mix
Town manager: Paul Lambert **– Referee:** Robert Lewis

Wycombe: Ryan Allsop, Joe Jacobson, Anthony Stewart, Giles Phillips, Darius Charles, David Wheeler, Matt Bloomfield, Paul Smyth (Adebayo Akinfenwa 65), Nick Freeman, Nnamdi Ofoborh, Alex Samuel (Scott Kashket 86)
Ipswich: Will Norris, Luke Chambers, Luke Garbutt, James Wilson, Luke Woolfenden, Gwion Edwards, Alan Judge (Teddy Bishop 88), Flynn Downes, Emyr Huws, James Norwood (Will Keane 79), Kayden Jackson

Ipswich Town 2 (Bishop 11; Edwards 80)
Wigan Athletic 0

Sunday, 13 September 2020, midday – League One
Portman Road – Attendance: 0 (COVID-19 restrictions)
Channels: Sky Sports Football and Sky Sports Main Event
Town manager: Paul Lambert **– Referee:** Thomas Bramall

Ipswich: Tomáš Holý, Luke Chambers, Stephen Ward, James Wilson, Toto Nsiala, Jon Nolan, Teddy Bishop (Emyr Huws 76), Alan Judge, Andre Dozzell, Freddie Sears (Gwion Edwards 80), Aaron Drinan (James Norwood 46)
Wigan: Jamie Jones, Tom Pearce, Emeka Obi, Adam Long, Kal Naismith, Lee Evans, Dan Gardner (Alex Perry 46), Viv Solomon-Otabor, Gary Roberts, Christopher Merrie (Oliver Crankshaw 82), Joe Garner

Ipswich Town 2 (Norwood 62; Judge 87)
Swindon Town 3 (Jaiyesimi 16, 74; Twine 67)

Saturday, 9 January 2021, 5.30pm – League One
Portman Road – Attendance: 0 (COVID-19 restrictions)
Channel: Sky Sports Football
Town manager: Paul Lambert – **Referee:** Seb Stockbridge

Ipswich: David Cornell, Luke Chambers, Stephen Ward, Mark McGuinness, Luke Woolfenden, Alan Judge, Andre Dozzell, Armando Dobra (Jack Lankester 78), Emyr Huws (Flynn Downes 46), Kayden Jackson, Aaron Drinan (James Norwood 62)
Swindon: Mark Travers, Paul Caddis, Zeki Fryers, Dion Conroy, Dominic Thompson, Diallang Jaiyesimi, Matthew Smith (Anthony Grant 89), Jordan Lyden, Matty Palmer, Brett Pitman, Scott Twine

Ipswich Town 0
Sunderland 1 (Wyke 45)

Tuesday, 26 January 2021, 7.45pm – League One
Portman Road – Attendance: 0 (COVID-19 restrictions)
Channels: Sky Sports Football and Sky Sports Main Event
Town manager: Paul Lambert – **Referee:** Charles Breakspear

Ipswich: Tomáš Holý, Luke Chambers, Stephen Ward (Myles Kenlock 87), Mark McGuinness, Luke Woolfenden, Gwion Edwards (Freddie Sears 87), Jon Nolan (Aaron Drinan 55), Flynn Downes, Andre Dozzell, Luke Thomas (Teddy Bishop 71), Kayden Jackson
Sunderland: Lee Burge, Jordan Willis, Bailey Wright (Dion Sanderson 65), Max Power, Josh Scowen, Grant Leadbitter, Callum McFadzean, Carl Winchester (Elliot Embleton 46), Aiden McGeady (Lynden Gooch 79), Charlie Wyke, Aiden O'Brien (Luke O'Nien 87)

Barrow 2 (Stevens 26; Gotts 35)
Ipswich Town 0

Wednesday, 15 December 2021, 7.45pm – FA Cup second round replay
The Dunes Hotel Stadium – Attendance: 2,756
Channel: ITV 4
Town Caretaker Manager: John McGreal – **Referee:** James Bell

Barrow: Paul Farman, Connor Brown (Remeao Hutton 79), Patrick Brough, Matthew Platt, James Jones, Joe Grayson, Tom White, Robbie Gotts (Mark Ellis 89), Ollie Banks, Josh Gordon (Offrande Zanzala 82), Jordan Stevens (Josh Kay 79)
Ipswich: Christian Walton, Kane Vincent-Young, Matt Penney, Toto Nsiala (Janoi Donacien 76), Cameron Burgess, Scott Fraser (Sam Morsy 46), Idris El Mizouni, Tom Carroll (Luke Woolfenden 46), Sone Aluko (Conor Chaplin 75), James Norwood (Joe Pigott 67), Kayden Jackson

Rotherham United 1 (Smith 78)
Ipswich Town 0

Saturday, 16 April 2022, 12.30pm – League One
AESSEAL New York Stadium – Attendance: 9,394
Channels: Sky Sports Football and Sky Sports Main Event
Town manager: Kieran McKenna **– Referee:** Peter Wright

Rotherham: Viktor Johansson, Wes Harding, Jordi Osei-Tutu (Richard Wood 89), Ben Wiles, Chiedozie Ogbene, Mickel Miller (Daniel Barlaser 23), Jamie Lindsay, Ollie Rathbone, Michael Ihiekwe, Rarmani Edmonds-Green, Michael Smith

Ipswich: Christian Walton, Janoi Donacien, Luke Woolfenden, Elkan Baggott, Wes Burns, Tyreeq Bakinson, Sam Morsy, Dominic Thompson, Sone Aluko (Conor Chaplin 66), Bersant Celina (Joe Pigott 79), James Norwood (Macauley Bonne 66)

STATISTICS SECTION

Abidallah to Zuiverloon

A-Z of Town's TV appearances and goals

The following is a list of appearances and goals by Ipswich players, in alphabetical order, live on television:

Surname	Forename	Starts	Subs	Total	Goals
Abidallah	Nabil		1	**1**	
Abou	Samassi	1		**1**	1
Adeyemi	Tom	1		**1**	
Ainsley	Jack	1		**1**	
Alexander	Neil	4		**4**	
Aluko	Sone	2		**2**	
Ambrose	Darren	4	4	**8**	2
Anderson	Paul	5	3	**8**	1
Andrews	Keith	3		**3**	4
Appleby	Richard		1	**1**	
Armstrong	Alun	10	12	**22**	4
Atkins	Ian	1		**1**	
Axeldal	Jonas		3	**3**	
Baggott	Elkan	1		**1**	
Bajner	Bálint	1	1	**2**	
Baker	Clive	3		**3**	
Bakinson	Tyreeq	1		**1**	
Balkestein	Pim	4		**4**	
Barber	Fred	1		**1**	
Barron	Scott	1		**1**	
Bart-Williams	Chris	2	1	**3**	
Bates	Matthew	1		**1**	
Beattie	Kevin	1		**1**	
Begović	Asmir	1		**1**	
Bent	Darren	21	4	**25**	6
Bent	Marcus	8	1	**9**	2
Berra	Christophe	25		**25**	
Best	Leon	1		**1**	
Białkowski	Bartosz	19	1	**20**	
Bishop	Teddy	11	7	**18**	1

Surname	Forename	Starts	Subs	Total	Goals
Bonne	Macauley		1	**1**	
Bowditch	Dean	5	6	**11**	5
Bowyer	Lee	2		**2**	
Bozinovski	Vlado		1	**1**	
Bramble	Titus	18	1	**19**	1
Bree	James	2		**2**	
Brennan	Mark	1		**1**	
Brown	Troy	1	1	**2**	
Brown	Wayne	4	4	**8**	
Bru	Kevin	6	6	**12**	
Bruce	Alex	15		**15**	
Bullard	Jimmy	2		**2**	2
Burchill	Mark	1	2	**3**	1
Burgess	Cameron	1		**1**	
Burley	George	1		**1**	
Burns	Wes	1		**1**	
Bywater	Stephen	1		**1**	
Campbell	DJ	1		**1**	1
Campo	Ivan	1	1	**2**	
Carroll	Tom	1		**1**	
Carson	Josh	1	1	**2**	
Carter-Vickers	Cameron	1		**1**	
Casement	Chris	1	1	**2**	
Celina	Bersant	2	1	**3**	
Chalobah	Trevoh	4	1	**5**	
Chambers	Luke	40		**40**	1
Chaplin	Conor		2	**2**	
Chaplow	Richard	1	1	**2**	
Chapman	Lee		1	**1**	
Chopra	Michael	3		**3**	1
Civelli	Luciano	1	1	**2**	
Clapham	Jamie	35	9	**44**	2
Clarke	Billy	4	4	**8**	
Clarke	Matt		1	**1**	
Clegg	Michael	1		**1**	
Coke	Giles		2	**2**	
Colback	Jack	5	1	**6**	
Collins	Aidan	1		**1**	

Surname	Forename	Starts	Subs	Total	Goals
Collins	Danny	2		**2**	1
Connolly	Callum	2		**2**	
Cooper	Paul	1		**1**	
Cornell	David	1		**1**	
Cotterell	Leo		1	**1**	
Couñago	Pablo	17	14	**31**	8
Cranson	Ian	1		**1**	
Cresswell	Aaron	6		**6**	
Croft	Gary	4	1	**5**	1
Cundy	Jason	5	1	**6**	
Currie	Darren	10	4	**14**	
Davis	Kelvin	18		**18**	
D'Avray	Mich	1		**1**	
Delaney	Damien	10	1	**11**	1
de Vos	Jason	23		**23**	2
Diagouraga	Toumani		1	**1**	
Diallo	Drissa	5	1	**6**	
Digby	Paul	1		**1**	
Dobra	Armando	1	1	**2**	
Donacien	Janoi	2	1	**3**	
Douglas	Jonathan	8		**8**	
Downes	Flynn	4	3	**7**	
Dozzell	Andre	5	3	**8**	
Dozzell	Jason	8		**8**	3
Drinan	Aaron	2	1	**3**	
Drury	Andy	1		**1**	
Dyer	Kieron	13	2	**15**	1
Edwards	Carlos	11	1	**12**	
Edwards	Gwion	5	2	**7**	1
Ellington	Nathan		2	**2**	
Elliott	Matt	6		**6**	
El Mizouni	Idris	1	1	**2**	
Emmanuel	Josh	3	1	**4**	
Emmanuel-Thomas	Jay	2	1	**3**	
Fallon	Rory	1	2	**3**	
Forrest	Craig	15		**15**	
Forster	Nicky	2		**2**	
Fraser	Ryan	1	1	**2**	

Surname	Forename	Starts	Subs	Total	Goals
Fraser	Scott	1		1	
Fryers	Zeki	1		1	
Fülöp	Márton	5		5	
Gaardsøe	Thomas	4	2	6	1
Garbutt	Luke	2		2	
Garner	Joe	3		3	1
Garvan	Owen	11	5	16	
Geddis	David	1		1	
George	Finidi	9		9	2
Georgiou	Anthony		1	1	
Gerken	Dean	15		15	
Gleeson	Stephen	1		1	
Gleghorn	Nigel		1	1	
Goddard	Paul	2	1	3	
Graham	Jordan	1		1	
Green	Paul	1		1	
Gregory	Neil	1	4	5	1
Gudmundsson	Niklas	2		2	1
Guentchev	Bontcho	2	3	5	
Hallworth	Jon	1		1	
Harbey	Graham	1		1	
Harding	Dan	7		7	
Harrison	Ellis		1	1	
Haynes	Danny	1	9	10	4
Healy	Colin	2	1	3	
Henshall	Alex		1	1	
Hewitt	Elliott	1		1	
Higginbotham	Danny	1		1	
Hodges	Lee		1	1	
Holland	Matt	50		50	7
Holster	Marco	1	1	2	
Holý	Tomáš	3		3	
Horlock	Kevin	7	2	9	
Hreidarsson	Hermann	26		26	2
Humes	Tony	1		1	1
Hunt	Noel		3	3	1
Hunt	Stephen	3	3	6	
Hunter	Allan	1		1	

Surname	Forename	Starts	Subs	Total	Goals
Huws	Emyr	4	2	**6**	
Hyam	Luke	6	1	**7**	1
Iorfa	Dominic	1		**1**	
Jackson	Kayden	8	1	**9**	1
John	Stern		1	**1**	
Johnson	David	20	1	**21**	6
Johnson	Gavin	10		**10**	1
Juan	Jimmy	2	1	**3**	2
Judge	Alan	7		**7**	1
Keane	Will	2	1	**3**	
Kenlock	Myles	5	1	**6**	
Kennedy	John	1		**1**	
Kennedy	Mark	4	1	**5**	
Kerslake	David		1	**1**	
Kiwomya	Chris	13		**13**	2
Knights	Darryl		1	**1**	
Knudsen	Jonas	15		**15**	2
Kuqi	Shefki	15	3	**18**	5
Lambert	Mick		1	**1**	
Lankester	Jack		2	**2**	
Lawrence	Tom	2		**2**	
Leadbitter	Grant	10		**10**	
Lee	Alan	9	1	**10**	5
Lee-Barrett	Arran	1		**1**	
Legg	Andrew	1		**1**	1
Legwinski	Sylvain	4	1	**5**	2
Le Pen	Ulrich		2	**2**	
Linighan	David	14		**14**	
Lisbie	Kevin	3	1	**4**	
Livermore	Jake		1	**1**	
Loach	Scott	1		**1**	
Lowe	David	1		**1**	
Luongo	Massimo		1	**1**	
Macken	Jon	1		**1**	
Magilton	Jim	51	3	**54**	2
Mahon	Alan	1		**1**	
Maitland-Niles	Ainsley	4	1	**5**	
Makin	Chris	15	1	**16**	

Surname	Forename	Starts	Subs	Total	Goals
Mariner	Paul	1		**1**	
Marshall	Andy	8		**8**	
Marshall	Ian	12		**12**	5
Martin	Lee	7		**7**	
Mason	Paul	10	2	**12**	2
Mathie	Alex	12	4	**16**	2
McAuley	Gareth	9	1	**10**	
McDonald	Dean		1	**1**	
McEveley	Jay	2		**2**	
McGoldrick	David	11	6	**17**	1
McGreal	John	28	1	**29**	
McGuinness	Mark	2		**2**	
Miller	Tommy	30	4	**34**	3
Mills	Mick	1		**1**	
Milton	Simon	17	2	**19**	3
Mings	Tyrone	11	1	**12**	
Mitchell	Scott		1	**1**	
Mohsni	Bilel		1	**1**	
Moore	Kieffer		2	**2**	
Morsy	Sam	2	1	**2**	
Mowbray	Tony	20		**20**	2
Murphy	Brian	1		**1**	
Murphy	Daryl	21	3	**24**	7
Murray	Ronan		1	**1**	
Naylor	Richard	30	20	**50**	7
Niven	Stuart	1		**1**	
Noble	Mark	2		**2**	
Nolan	John	6		**6**	
Norris	David	11		**11**	2
Norris	Will	1		**1**	
Norwood	James	3	2	**5**	2
Nouble	Frank		2	**2**	
Nsiala	Toto	6		**6**	
Nydam	Tristan	1		**1**	
Oar	Tommy		1	**1**	
O'Connor	Shane	1	2	**3**	
O'Dea	Darren	4	1	**5**	
Osborne	Roger	1		**1**	1

Surname	Forename	Starts	Subs	Total	Goals
Palmer	Steve	7	1	8	1
Parkin	Sam	2		2	
Parr	Jonathan	6	3	9	
Paz	Adrian	1		1	
Penney	Matt	1		1	
Pennington	Matthew	2		2	
Peralta	Sixto	5	4	9	
Peters	Jaime	4	4	8	1
Petta	Bobby	9	1	10	
Pigott	Joe		2	2	
Pitman	Brett	6		6	3
Pollitt	Mike	1		1	
Price	Lewis	7		7	
Priskin	Tamás	6	3	9	1
Proudlock	Adam		1	1	
Quinn	Alan	3	2	5	
Reuser	Martijn	16	11	27	6
Rhodes	Jordan		2	2	
Richards	Matt	20	1	21	1
Richardson	Frazer	1		1	
Roberts	Gary	3	2	5	
Roberts	Jordan	1		1	
Rosenior	Liam	2	1	3	
Rowe	Danny	1	1	2	
Sammon	Conor	1	2	3	1
Samuel	Dominic	1		1	
Santos	Georges	2	1	3	
Scotland	Jason	6	2	8	4
Scowcroft	James	25	7	32	4
Sears	Freddie	20	5	25	3
Sedgley	Steve	13		13	1
Sereni	Matteo	12		12	
Simpson	Danny	1		1	
Sito	Castro	4	1	5	
Skuse	Cole	32	1	33	
Slater	Stuart	7		7	
Smith	Tommy	24	4	28	1
Sonko	Ibrahima	2		2	

Surname	Forename	Starts	Subs	Total	Goals
Sonner	Danny	1	4	**5**	1
Spence	Jordan	5	1	**6**	
Stead	Jon	4	3	**7**	2
Stein	Mark	1		**1**	1
Stewart	Cameron		1	**1**	
Stewart	Marcus	17	2	**19**	12
Stockdale	David	3		**3**	
Stockwell	Mick	34	3	**37**	2
Šumulikoski	Veliče	3	2	**5**	
Supple	Shane	1		**1**	
Swailes	Chris	3		**3**	
Tabb	Jay	9	3	**12**	
Talbot	Brian	1		**1**	
Tanner	Adam	2	3	**5**	
Taricco	Mauricio	14		**14**	1
Taylor	Paul		2	**2**	
Thatcher	Ben	2		**2**	
Thétis	Manuel	9	1	**10**	
Thomas	Luke	1		**1**	
Thompson	Dominic	1		**1**	
Thompson	Neil	10		**10**	1
Thomsen	Claus	9		**9**	
Touré	Larsen	1		**1**	
Townsend	Andros	1		**1**	1
Trotter	Liam	4	2	**6**	
Tunnicliffe	Ryan	1		**1**	
Uhlenbeek	Gus	8	4	**12**	
Unsworth	David	4		**4**	
Varney	Luke	2	5	**7**	
Vaughan	Tony	6	2	**8**	
Venus	Mark	30	1	**31**	
Vincent-Young	Kane	1		**1**	
Volz	Moritz	3		**3**	
Wabara	Reece		1	**1**	
Waghorn	Martyn	3		**3**	1
Walters	Jon	14	1	**15**	4
Walton	Christian	2		**2**	
Walton	Simon	4		**4**	1

Surname	Forename	Starts	Subs	Total	Goals
Ward	Grant	7	1	**8**	
Ward	Stephen	3		**3**	
Wark	John	19		**19**	5
Webster	Adam	4	1	**5**	
Wellens	Richie	1		**1**	
Westlake	Ian	17	4	**21**	1
Whelan	Phil	6	1	**7**	
Whitton	Steve	6	1	**7**	
Wickham	Connor	5	2	**7**	
Williams	Gavin	3	1	**4**	
Williams	Geraint	24		**24**	
Williams	Jonny	1	1	**2**	
Wilnis	Fabian	45	6	**51**	1
Wilson	James	2		**2**	
Wood	Chris		4	**4**	
Woods	Clive	1		**1**	
Woolfenden	Luke	5	1	**6**	
Wordsworth	Anthony		1	**1**	
Wright	David	11		**11**	
Wright	Jermaine	30	9	**39**	1
Wright	Richard	45		**45**	
Yallop	Frank	5		**5**	
Youds	Eddie	3	2	**5**	
Zondervan	Romeo	1	1	**2**	
Zuiverloon	Gianni	3		**3**	
Own Goals					6

TOWN'S TV TEN APPEARANCES

The following is a list of the top ten players for appearances by Ipswich players, live on television:

Surname	Forename	Starts	Subs	Total
Magilton	Jim	51	3	**54**
Wilnis	Fabian	45	6	**51**
Holland	Matt	50		**50**
Naylor	Richard	30	20	**50**
Wright	Richard	45		**45**
Clapham	Jamie	35	9	**44**
Chambers	Luke	40		**40**
Wright	Jermaine	30	9	**39**
Stockwell	Mick	34	3	**37**
Miller	Tommy	30	4	**34**

GOALS

The following is a list of the top ten players for goals scored by Ipswich players, live on television:

Surname	Forename	Goals
Stewart	Marcus	**12**
Couñago	Pablo	**8**
Holland	Matt	7
Murphy	Daryl	7
Naylor	Richard	7
Bent	Darren	**6**
Johnson	David	**6**
Reuser	Martijn	**6**
Bowditch	Dean	5
Kuqi	Shefki	5
Lee	Alan	5
Marshall	Ian	5
Wark	John	5

SIR BOBBY TO MCKENNA

Town managers' TV record

The below is a complete record of all managers to oversee an Ipswich game live on television:

Manager	P	W	D	L	F	A	TV win per cent
Sir Bobby Robson	1	1	0	0	1	0	100
John Duncan	1	0	0	1	1	2	0
John Lyall	14	3	4	7	17	19	21
George Burley	60	24	12	24	82	80	40
Joe Royle	25	10	6	9	32	35	40
Jim Magilton	14	7	2	5	25	15	50
Roy Keane	8	1	2	5	7	16	13
Ian McParland (Caretaker)	1	1	0	0	1	0	100
Paul Jewell	6	3	0	3	12	15	50
Mick McCarthy	29	5	9	15	25	44	17
Paul Hurst	1	0	0	1	0	2	0
Paul Lambert	9	1	2	6	7	15	11
John McGreal (Caretaker)	1	0	0	1	0	2	0
Kieran McKenna	1	0	0	1	0	1	0
Total	171	56	37	78	210	246	33 per cent

THE OPPOSITION

Town's opponents live on TV

The below is a complete record of all 63 opponents faced to date and the number of times played live on TV:

Opposition	Games
Norwich City	24
Coventry City	7
Sheffield United	6
Sunderland	6
Charlton Athletic	5
Leicester City	5
West Ham United	5
Arsenal	4
Cardiff City	4
Manchester City	4
Nottingham Forest	4
West Bromwich Albion	4
Wigan Athletic	4
Wolverhampton Wanderers	4
Barnsley	3
Birmingham City	3
Blackburn Rovers	3
Bolton Wanderers	3
Crystal Palace	3
Liverpool	3
Manchester United	3

Opposition	Games
Middlesbrough	3
Reading	3
Sheffield Wednesday	3
Southampton	3
Tottenham Hotspur	3
Helsingborgs IF	2
Inter Milan	2
Leeds United	2
Luton Town	2
Millwall	2
Newcastle United	2
Preston North End	2
Queens Park Rangers	2
Stoke City	2
Swindon Town	2
Torpedo Moscow	2
Watford	2

The following teams have all been faced once by Ipswich live on TV:

Accrington Stanley, Aston Villa, Barrow, Bournemouth, Bradford City, Brentford, Brighton & Hove Albion, Bristol City, Burnley, Colchester United, Derby County, Doncaster Rovers, Fulham, Grimsby Town, Hull City, Lincoln City, MK Dons, Peterborough United, Portsmouth, Rotherham United, Stockport County, Swansea City, Walsall, Wimbledon, and Wycombe Wanderers

TOWN'S TV HIGHLIGHTS

Records from Town on TV

The below is a selection of records and statistics from Ipswich games shown live on television:

ATTENDANCE RECORDS

Highest attendance on TV

Saturday, 6 May 1978 – 100,000

Arsenal 0 Ipswich Town 1 – FA Cup Final

Highest Portman Road attendance on TV

Wednesday, 18 May 2005 – 30,010

Ipswich Town 0 West Ham 2 – play-off semi-final

Highest away attendance on TV

Tuesday, 25 January 2011 – 59,387

Arsenal 3 Ipswich Town 0 – League Cup semi-final

Lowest attendance on TV (outside of COVID-19)

Wednesday, 15 December 2021 – 2,756

Barrow 2 Ipswich Town 0 – FA Cup second round replay

Lowest Portman Road attendance on TV (outside of COVID-19)

Sunday, 22 October 1995 – 9,123

Ipswich Town 0 Luton Town 1 – Division One

WIN AND LOSS RECORD

Biggest win on TV

Sunday, 29 October 2006

Ipswich Town 5 Luton Town 0

Heaviest defeat on TV

Saturday, 20 August 2011

Peterborough United 7 Ipswich Town 1

IPSWICH TOWN HAT-TRICKS ON TV

Marcus Stewart

Monday, 2 April 2001

Southampton 0 Ipswich Town 3 – FA Premier League

Dean Bowditch

Saturday, 20 March 2004

Ipswich Town 4 Watford 1 – Division One

Alan Lee

Sunday, 29 October 2006

Ipswich Town 5 Luton Town 0 – Championship

IPSWICH TOWN PLAYERS SENT OFF ON TV

John Wark (44th minute)

Monday, 20 March 1995

Norwich City 3 Ipswich Town 0 – FA Premier League

Fabian Wilnis (13th minute)

Monday, 28 November 2005

Cardiff City 2 Ipswich Town 1 – Championship

Tommy Miller (86th minute)

Saturday, 29 December 2007

Coventry City 2 Ipswich Town 1 – Championship

Damien Delaney (36th minute)

Sunday, 28 November 2010

Norwich City 4 Ipswich Town 1 – Championship

Lee Martin (44th minute)

Saturday, 20 August 2011

Peterborough Utd 7 Ipswich Town 1 – Championship

Tommy Smith (46th minute)

Saturday, 20 August 2011

Peterborough Utd 7 Ipswich Town 1 – Championship

Aaron Cresswell (90th minute)

Friday, 1 November 2013

Ipswich Town 1 Barnsley 1 – Championship

Christophe Berra (48th minute)

Saturday, 16 May 2015

Norwich City 3 Ipswich Town 1 – Championship play-off

Armando Dobra (79th minute)

Sunday, 20 October 2019

Accrington Stanley 2 Ipswich Town 0 – League One

Kayden Jackson (10th minute)

Tuesday, 26 January 2021

Ipswich Town 0 Sunderland 1 – League One

TOWN'S TV MILESTONES

Key moments from Town on TV

Listed below are some of the key milestone moments achieved by the team and the players live on television:

6 May 1978

First full, live TV game for Ipswich

Roger Osborne scores Town's first live TV goal

Mick Lambert is Town's first live TV substitute

10 January 1988

First live TV game to be played at Portman Road

16 February 1992

Ipswich's first live Sky Sports game is screened

30 August 1992

First Ipswich league game is screened live

26 September 1993

The first player to be sent off in an Ipswich live TV game is Tottenham's Colin Calderwood

20 March 1995

The first Ipswich player to be sent off in a live TV game is John Wark as he sees red at Norwich

9 November 1997

Neil Gregory becomes the first Ipswich substitute to score a live TV goal

9 August 1998

Alex Mathie becomes Ipswich's 50th live TV substitution

11 August 1999

David Johnson scores Ipswich's 50th live TV goal

14 May 2000

Ipswich play their 50th live TV game

2 April 2001

Marcus Stewart becomes the first Ipswich player to score a live TV hat-trick

7 May 2001

Richard Naylor becomes Ipswich's 100th live TV substitution

18 October 2001

Sixto Peralta becomes the 100th Ipswich player to appear live on TV

28 October 2001

Ipswich score their 50th live TV home goal

18 November 2001

George Burley becomes the first and only Ipswich manager to reach 50 live TV games in charge

10 August 2002

Our second goal scored in the game – scored by Marcus Bent – is Ipswich's 100th live TV goal

Also in the same game, Alun Armstrong becomes Ipswich's 150th live TV substitution

18 April 2003

Matt Holland becomes the first Ipswich player to play 50 live TV games. It is also his final live TV game

30 April 2003

Ian Westlake becomes the 50th different Ipswich player to score in a live TV game

20 March 2004

Seventeen-year-old Dean Bowditch scores Ipswich's second live TV hat-trick and at the time of writing, he remains the only teenager to score a hat-trick in a live game for Ipswich

28 December 2004

Ipswich play their 50th live TV home game

16 October 2005

Dean Bowditch becomes Ipswich's 200th live TV substitution

14 May 2005

Jim Magilton becomes the second Ipswich player to play in 50 live TV games

In the same game, Ipswich score their 50th away goal in live TV games

28 November 2005

Ipswich play their 100th live TV game

In this game, Jim Magilton plays his 54th and final live TV game, setting the record as the Ipswich player to appear the most live on TV

27 August 2007

David Wright becomes the 150th Ipswich player to appear live on TV

4 November 2007

Fabian Wilnis becomes the third Ipswich player to play in 50 live TV games

In the same game, Alan Lee scores Ipswich's 150th live TV goal

29 December 2007
Ipswich play their 50th live TV away game

7 December 2008
Richard Naylor becomes the fourth and last Ipswich player to play in 50 live TV games

22 August 2009
Tamás Priskin becomes Ipswich's 250th live TV substitution

20 August 2011
The 200th player appears as David Stockdale, Josh Carson, Aaron Cresswell, Jack Ainsley, Jay Emmanuel-Thomas, Keith Andrews, Michael Chopra, and Nathan Ellington all play in their first live TV games for Ipswich

22 September 2004
Tommy Smith becomes Ipswich's 300th live TV substitution

9 August 2014
Ipswich score their 100th live TV home goal

11 September 2015
The 250th Ipswich player appears live on TV as Jonas Knudsen, Jonathan Douglas, Ryan Fraser, Brett Pitman, and Ainsley Maitland-Niles all play in their first live TV games for Town

12 December 2015
Ipswich play their 150th live TV game

26 February 2017
Jonas Knudsen scores Ipswich's 200th live TV goal
Tommy Smith becomes Ipswich's 350th live TV substitution

1 January 2020
The 300th Ipswich player appears live on TV as Will Norris, James Wilson and James Norwood all play in their first live TV games for Town

ACKNOWLEDGEMENTS

When I first set out to write this book, I had no idea where to start, how I would achieve my end goal, and who would help me along the way. There is a multitude of people to thank and there is no order to any of the following people that I must accord a heartfelt acknowledgement to.

I have in the main used my own memories to tell as many stories around Ipswich's live TV games as possible. To help me fill in some gaps, I am indebted to the wonderful website prideofanglia.com, and in turn, my thanks to Ralph Morris for allowing me to use some material from his website.

I have learnt that there are a whole lot of hoops to jump through in using photos. So, please forgive me for sharing photos of players in their civvies rather than on the pitch and I thank Pat for sharing just a few pictures from her exceptionally ample collection taken over the last 40 years or more.

When I first started to collate all of Ipswich live TV games on my website a few years ago, I could not have done so without the tremendous help from Paul Bloomfield and Seán Salter who is otherwise known as the Renegade Statman on Twitter. Their knowledge helped to compile the full list of games from which I could turn into this book.

Seán has also been a tremendous help with proofreading the book for me and checking all the important stats. Graeme Brooke has also helped with proofreading, and I thank both great Ipswich Town fans for all their help.

None of this would have been possible without Steve Caron at JMD Media and Michelle Grainger agreeing to take my project on and publishing into this book. I cannot thank you and your team enough for making my own personal dream come true.

I go back really to where all my writing started as far as local media and ultimately this Ipswich book is concerned. My dear friend Dave Allard both encouraged and inspired me to want to write. His guidance, advice and little black book over the years have been a massive help.

Mike Bacon gave me a break in the *Green 'Un* all those years ago by allowing me to write a full-page non-league column and has continued to do so right up until the present day by continuing to accept my feature articles for the *Kings of Anglia* magazine.

And the *EADT*'s sports editor Mark Heath gave me the opportunity to fulfil another ambition of writing a weekly Ipswich Town column in the *East Anglian Daily Times* and *Ipswich Star* – a privileged position that I have now held for around ten years at the time of writing. Mike and Mark are two top guys who have been amazing towards me.

When Brad Lloyd of Glory Days Artwork sent me his illustration of the cover for this book, I was truly gobsmacked. Brad serves the *East Anglian Daily Times* as well as illustrating merchandise that can be found in the Ipswich Town club shop. To add my book to his portfolio is a real honour I cannot thank Brad enough. Everyone who has seen the cover says how great it looks.

His website is well worth a visit where he has some excellent Ipswich Town illustrations and so much more. Please pay the site a visit at glorydaysartwork.co.uk.

I list Matt Holland as one of my favourite all-time Ipswich players, up there with the likes of Paul Mariner, Terry Butcher, John Wark and Kevin Beattie.

For Matt to therefore write the foreword in this book is a gesture by which I am truly humbled. He is one of only four players to achieve the feat of playing in 50 or more live TV games for Ipswich. In fact, he was also the first to do so. Not only was he a fantastic captain for the club, but he is also a fantastic person which I am sure you already know. Matt's generosity towards me will never be forgotten.

And finally, to my family and friends who have either shared my life of watching Ipswich with me or at the very least, put up with me watching the Town and then talking about them on an almost daily basis.

This category has far too many people to mention. But thank you to my boys Karl and Craig, both fellow ITFC season ticket holders, for sharing your company at the games we go to, and to my brother Shaun who if he had not have threatened to beat me up when I was six years old if I did not change my allegiance from Liverpool to Ipswich, none of this would have been possible.

Lastly, to my wife Pegga and my twin daughters Lola and Angel. Pegga and Lola do not like football. So, they put up with a lot from me. Thankfully, Angel likes the game and is an Ipswich fan – she still must put up with more from me than she has or wants to.

Thank you to everyone else I have not specifically mentioned, and here is to many more years of watching Ipswich Town together.

ND - #0285 - 270225 - C0 - 234/156/13 - PB - 9781780916378 - Gloss Lamination